The Flash #750

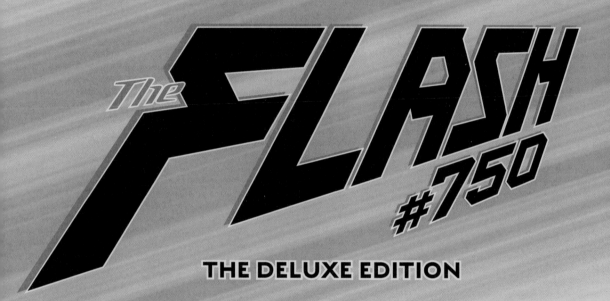

THE DELUXE EDITION

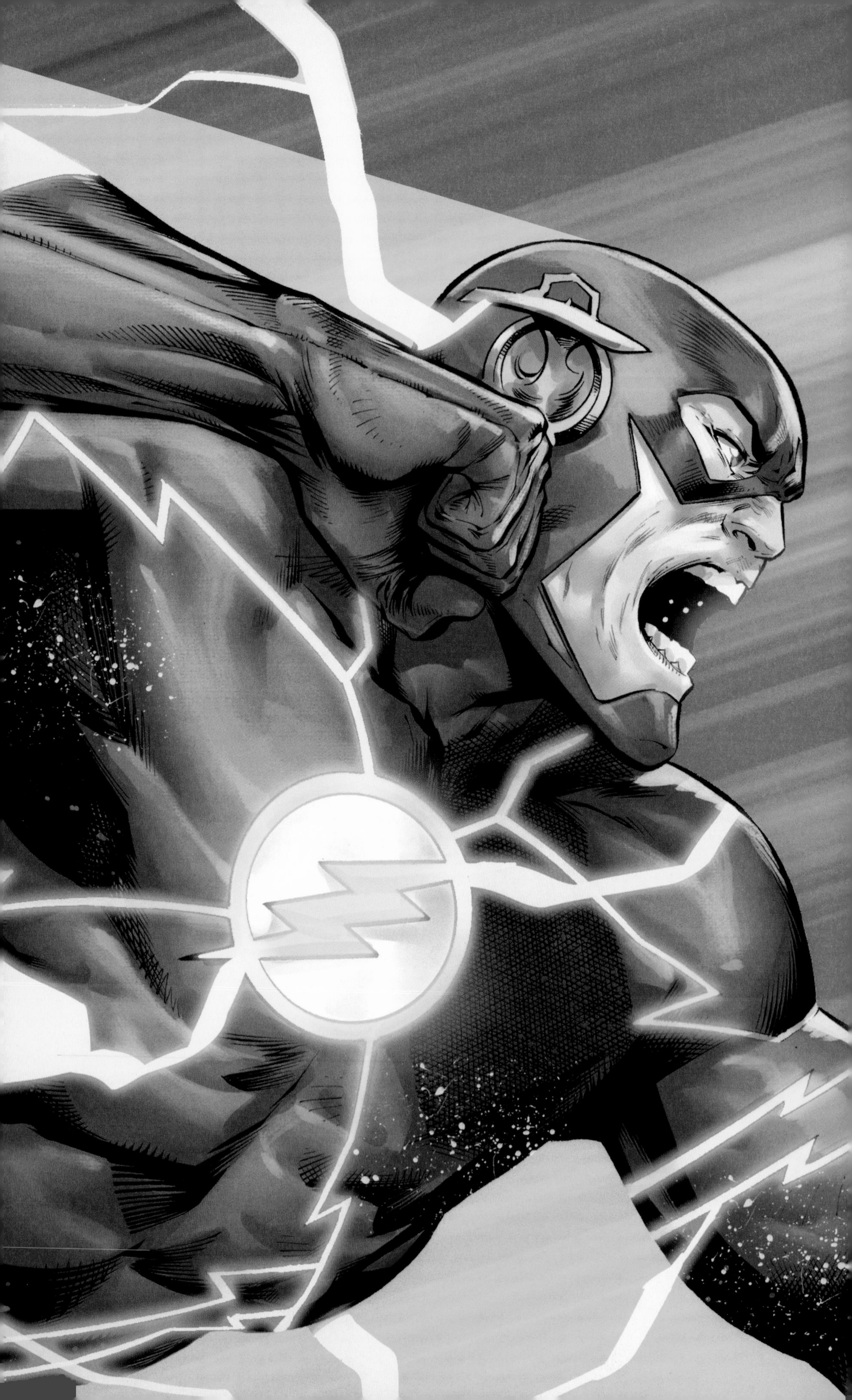

THE FLASH #750

THE DELUXE EDITION

THE FLASH/JAY GARRICK created by
GARDNER FOX

SUPERMAN created by
JERRY SIEGEL and **JOE SHUSTER**
By special arrangement with the **JERRY SIEGEL** family

Collection cover art by
HOWARD PORTER and **HI-FI**

JULIUS SCHWARTZ MIKE COTTON Editors – Original Series
BEN MEARES MARQUIS DRAPER Assistant Editors – Original Series
JEB WOODARD Group Editor – Collected Editions
REZA LOKMAN Editor – Collected Edition
STEVE COOK Design Director – Books
DAMIAN RYLAND Publication Design
SUZANNAH ROWNTREE Publication Production

BOB HARRAS Senior VP – Editor-in-Chief, DC Comics

DAN DiDIO Publisher
JIM LEE Publisher & Chief Creative Officer
BOBBIE CHASE VP – New Publishing Initiatives
DON FALLETTI VP – Manufacturing Operations & Workflow Management
LAWRENCE GANEM VP – Talent Services
ALISON GILL Senior VP – Manufacturing & Operations
HANK KANALZ Senior VP – Publishing Strategy & Support Services
DAN MIRON VP – Publishing Operations
NICK J. NAPOLITANO VP – Manufacturing Administration & Design
NANCY SPEARS VP – Sales
JONAH WEILAND VP – Marketing & Creative Services
MICHELE R. WELLS VP & Executive Editor, Young Reader

THE FLASH #750: THE DELUXE EDITION

DC Comics, 2900 West Alameda Ave., Burbank, CA 91505
Printed by Transcontinental Interglobe, Beauceville, QC, Canada. 5/29/20. First Printing.
ISBN: 978-1-77950-507-1

Library of Congress Cataloging-in-Publication Data is available.

PEFC Certified
This product is from sustainably managed forests and controlled sources
PEFC
PEFC/01-31-106
www.pefc.org

TABLE OF CONTENTS

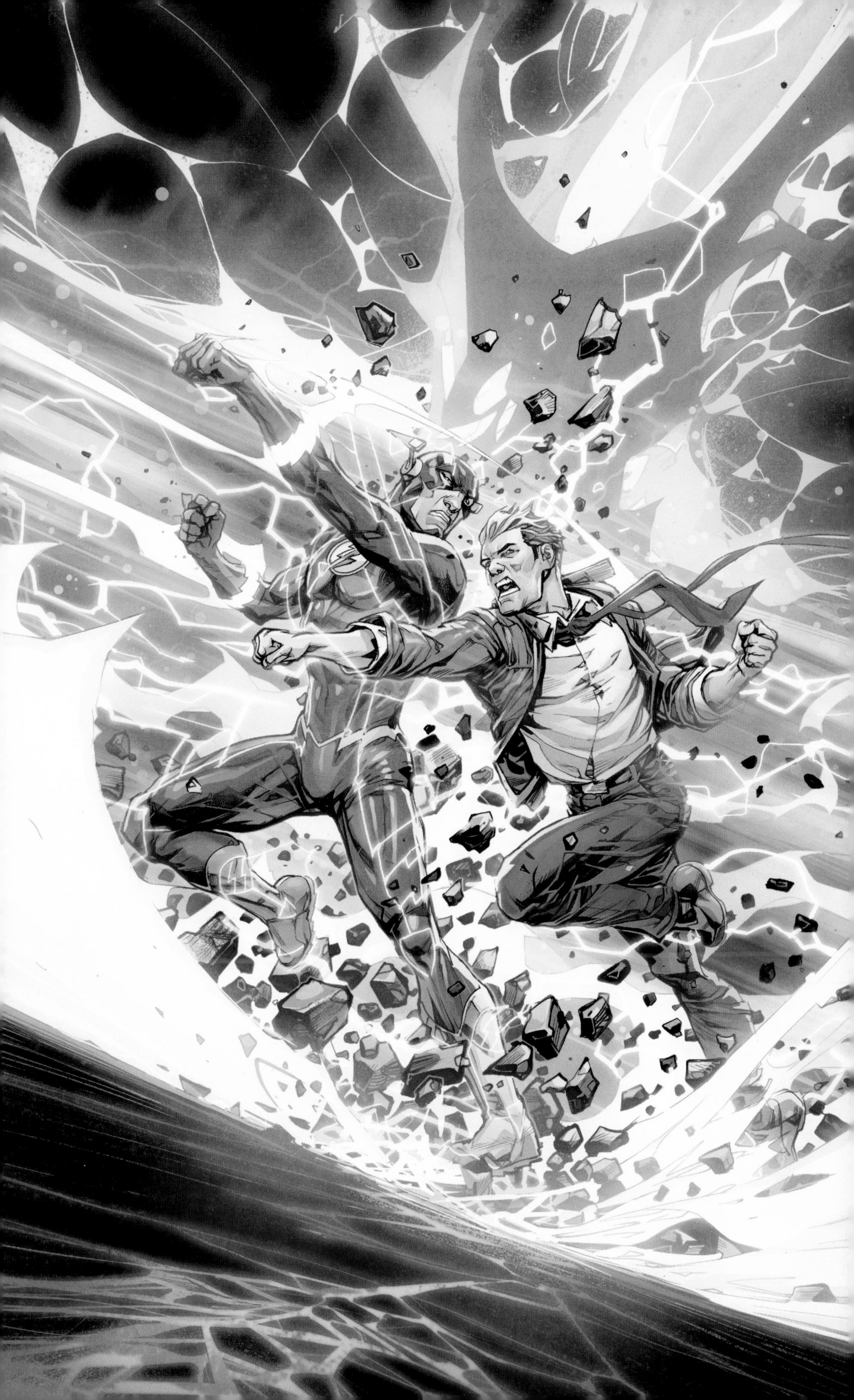

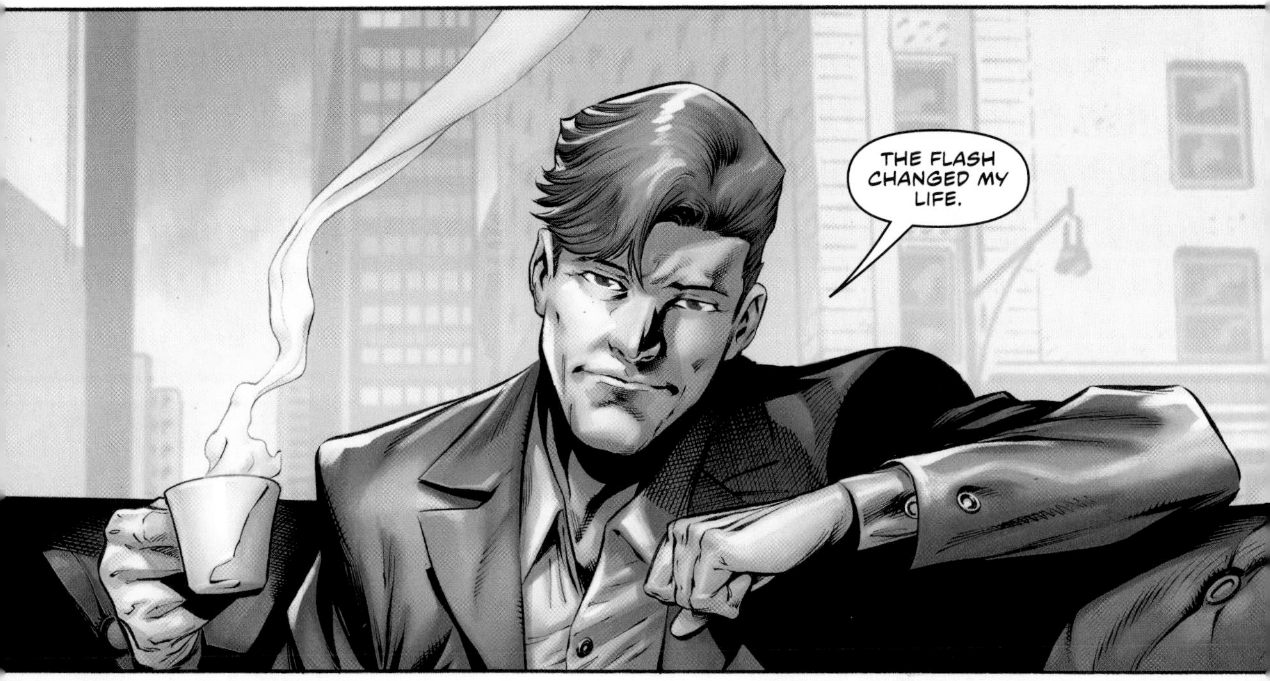
THE FLASH CHANGED MY LIFE.

THE FLASH AGE

PART ONE

JOSHUA WILLIAMSON WRITER
RAFA SANDOVAL & JORDI TARRAGONA (1-7,10-15,20-25,28-30)
STEPHEN SEGOVIA (8-9,16-19,26-27) ARTISTS
ARIF PRIANTO COLORS **STEVE WANDS** LETTERER

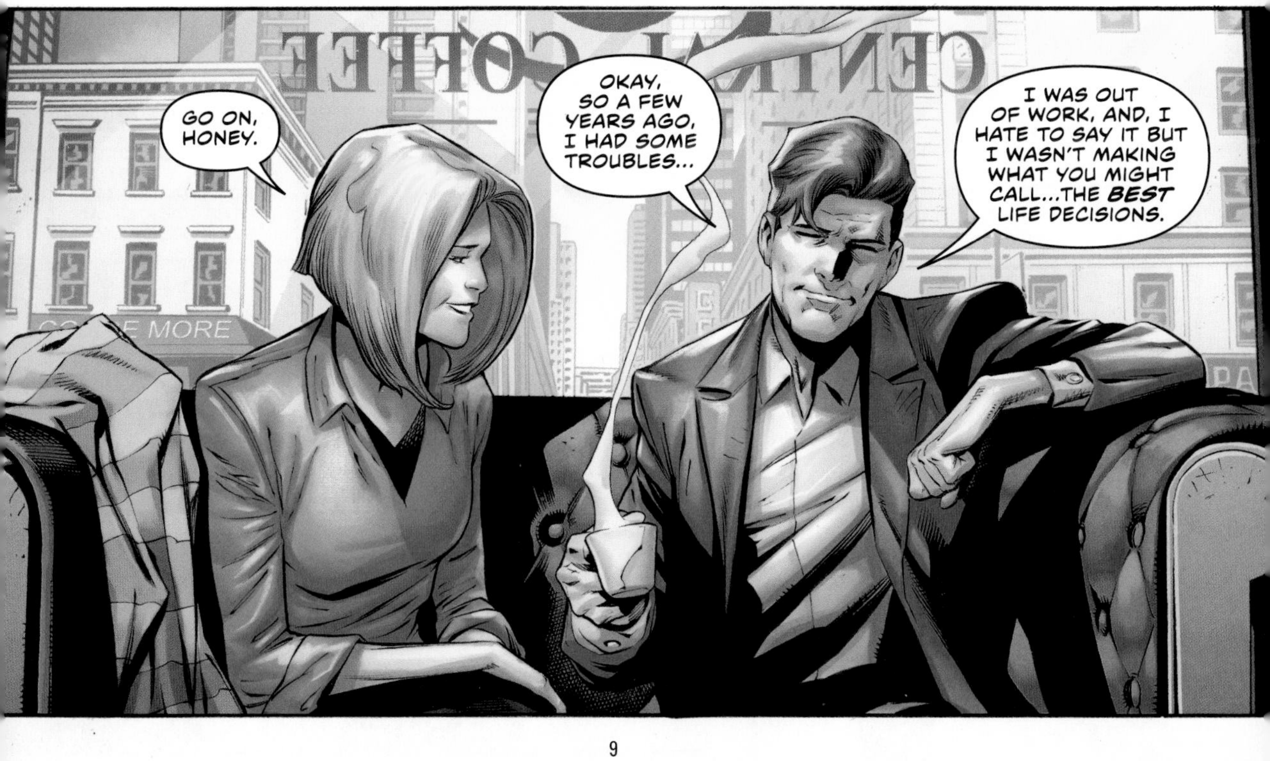
GO ON, HONEY.
OKAY, SO A FEW YEARS AGO, I HAD SOME TROUBLES...
I WAS OUT OF WORK, AND, I HATE TO SAY IT BUT I WASN'T MAKING WHAT YOU MIGHT CALL...THE *BEST* LIFE DECISIONS.

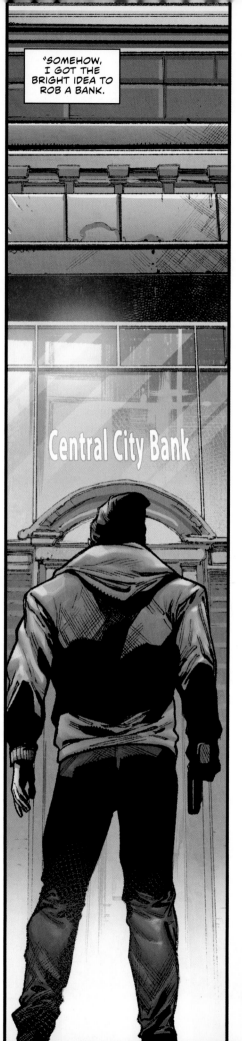

"SOMEHOW, I GOT THE BRIGHT IDEA TO ROB A BANK.

Central City Bank

"BUT WHEN I GOT INSIDE, AND I SAW THE PEOPLE AROUND ME, I REALIZED...I CAN'T DO THIS. I'M NOT THIS PERSON.

"SO I TURN AROUND TO LEAVE...

"...I'M ABOUT TO PAY WITH MY LIFE!

"I FELT IT BEFORE I SAW HIM. A GUST OF WIND, AND THE HAIR ON THE BACK OF MY NECK STUCK UP.

"...AND THEN, *BOOM...* HEAT WAVE SHOWS UP.

"THERE'S FIRE *EVERYWHERE* AND *HE'S* ROBBING THE BANK. I CAME IN TO ROB IT, AND NOW...

"NEXT THING I KNOW, HEAT WAVE IS DOWN.

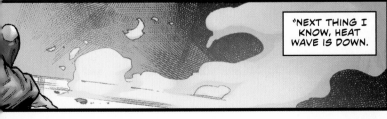

CENTRAL CITY CAREER CENTER

"THEN I BLINK AND I'M OUTSIDE THE CENTRAL CITY CAREER CENTER AND MY GUN IS GONE.

"AND I DON'T KNOW HOW FLASH KNEW WHAT I NEEDED.

"BUT I WENT IN AND GOT A JOB. WHICH IS HOW I MET MY WIFE.

"FLASH SAVED MY LIFE IN MORE WAYS THAN ONE THAT DAY..."

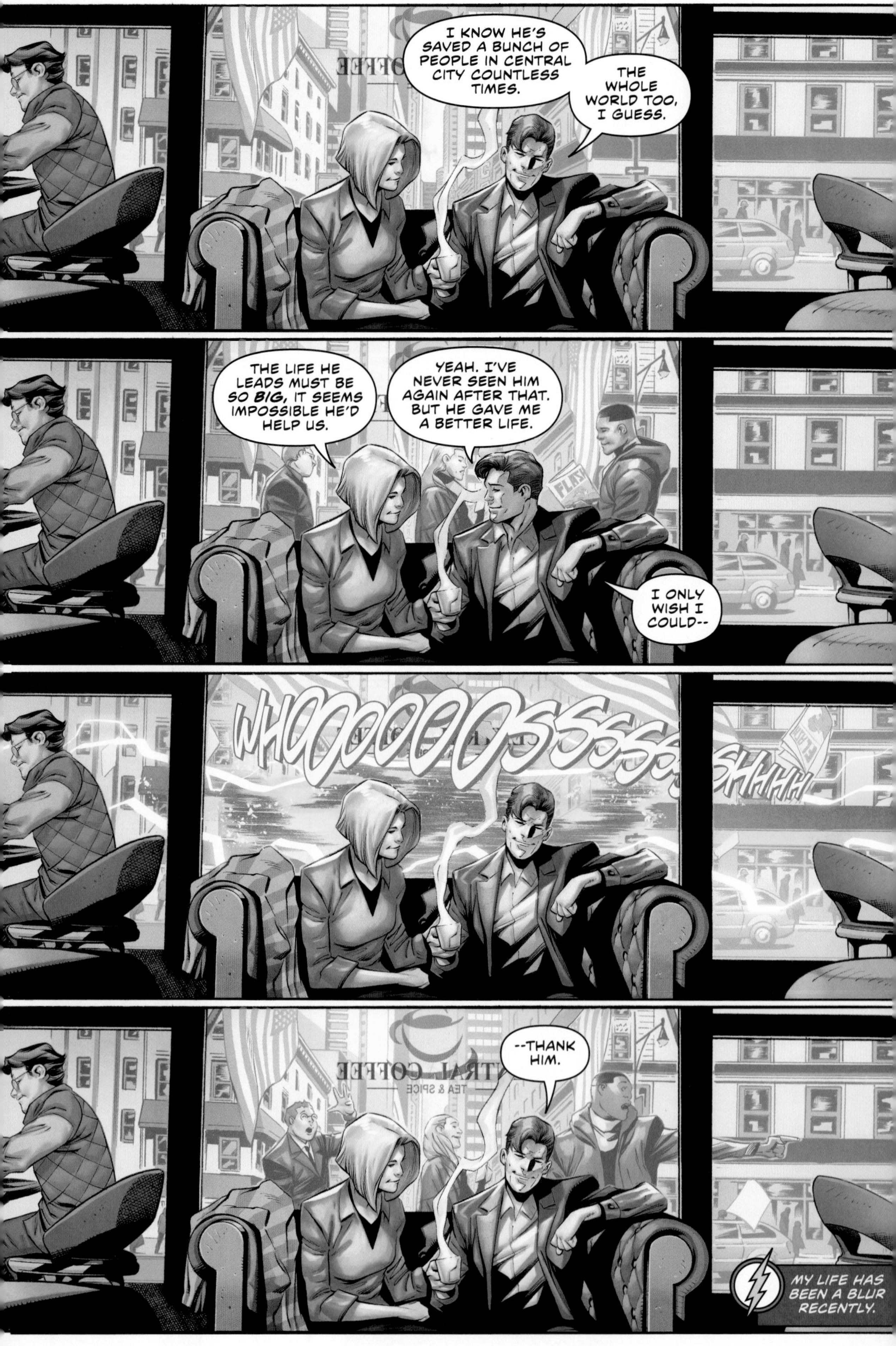

I KNOW HE'S SAVED A BUNCH OF PEOPLE IN CENTRAL CITY COUNTLESS TIMES.
THE WHOLE WORLD TOO, I GUESS.
THE LIFE HE LEADS MUST BE SO BIG, IT SEEMS IMPOSSIBLE HE'D HELP US.
YEAH. I'VE NEVER SEEN HIM AGAIN AFTER THAT. BUT HE GAVE ME A BETTER LIFE.
I ONLY WISH I COULD--
WHOOOOOOSSSSSSHHHH
--THANK HIM.
MY LIFE HAS BEEN A BLUR RECENTLY.

FUERZA AND STEADFAST WENT TO INVESTIGATE THE STRENGTH AND STILL FORCES ON THEIR OWN. IT WAS TIME THEY MOVED ON AND FOUND THEIR OWN WAY. I WISHED THEM WELL.

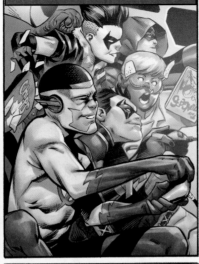

KID FLASH IS WITH THE TEEN TITANS. BEING A KID AGAIN. THE LAST YEAR HAS BEEN HARD ON HIM, BUT I HOPE HE'S HAPPY WITH HIS FRIENDS.

AVERY WENT BACK TO CHINA. EVERY TIME WE GET CLOSE TO KNOWING EACH OTHER, SHE TAKES OFF AGAIN.

I MANAGED TO RETRIEVE COMMANDER COLD'S BODY AND GIVE HIM A PROPER BURIAL.

TRICKSTER TRIED TO PULL A FAST ONE DURING ALL THE CHAOS, BUT I CAUGHT UP TO HIM AT THE CITY LINE. THANKFULLY A BRAND-NEW IRON HEIGHTS WAS READY FOR GUESTS.

THE ROGUES ARE STILL ON THE RUN.

MY SPEED FORCE WAS SUPERCHARGED AND OUT OF CONTROL...

HOWEVER, PIED PIPER WAS ABLE TO GET ME BACK ON FREQUENCY ENOUGH THAT I CAN FUNCTION. BUT I NEED TO BE CAREFUL.

AND THEN...

PARADOX IS COMING FOR YOU...

IT'S BEEN A LOT. BUT YOU KNOW WHAT?

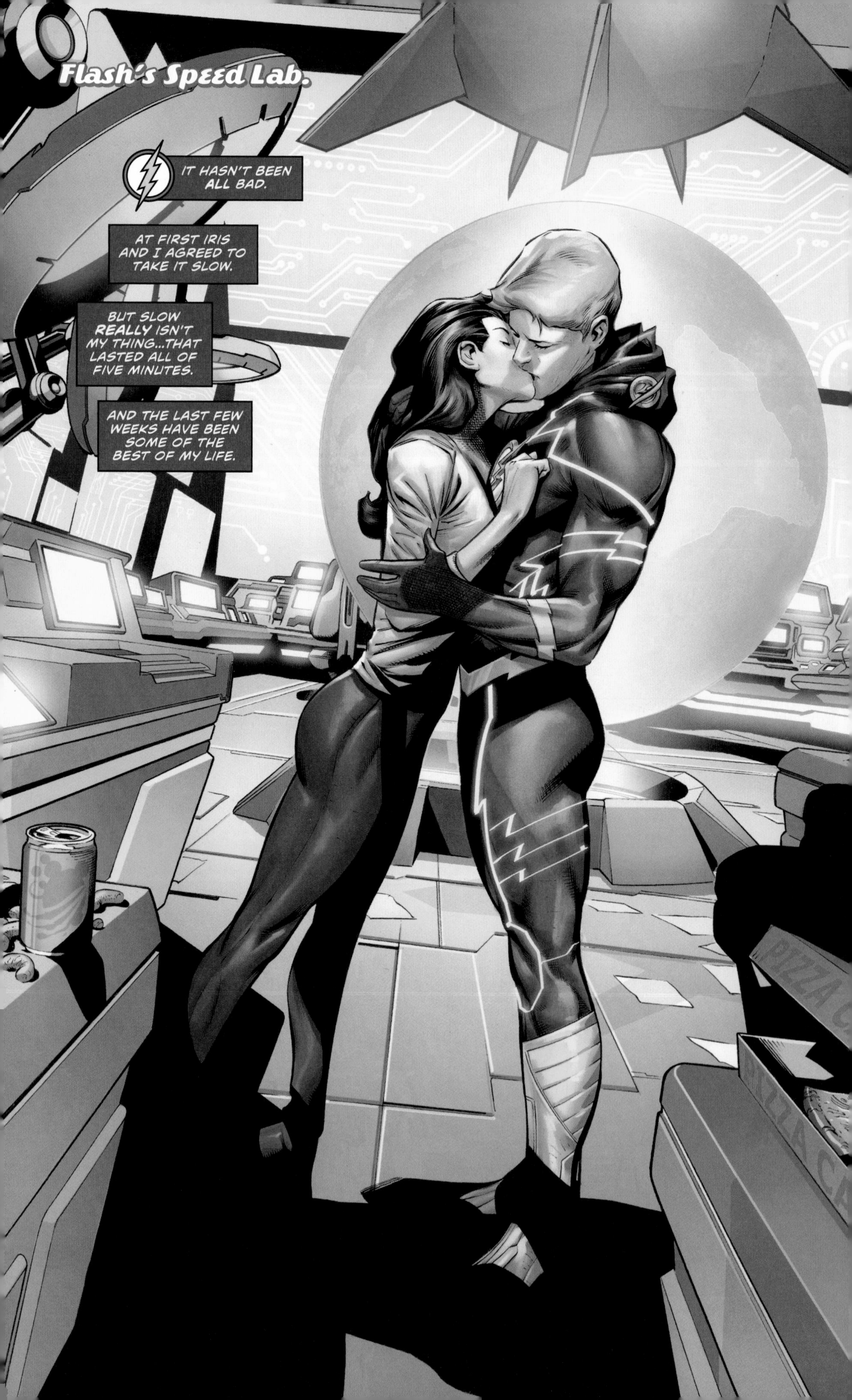
Flash's Speed Lab.
IT HASN'T BEEN ALL BAD.
AT FIRST IRIS AND I AGREED TO TAKE IT SLOW.
BUT SLOW REALLY ISN'T MY THING...THAT LASTED ALL OF FIVE MINUTES.
AND THE LAST FEW WEEKS HAVE BEEN SOME OF THE BEST OF MY LIFE.

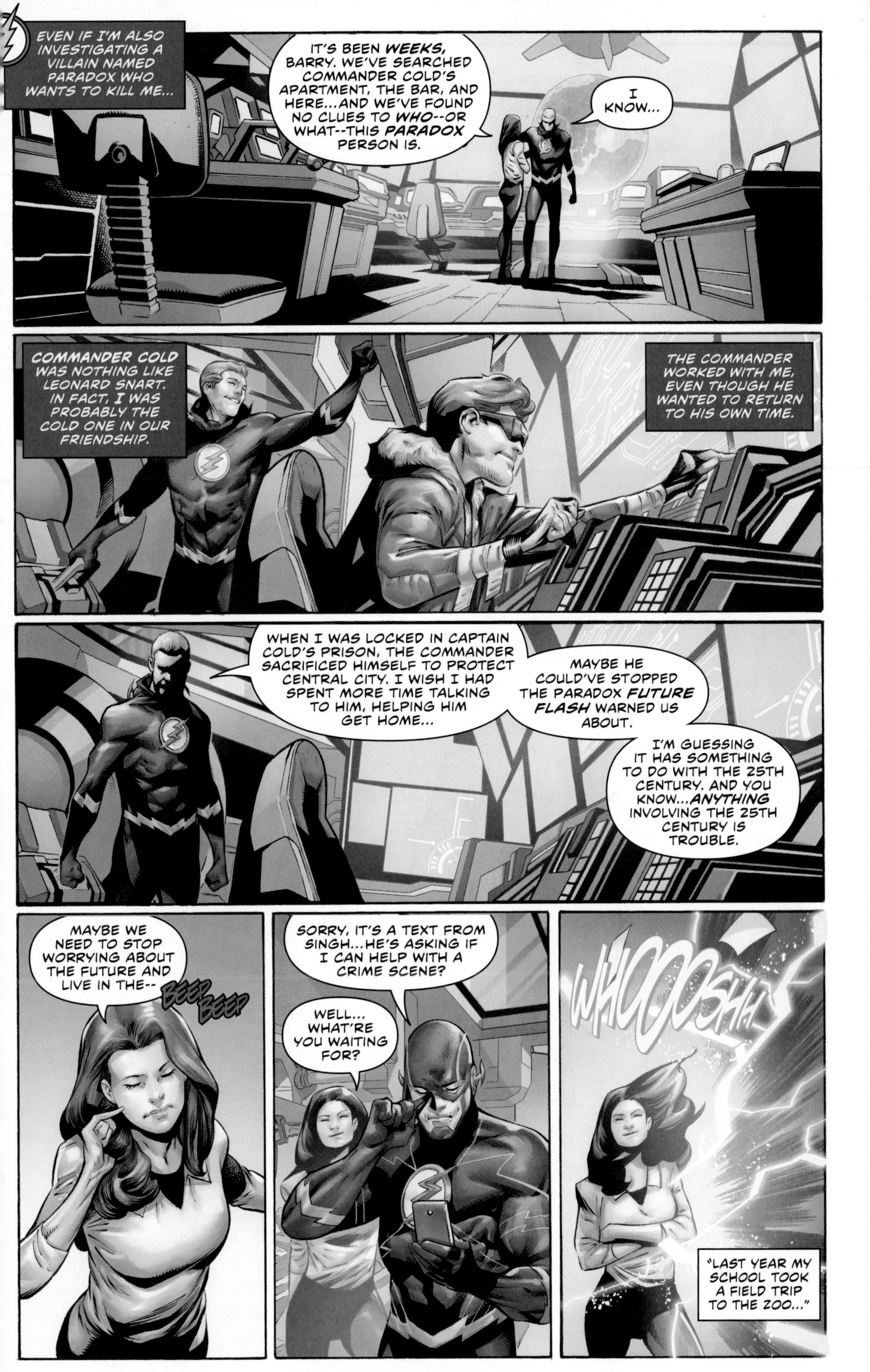
EVEN IF I'M ALSO INVESTIGATING A VILLAIN NAMED PARADOX WHO WANTS TO KILL ME...
IT'S BEEN WEEKS, BARRY. WE'VE SEARCHED COMMANDER COLD'S APARTMENT, THE BAR, AND HERE...AND WE'VE FOUND NO CLUES TO WHO--OR WHAT--THIS PARADOX PERSON IS.
I KNOW...
COMMANDER COLD WAS NOTHING LIKE LEONARD SNART. IN FACT, I WAS PROBABLY THE COLD ONE IN OUR FRIENDSHIP.
THE COMMANDER WORKED WITH ME, EVEN THOUGH HE WANTED TO RETURN TO HIS OWN TIME.
WHEN I WAS LOCKED IN CAPTAIN COLD'S PRISON, THE COMMANDER SACRIFICED HIMSELF TO PROTECT CENTRAL CITY. I WISH I HAD SPENT MORE TIME TALKING TO HIM, HELPING HIM GET HOME...
MAYBE HE COULD'VE STOPPED THE PARADOX FUTURE FLASH WARNED US ABOUT.
I'M GUESSING IT HAS SOMETHING TO DO WITH THE 25TH CENTURY. AND YOU KNOW...ANYTHING INVOLVING THE 25TH CENTURY IS TROUBLE.
MAYBE WE NEED TO STOP WORRYING ABOUT THE FUTURE AND LIVE IN THE--
BEEP BEEP
SORRY, IT'S A TEXT FROM SINGH...HE'S ASKING IF I CAN HELP WITH A CRIME SCENE?
WELL... WHAT'RE YOU WAITING FOR?
WHOOOSHH
"LAST YEAR MY SCHOOL TOOK A FIELD TRIP TO THE ZOO..."

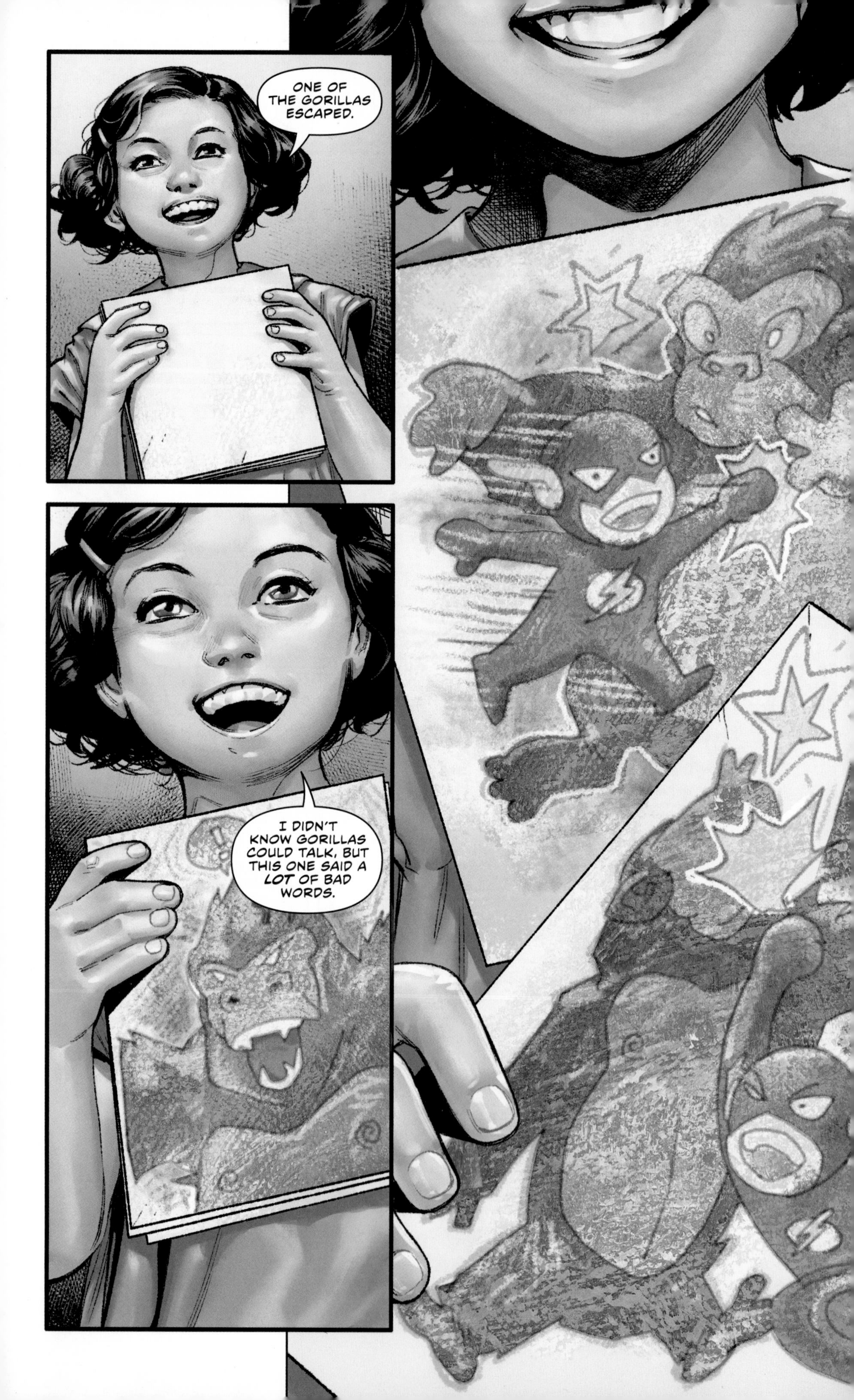
ONE OF THE GORILLAS ESCAPED.
I DIDN'T KNOW GORILLAS COULD TALK, BUT THIS ONE SAID A *LOT* OF BAD WORDS.

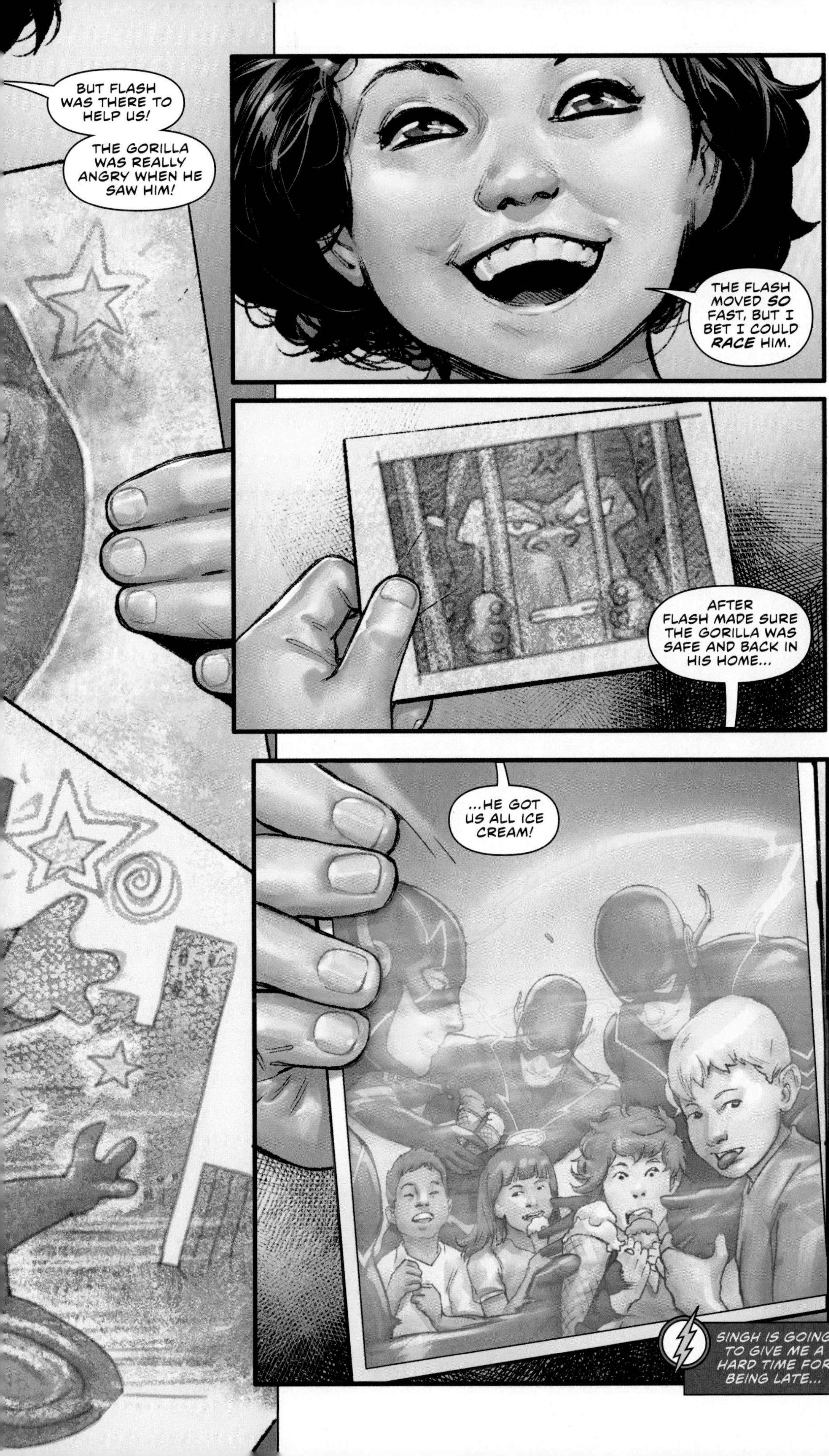

BUT FLASH WAS THERE TO HELP US!
THE GORILLA WAS REALLY ANGRY WHEN HE SAW HIM!
THE FLASH MOVED *SO* FAST, BUT I BET I COULD *RACE* HIM.
AFTER FLASH MADE SURE THE GORILLA WAS SAFE AND BACK IN HIS HOME...
...HE GOT US ALL ICE CREAM!
SINGH IS GOING TO GIVE ME A HARD TIME FOR BEING LATE...

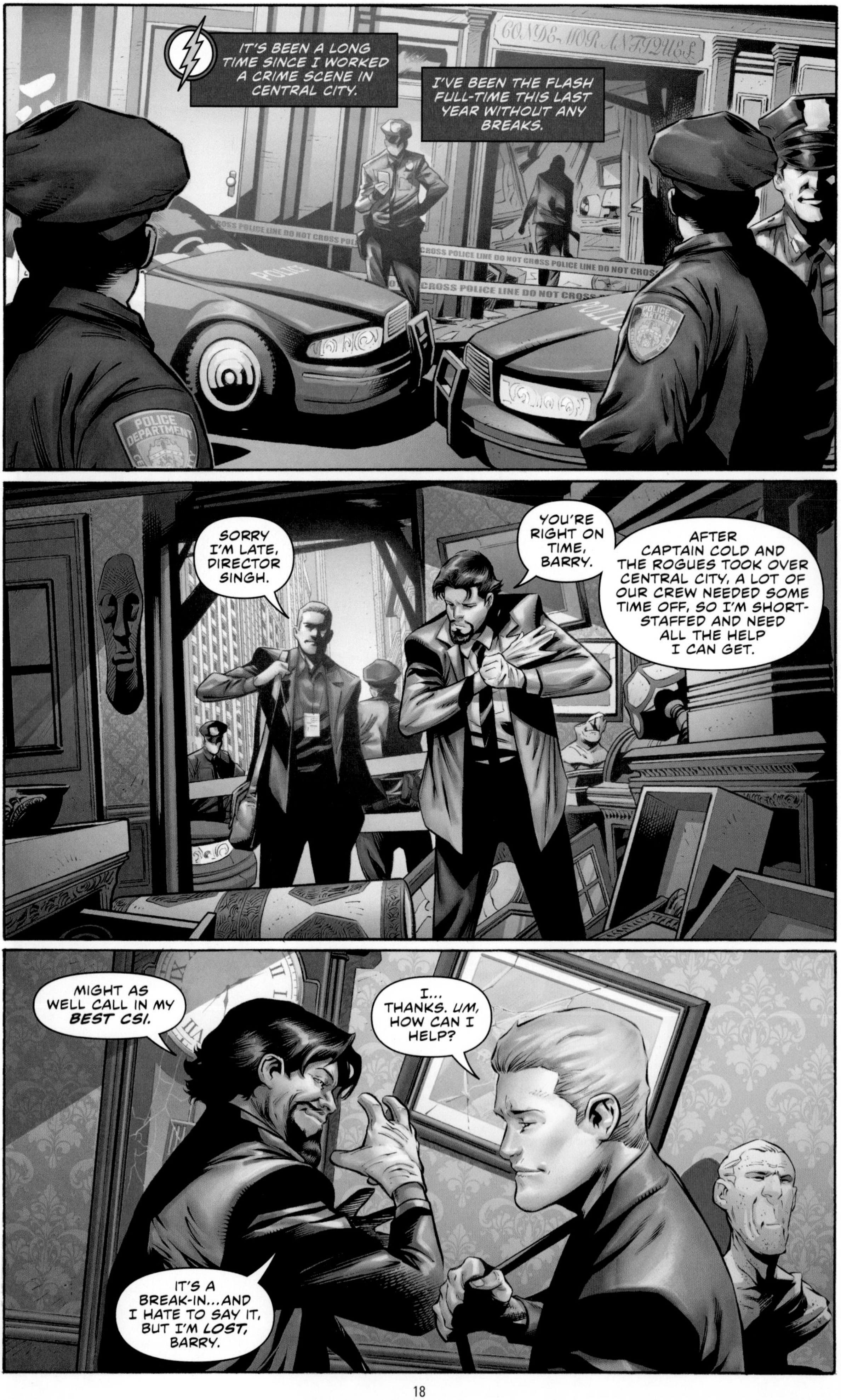
IT'S BEEN A LONG TIME SINCE I WORKED A CRIME SCENE IN CENTRAL CITY.
I'VE BEEN THE FLASH FULL-TIME THIS LAST YEAR WITHOUT ANY BREAKS.
SORRY I'M LATE, DIRECTOR SINGH.
YOU'RE RIGHT ON TIME, BARRY.
AFTER CAPTAIN COLD AND THE ROGUES TOOK OVER CENTRAL CITY, A LOT OF OUR CREW NEEDED SOME TIME OFF, SO I'M SHORT-STAFFED AND NEED ALL THE HELP I CAN GET.
MIGHT AS WELL CALL IN MY *BEST CSI*.
I... THANKS. *UM,* HOW CAN I HELP?
IT'S A BREAK-IN...AND I HATE TO SAY IT, BUT I'M *LOST,* BARRY.

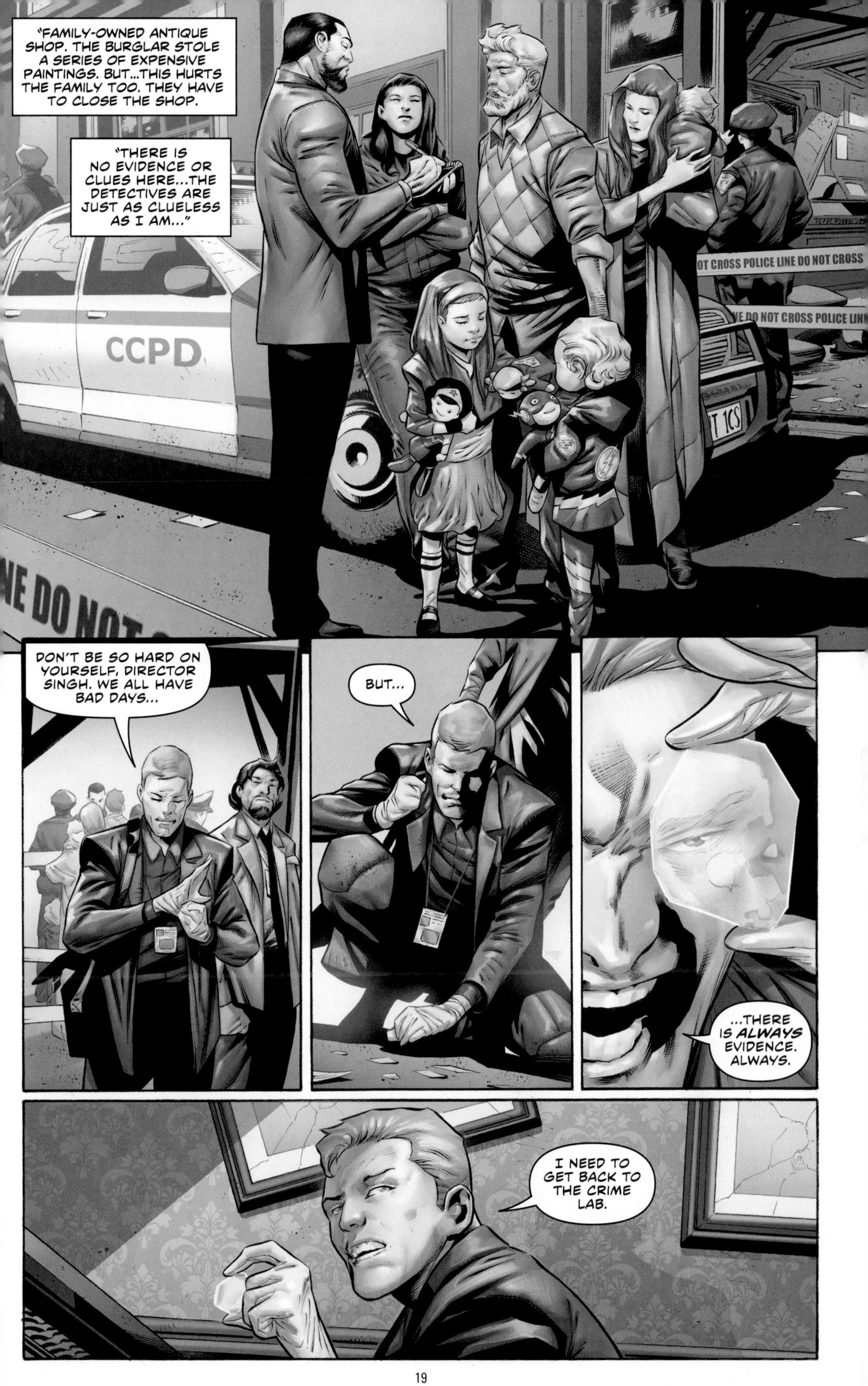
"FAMILY-OWNED ANTIQUE SHOP. THE BURGLAR STOLE A SERIES OF EXPENSIVE PAINTINGS. BUT...THIS HURTS THE FAMILY TOO. THEY HAVE TO CLOSE THE SHOP.
"THERE IS NO EVIDENCE OR CLUES HERE...THE DETECTIVES ARE JUST AS CLUELESS AS I AM..."
CCPD
OT CROSS POLICE LINE DO NOT CROSS
NE DO NOT CROSS POLICE LINE
DON'T BE SO HARD ON YOURSELF, DIRECTOR SINGH. WE ALL HAVE BAD DAYS...
BUT...
...THERE IS *ALWAYS* EVIDENCE. ALWAYS.
I NEED TO GET BACK TO THE CRIME LAB.

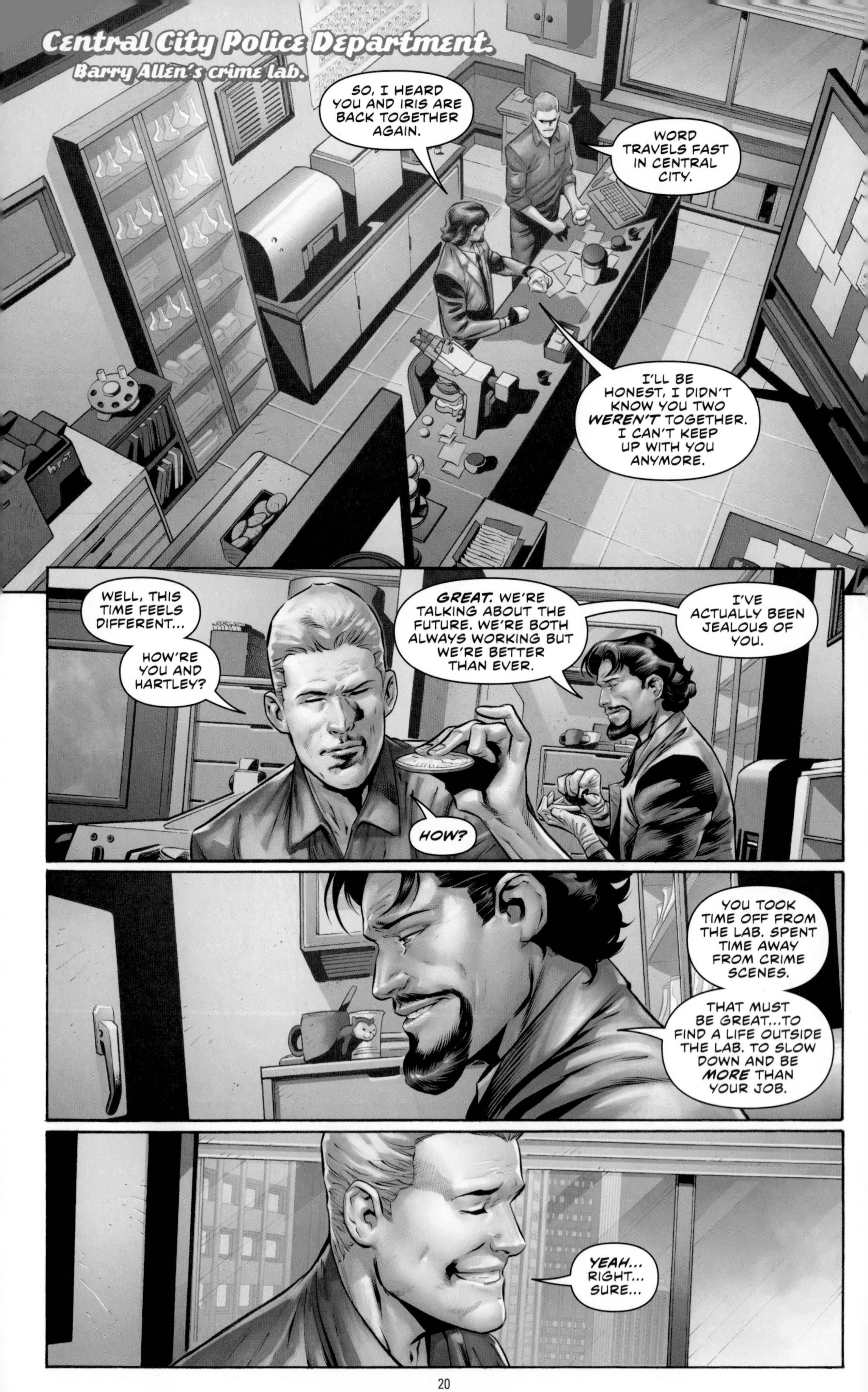
Central City Police Department.
Barry Allen's crime lab.
SO, I HEARD YOU AND IRIS ARE BACK TOGETHER AGAIN.
WORD TRAVELS FAST IN CENTRAL CITY.
I'LL BE HONEST, I DIDN'T KNOW YOU TWO *WEREN'T* TOGETHER. I CAN'T KEEP UP WITH YOU ANYMORE.
WELL, THIS TIME FEELS DIFFERENT...
HOW'RE YOU AND HARTLEY?
GREAT. WE'RE TALKING ABOUT THE FUTURE. WE'RE BOTH ALWAYS WORKING BUT WE'RE BETTER THAN EVER.
I'VE ACTUALLY BEEN JEALOUS OF YOU.
HOW?
YOU TOOK TIME OFF FROM THE LAB. SPENT TIME AWAY FROM CRIME SCENES.
THAT MUST BE GREAT...TO FIND A LIFE OUTSIDE THE LAB. TO SLOW DOWN AND BE *MORE* THAN YOUR JOB.
YEAH... RIGHT... SURE...

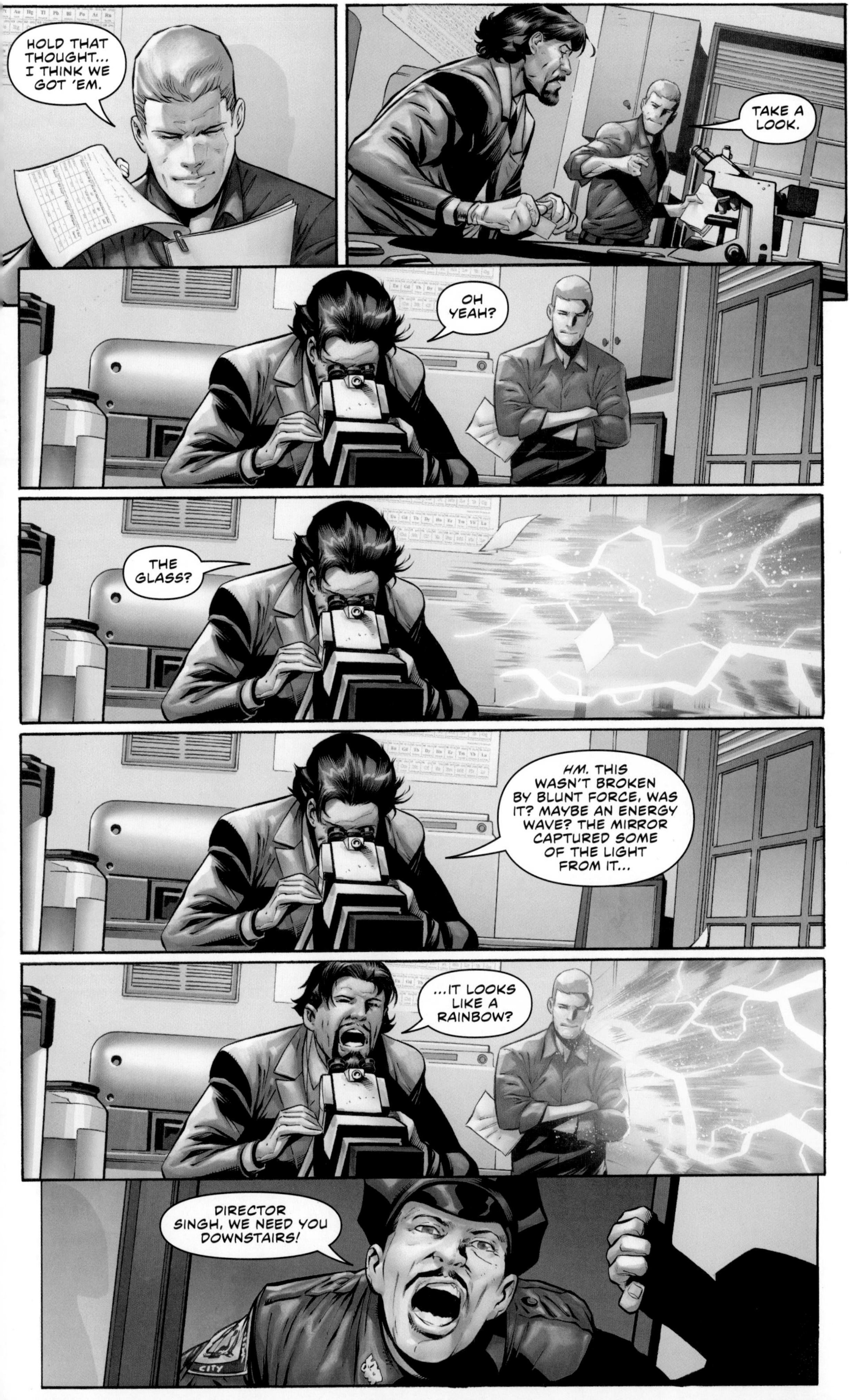
HOLD THAT THOUGHT... I THINK WE GOT 'EM.
TAKE A LOOK.
OH YEAH?
THE GLASS?
HM. THIS WASN'T BROKEN BY BLUNT FORCE, WAS IT? MAYBE AN ENERGY WAVE? THE MIRROR CAPTURED SOME OF THE LIGHT FROM IT...
...IT LOOKS LIKE A RAINBOW?
DIRECTOR SINGH, WE NEED YOU DOWNSTAIRS!

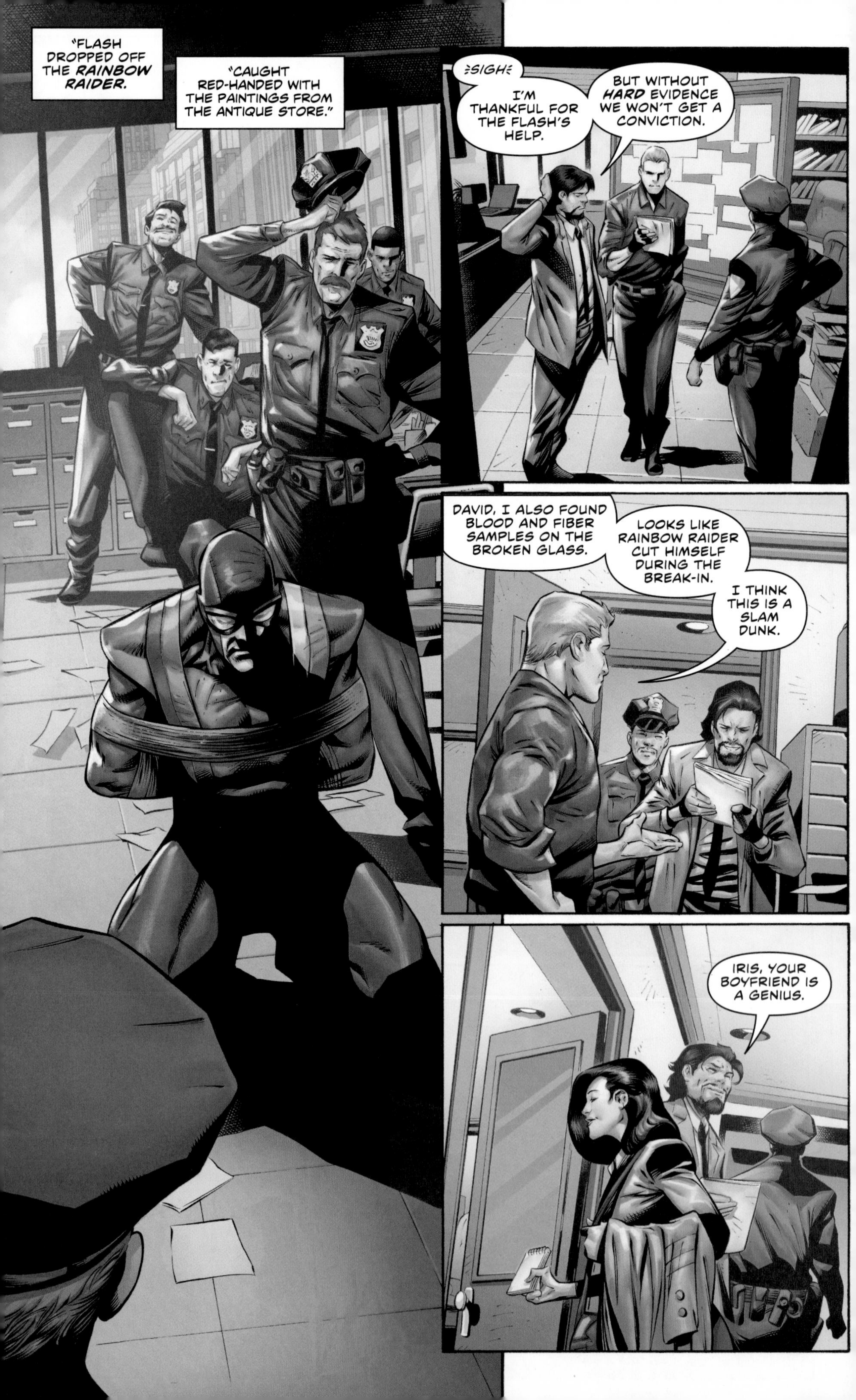
"FLASH DROPPED OFF THE *RAINBOW RAIDER.*
"CAUGHT RED-HANDED WITH THE PAINTINGS FROM THE ANTIQUE STORE."
SIGH
I'M THANKFUL FOR THE FLASH'S HELP.
BUT WITHOUT *HARD* EVIDENCE WE WON'T GET A CONVICTION.
DAVID, I ALSO FOUND BLOOD AND FIBER SAMPLES ON THE BROKEN GLASS.
LOOKS LIKE RAINBOW RAIDER CUT HIMSELF DURING THE BREAK-IN.
I THINK THIS IS A SLAM DUNK.
IRIS, YOUR BOYFRIEND IS A GENIUS.

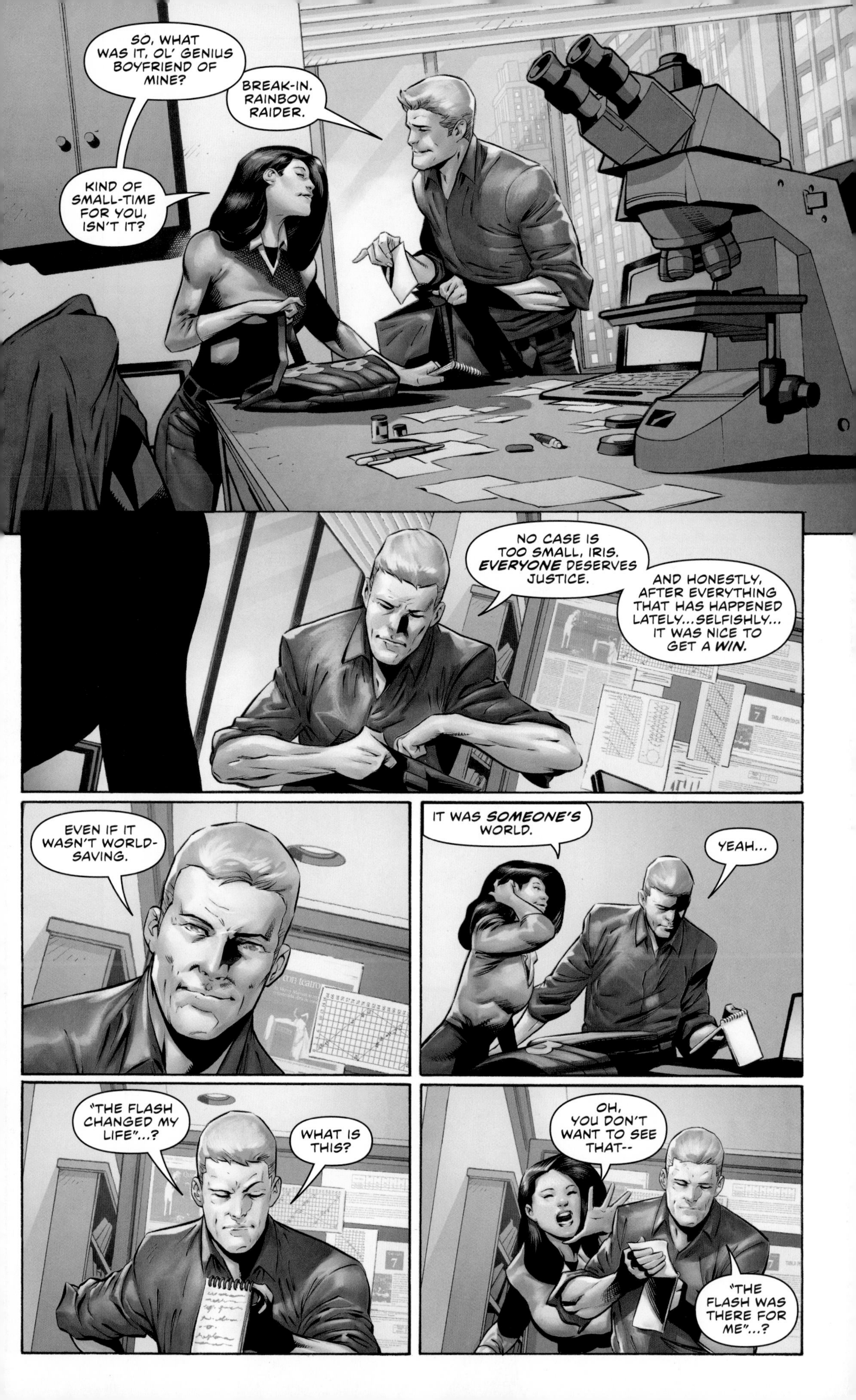
SO, WHAT WAS IT, OL' GENIUS BOYFRIEND OF MINE?
BREAK-IN. RAINBOW RAIDER.
KIND OF SMALL-TIME FOR YOU, ISN'T IT?
NO CASE IS TOO SMALL, IRIS. *EVERYONE* DESERVES JUSTICE.
AND HONESTLY, AFTER EVERYTHING THAT HAS HAPPENED LATELY...SELFISHLY... IT WAS NICE TO GET A *WIN.*
EVEN IF IT WASN'T WORLD-SAVING.
IT WAS *SOMEONE'S* WORLD.
YEAH...
"THE FLASH CHANGED MY LIFE"...?
WHAT IS THIS?
OH, YOU DON'T WANT TO SEE THAT--
"THE FLASH WAS THERE FOR ME"...?

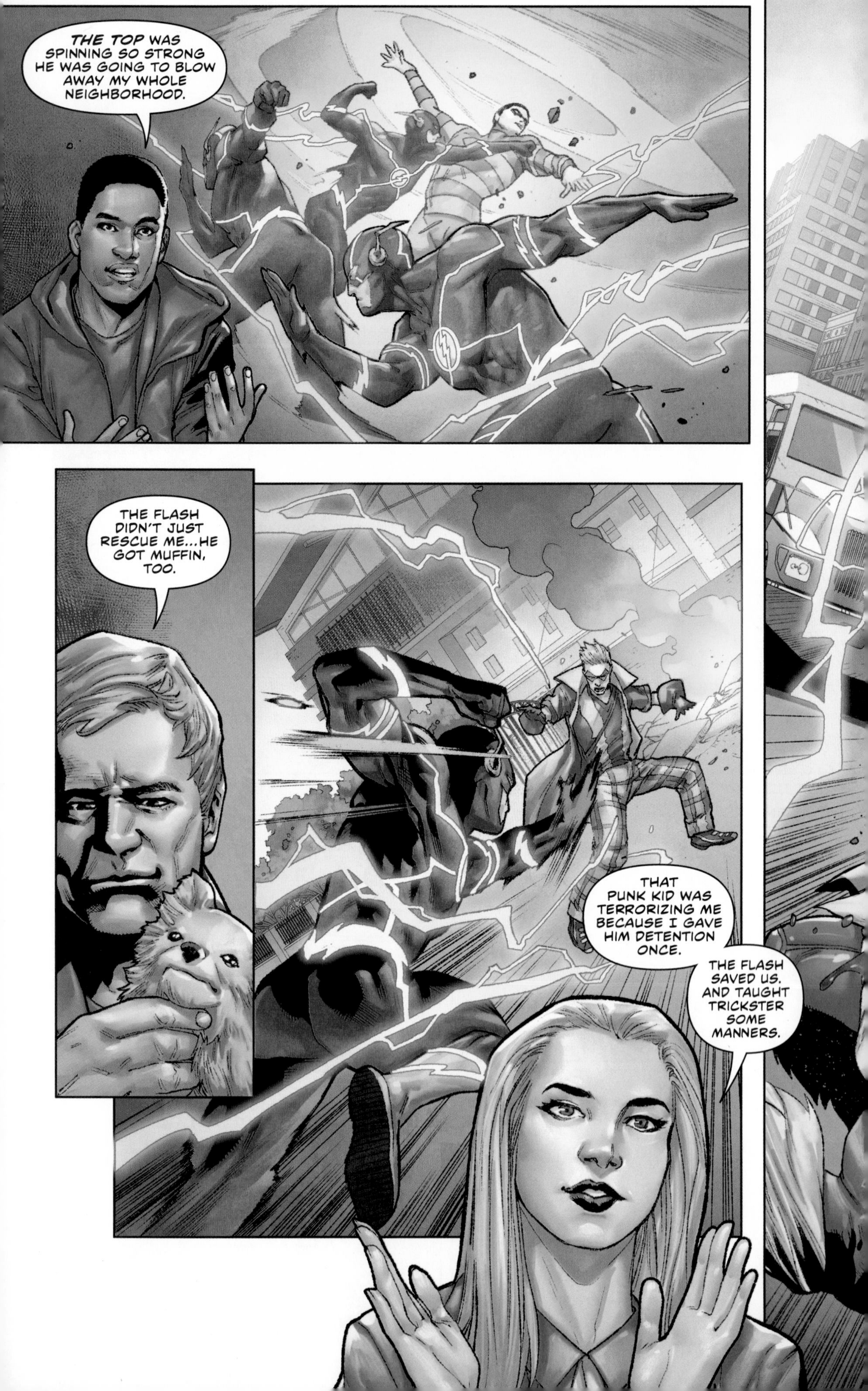

THE TOP WAS SPINNING SO STRONG HE WAS GOING TO BLOW AWAY MY WHOLE NEIGHBORHOOD.
THE FLASH DIDN'T JUST RESCUE ME...HE GOT MUFFIN, TOO.
THAT PUNK KID WAS TERRORIZING ME BECAUSE I GAVE HIM DETENTION ONCE.
THE FLASH SAVED US. AND TAUGHT TRICKSTER SOME MANNERS.

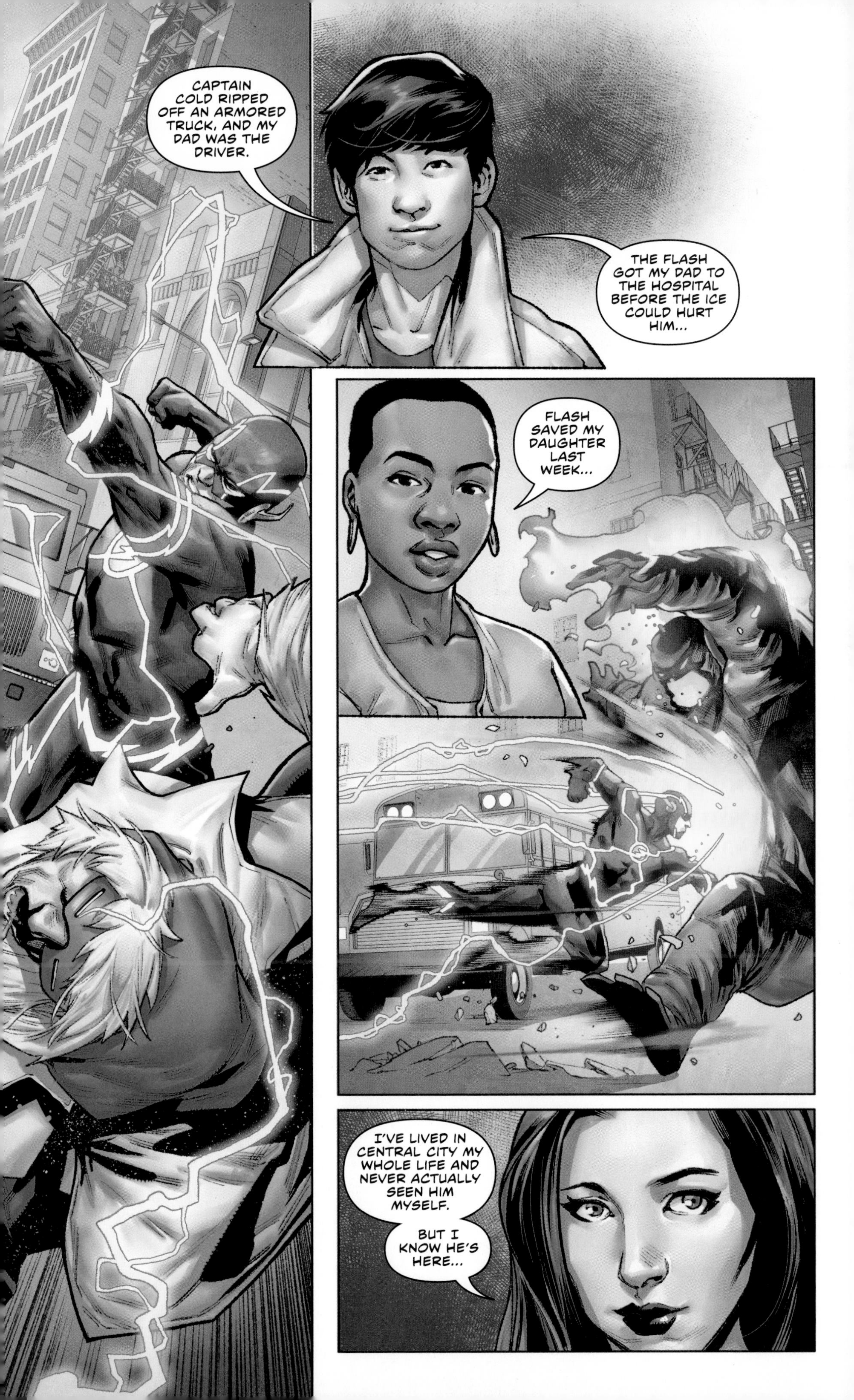
CAPTAIN COLD RIPPED OFF AN ARMORED TRUCK, AND MY DAD WAS THE DRIVER.
THE FLASH GOT MY DAD TO THE HOSPITAL BEFORE THE ICE COULD HURT HIM...
FLASH SAVED MY DAUGHTER LAST WEEK...
I'VE LIVED IN CENTRAL CITY MY WHOLE LIFE AND NEVER ACTUALLY SEEN HIM MYSELF.
BUT I KNOW HE'S HERE...

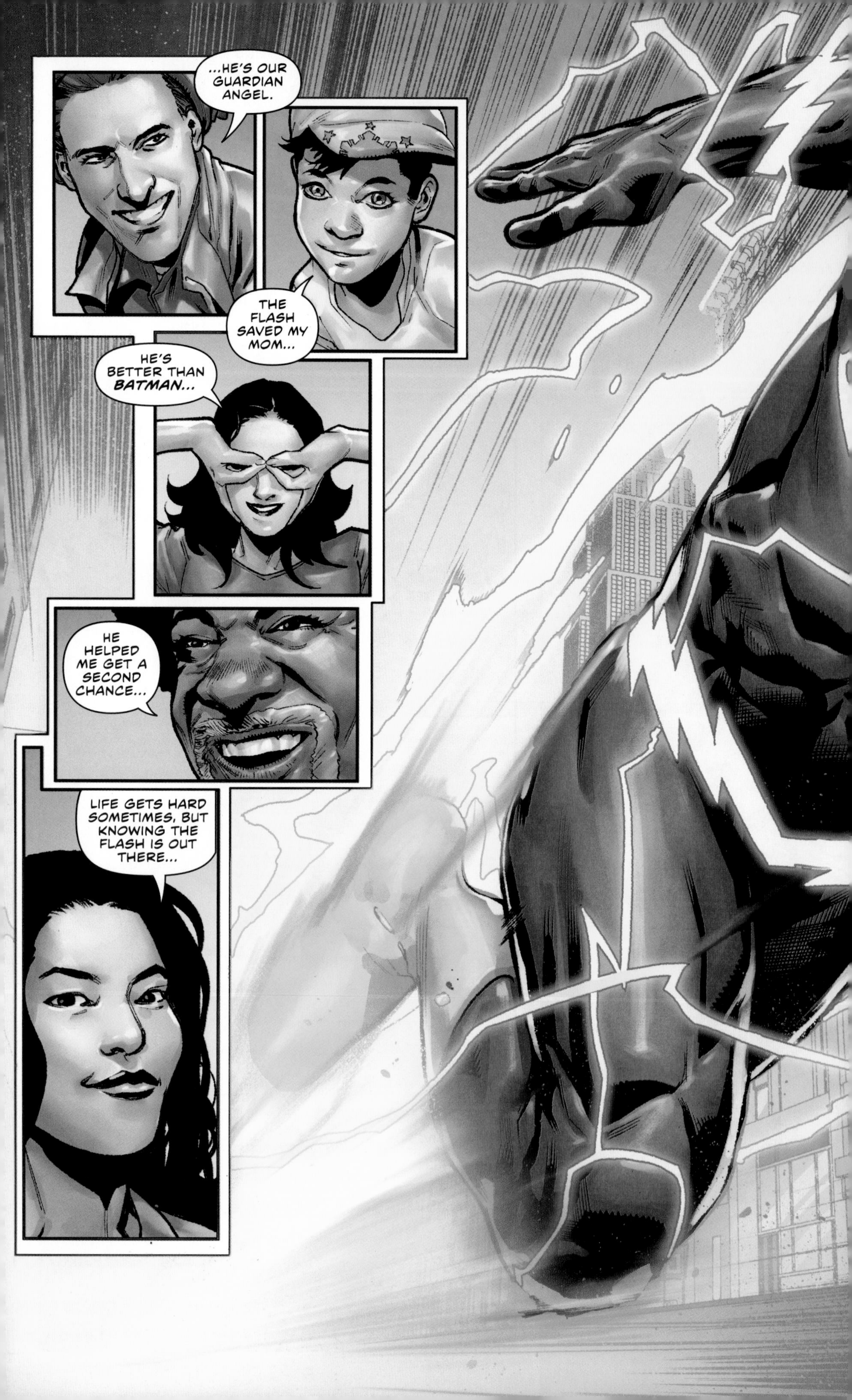
...HE'S OUR GUARDIAN ANGEL.
THE FLASH SAVED MY MOM...
HE'S BETTER THAN BATMAN...
HE HELPED ME GET A SECOND CHANCE...
LIFE GETS HARD SOMETIMES, BUT KNOWING THE FLASH IS OUT THERE...

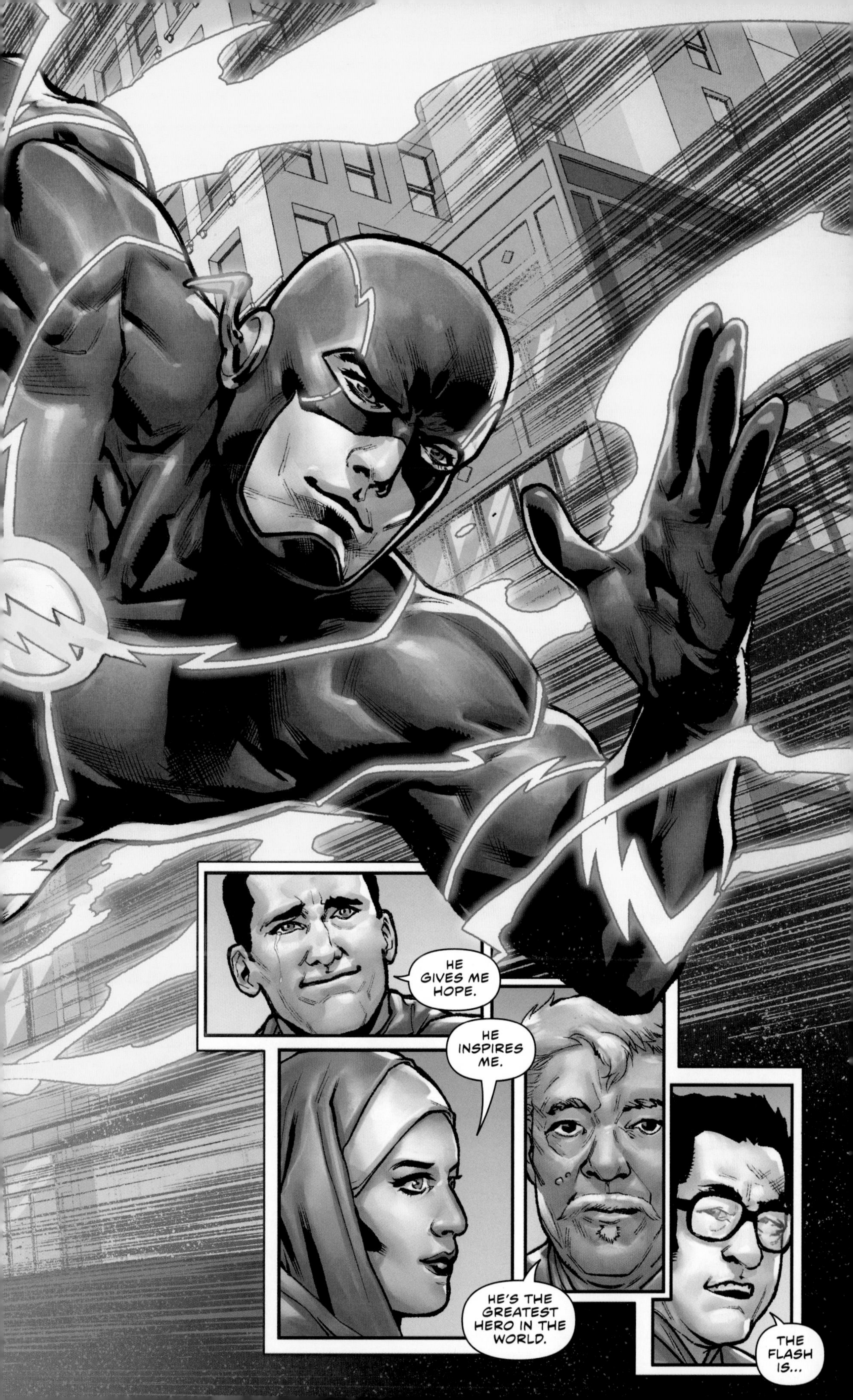
HE GIVES ME HOPE.
HE INSPIRES ME.
HE'S THE GREATEST HERO IN THE WORLD.
THE FLASH IS...

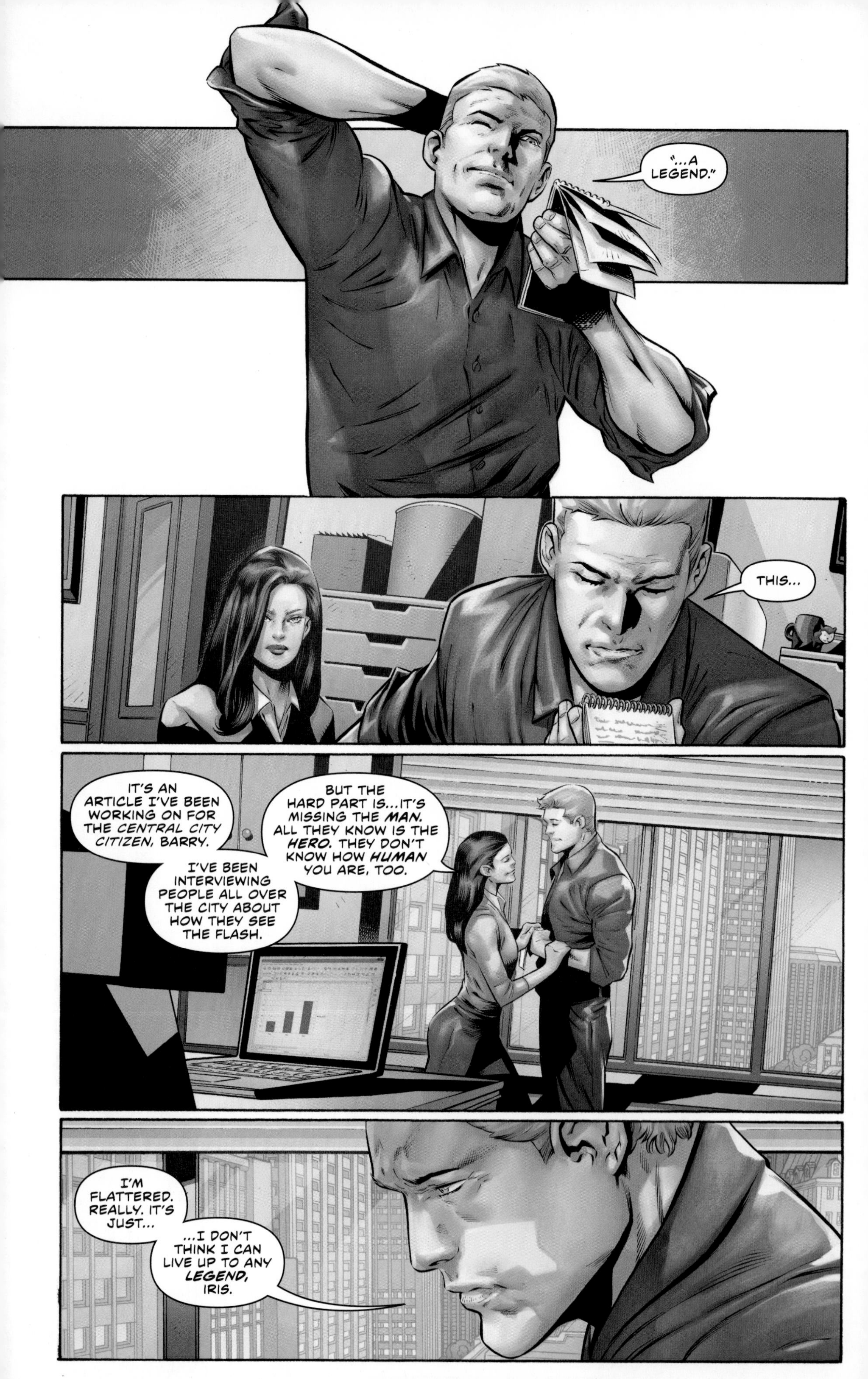
"...A LEGEND."
THIS...
IT'S AN ARTICLE I'VE BEEN WORKING ON FOR THE CENTRAL CITY CITIZEN, BARRY.
I'VE BEEN INTERVIEWING PEOPLE ALL OVER THE CITY ABOUT HOW THEY SEE THE FLASH.
BUT THE HARD PART IS...IT'S MISSING THE MAN. ALL THEY KNOW IS THE HERO. THEY DON'T KNOW HOW HUMAN YOU ARE, TOO.
I'M FLATTERED. REALLY. IT'S JUST...
...I DON'T THINK I CAN LIVE UP TO ANY LEGEND, IRIS.

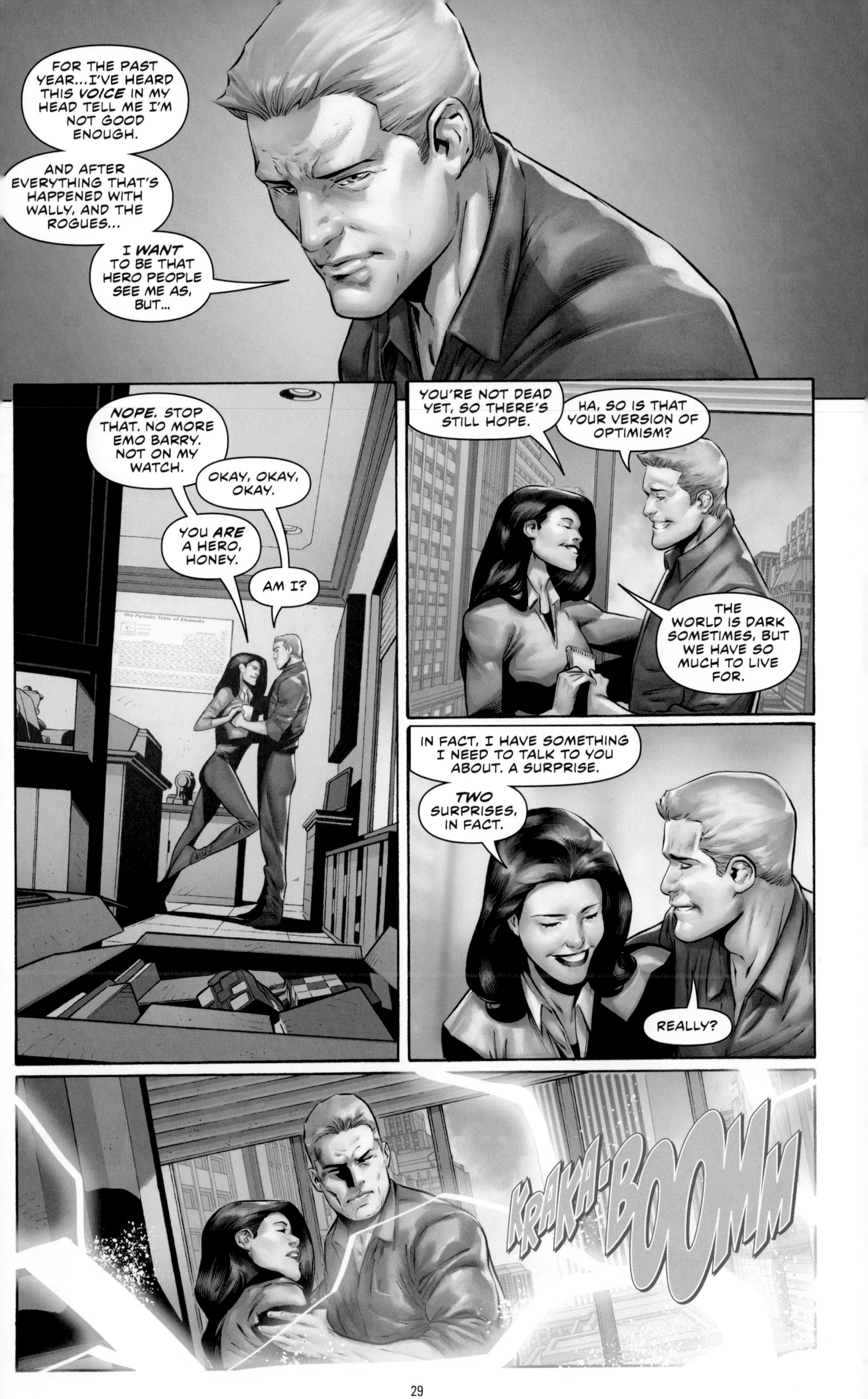
FOR THE PAST YEAR...I'VE HEARD THIS VOICE IN MY HEAD TELL ME I'M NOT GOOD ENOUGH.
AND AFTER EVERYTHING THAT'S HAPPENED WITH WALLY, AND THE ROGUES...
I WANT TO BE THAT HERO PEOPLE SEE ME AS, BUT...
NOPE. STOP THAT. NO MORE EMO BARRY. NOT ON MY WATCH.
OKAY, OKAY, OKAY.
YOU ARE A HERO, HONEY.
AM I?
The Periodic Table of Elements
YOU'RE NOT DEAD YET, SO THERE'S STILL HOPE.
HA, SO IS THAT YOUR VERSION OF OPTIMISM?
THE WORLD IS DARK SOMETIMES, BUT WE HAVE SO MUCH TO LIVE FOR.
IN FACT, I HAVE SOMETHING I NEED TO TALK TO YOU ABOUT. A SURPRISE.
TWO SURPRISES, IN FACT.
REALLY?
KRAKA-BOOMM

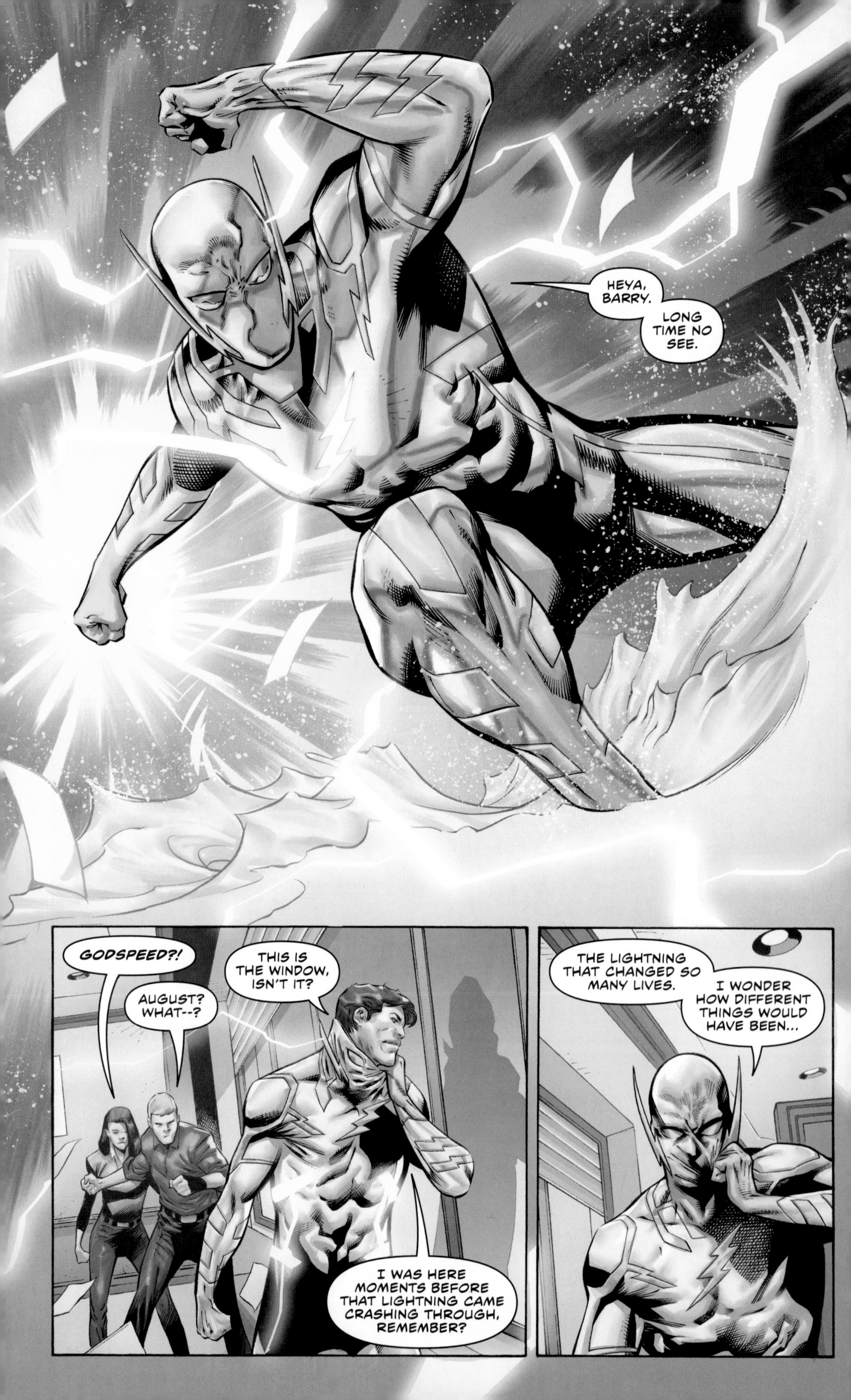
HEYA, BARRY.
LONG TIME NO SEE.
GODSPEED?!
AUGUST? WHAT--?
THIS IS THE WINDOW, ISN'T IT?
I WAS HERE MOMENTS BEFORE THAT LIGHTNING CAME CRASHING THROUGH, REMEMBER?
THE LIGHTNING THAT CHANGED SO MANY LIVES.
I WONDER HOW DIFFERENT THINGS WOULD HAVE BEEN...

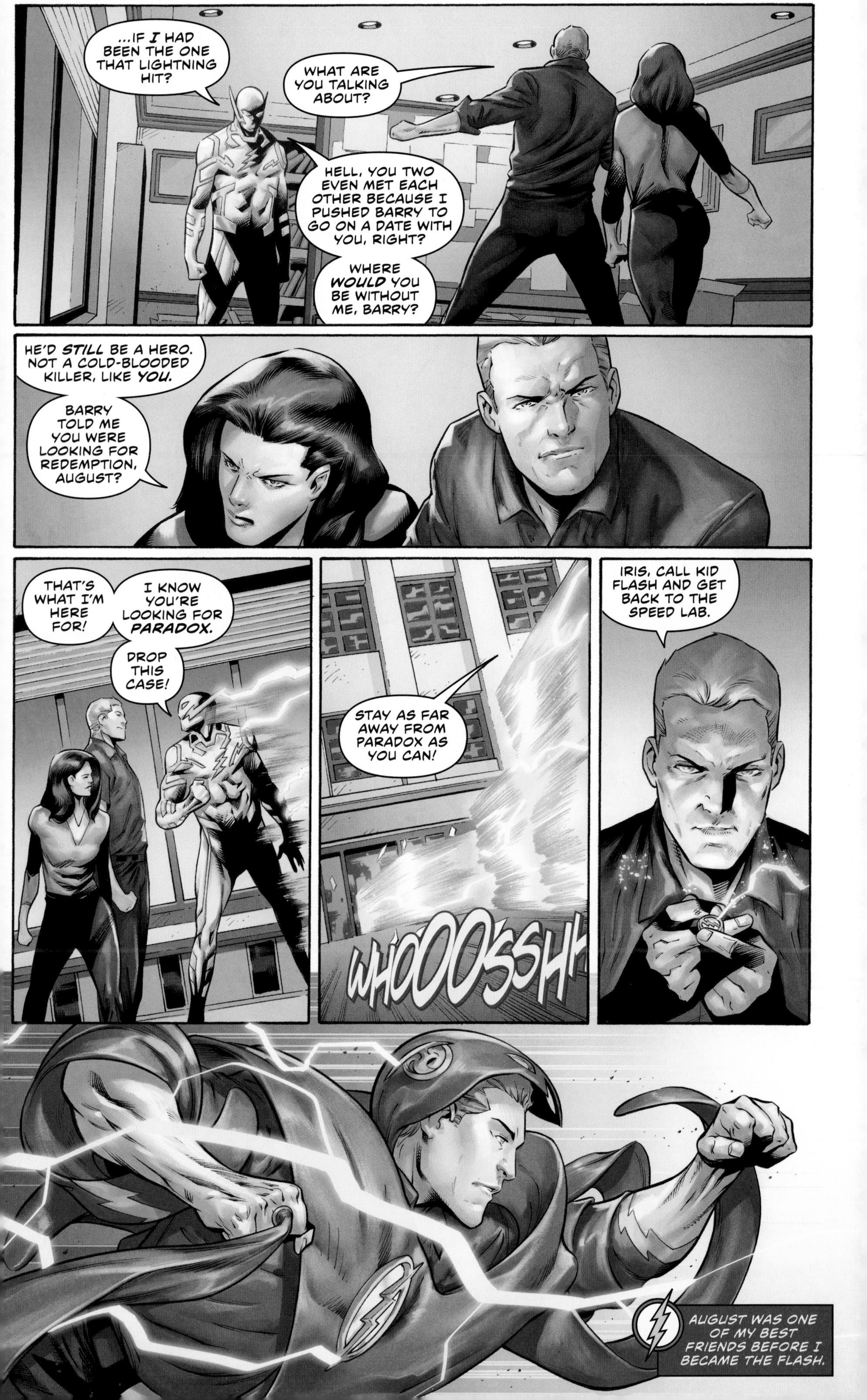
...IF I HAD BEEN THE ONE THAT LIGHTNING HIT?
WHAT ARE YOU TALKING ABOUT?
HELL, YOU TWO EVEN MET EACH OTHER BECAUSE I PUSHED BARRY TO GO ON A DATE WITH YOU, RIGHT?
WHERE WOULD YOU BE WITHOUT ME, BARRY?
HE'D STILL BE A HERO. NOT A COLD-BLOODED KILLER, LIKE YOU.
BARRY TOLD ME YOU WERE LOOKING FOR REDEMPTION, AUGUST?
THAT'S WHAT I'M HERE FOR!
I KNOW YOU'RE LOOKING FOR PARADOX.
DROP THIS CASE!
STAY AS FAR AWAY FROM PARADOX AS YOU CAN!
WHOOOOSSH
IRIS, CALL KID FLASH AND GET BACK TO THE SPEED LAB.
AUGUST WAS ONE OF MY BEST FRIENDS BEFORE I BECAME THE FLASH.

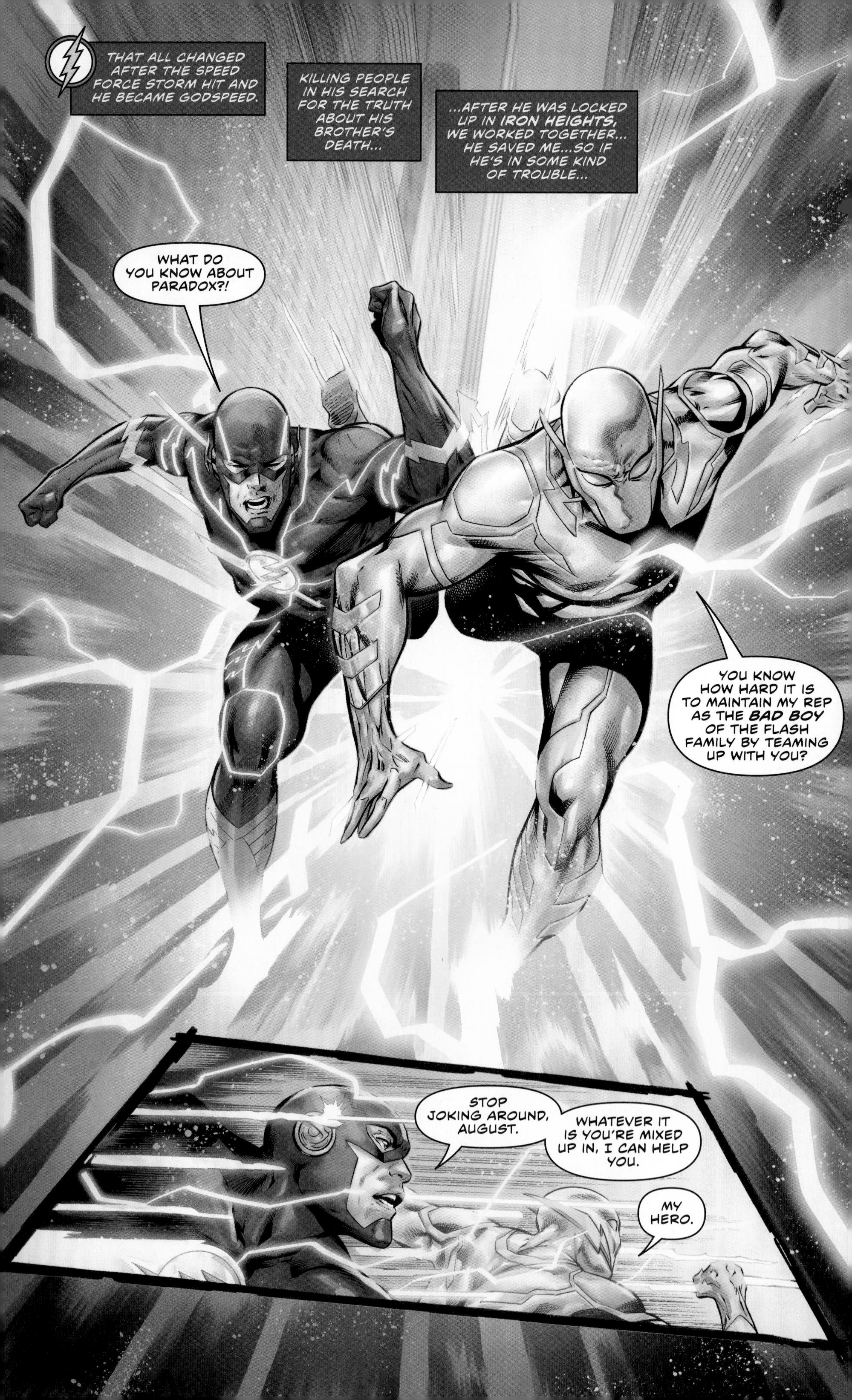
THAT ALL CHANGED AFTER THE SPEED FORCE STORM HIT AND HE BECAME GODSPEED.
KILLING PEOPLE IN HIS SEARCH FOR THE TRUTH ABOUT HIS BROTHER'S DEATH...
...AFTER HE WAS LOCKED UP IN IRON HEIGHTS, WE WORKED TOGETHER... HE SAVED ME...SO IF HE'S IN SOME KIND OF TROUBLE...
WHAT DO YOU KNOW ABOUT PARADOX?!
YOU KNOW HOW HARD IT IS TO MAINTAIN MY REP AS THE BAD BOY OF THE FLASH FAMILY BY TEAMING UP WITH YOU?
STOP JOKING AROUND, AUGUST.
WHATEVER IT IS YOU'RE MIXED UP IN, I CAN HELP YOU.
MY HERO.

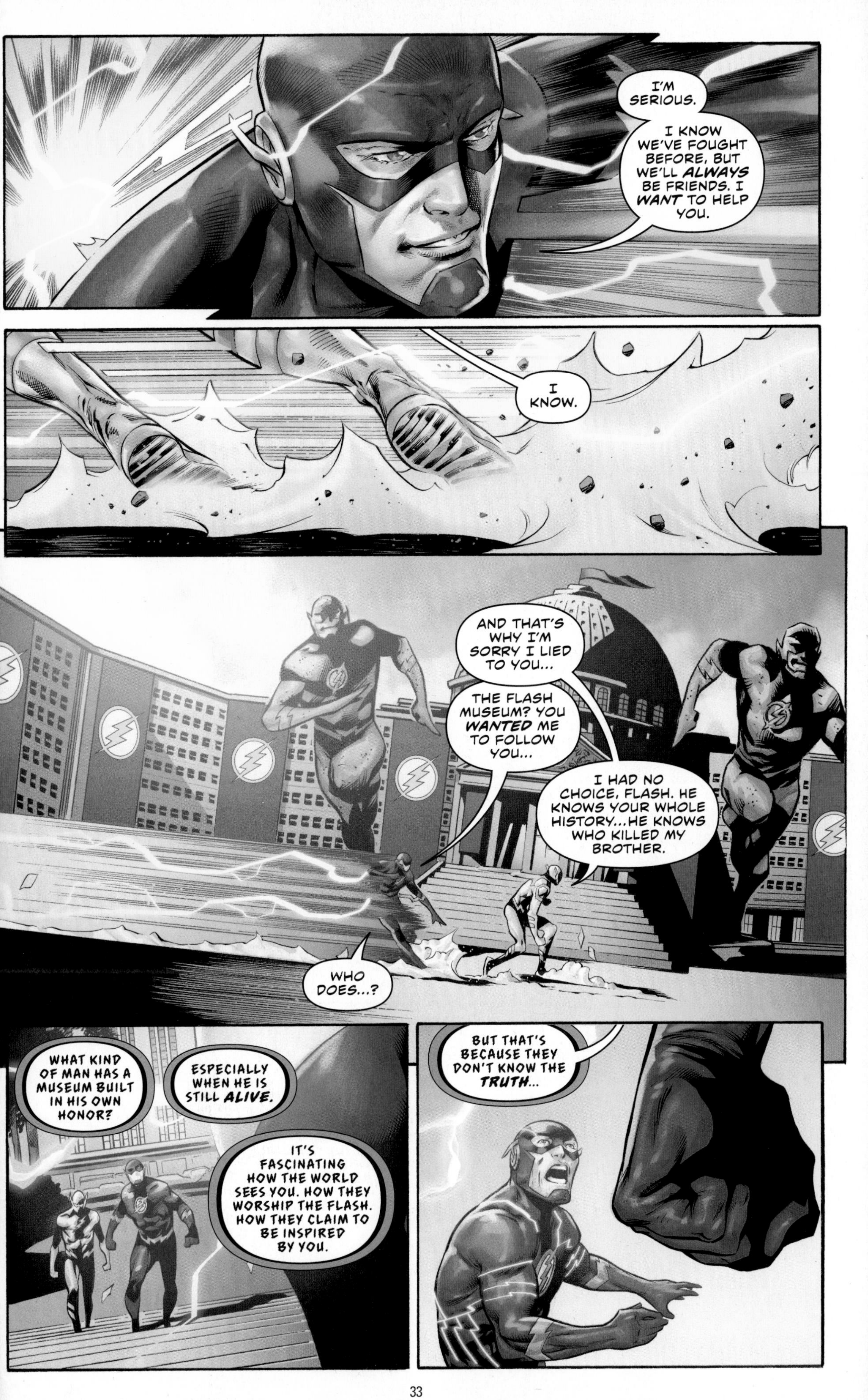
I'M SERIOUS.
I KNOW WE'VE FOUGHT BEFORE, BUT WE'LL ALWAYS BE FRIENDS. I WANT TO HELP YOU.
I KNOW.
AND THAT'S WHY I'M SORRY I LIED TO YOU...
THE FLASH MUSEUM? YOU WANTED ME TO FOLLOW YOU...
I HAD NO CHOICE, FLASH. HE KNOWS YOUR WHOLE HISTORY...HE KNOWS WHO KILLED MY BROTHER.
WHO DOES...?
WHAT KIND OF MAN HAS A MUSEUM BUILT IN HIS OWN HONOR?
ESPECIALLY WHEN HE IS STILL ALIVE.
IT'S FASCINATING HOW THE WORLD SEES YOU. HOW THEY WORSHIP THE FLASH. HOW THEY CLAIM TO BE INSPIRED BY YOU.
BUT THAT'S BECAUSE THEY DON'T KNOW THE TRUTH...

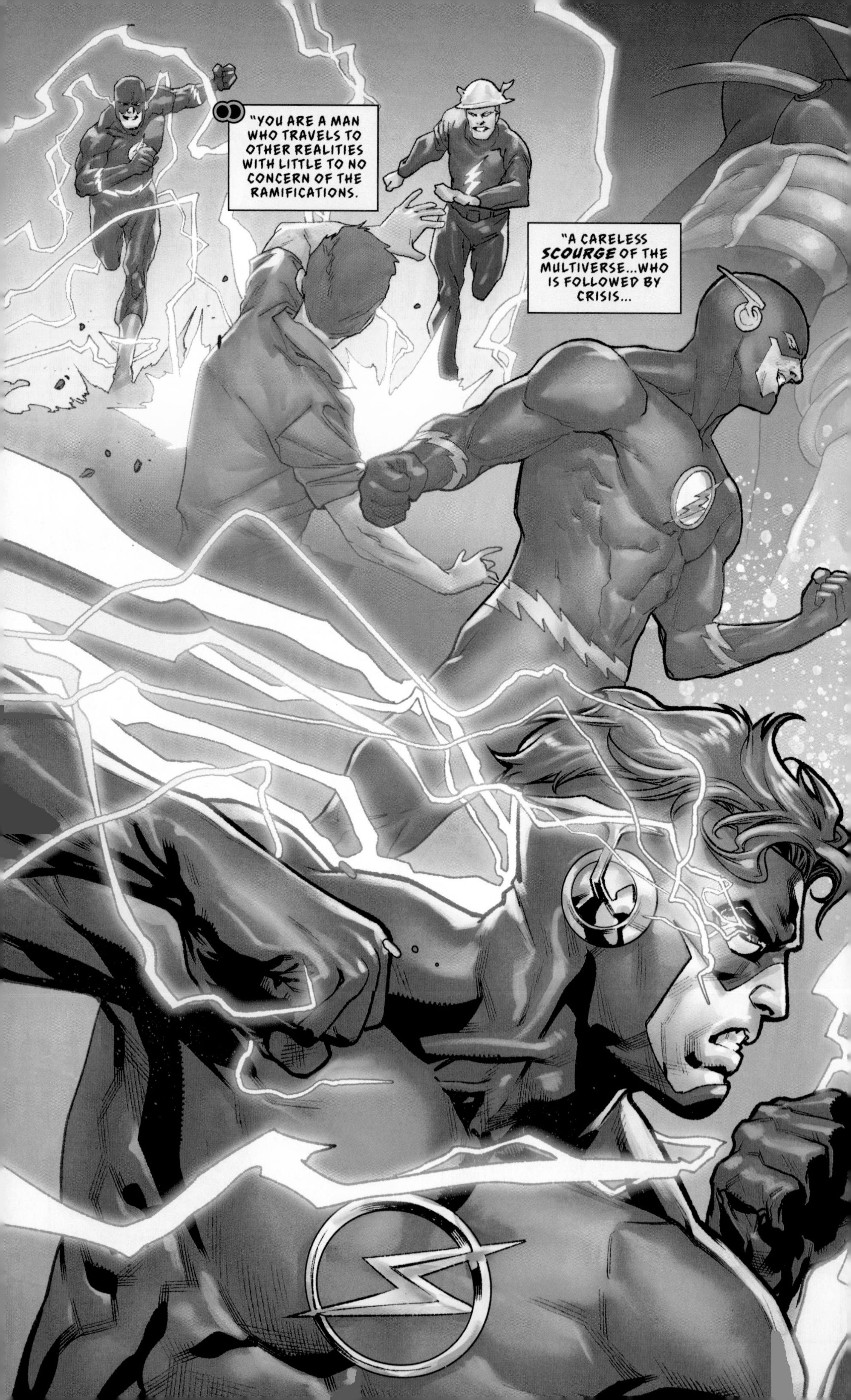
"YOU ARE A MAN WHO TRAVELS TO OTHER REALITIES WITH LITTLE TO NO CONCERN OF THE RAMIFICATIONS.
"A CARELESS SCOURGE OF THE MULTIVERSE...WHO IS FOLLOWED BY CRISIS...

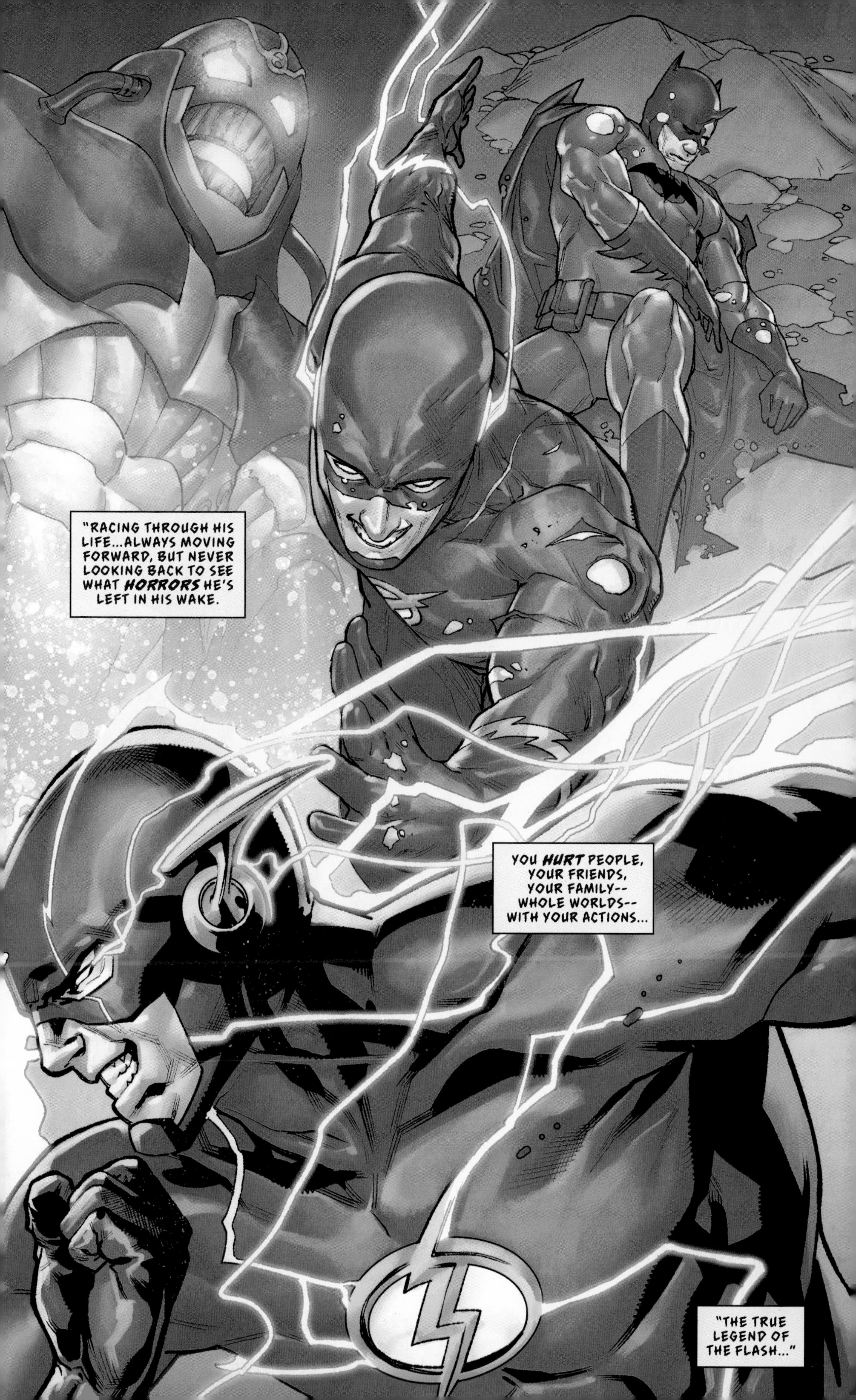
"RACING THROUGH HIS LIFE...ALWAYS MOVING FORWARD, BUT NEVER LOOKING BACK TO SEE WHAT HORRORS HE'S LEFT IN HIS WAKE.
YOU HURT PEOPLE, YOUR FRIENDS, YOUR FAMILY-- WHOLE WORLDS-- WITH YOUR ACTIONS...
"THE TRUE LEGEND OF THE FLASH..."

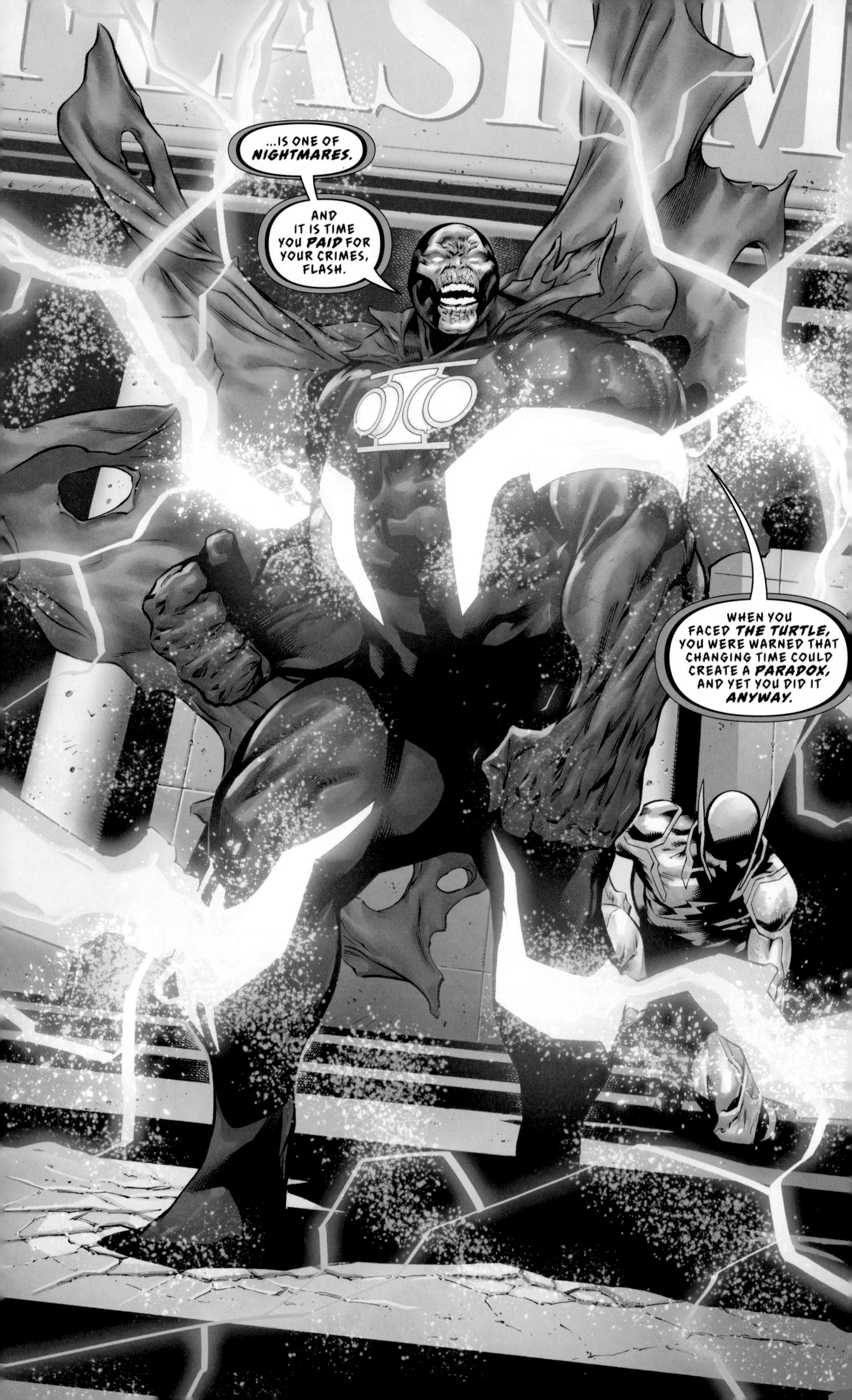
...IS ONE OF NIGHTMARES.
AND IT IS TIME YOU PAID FOR YOUR CRIMES, FLASH.
WHEN YOU FACED THE TURTLE, YOU WERE WARNED THAT CHANGING TIME COULD CREATE A PARADOX, AND YET YOU DID IT ANYWAY.

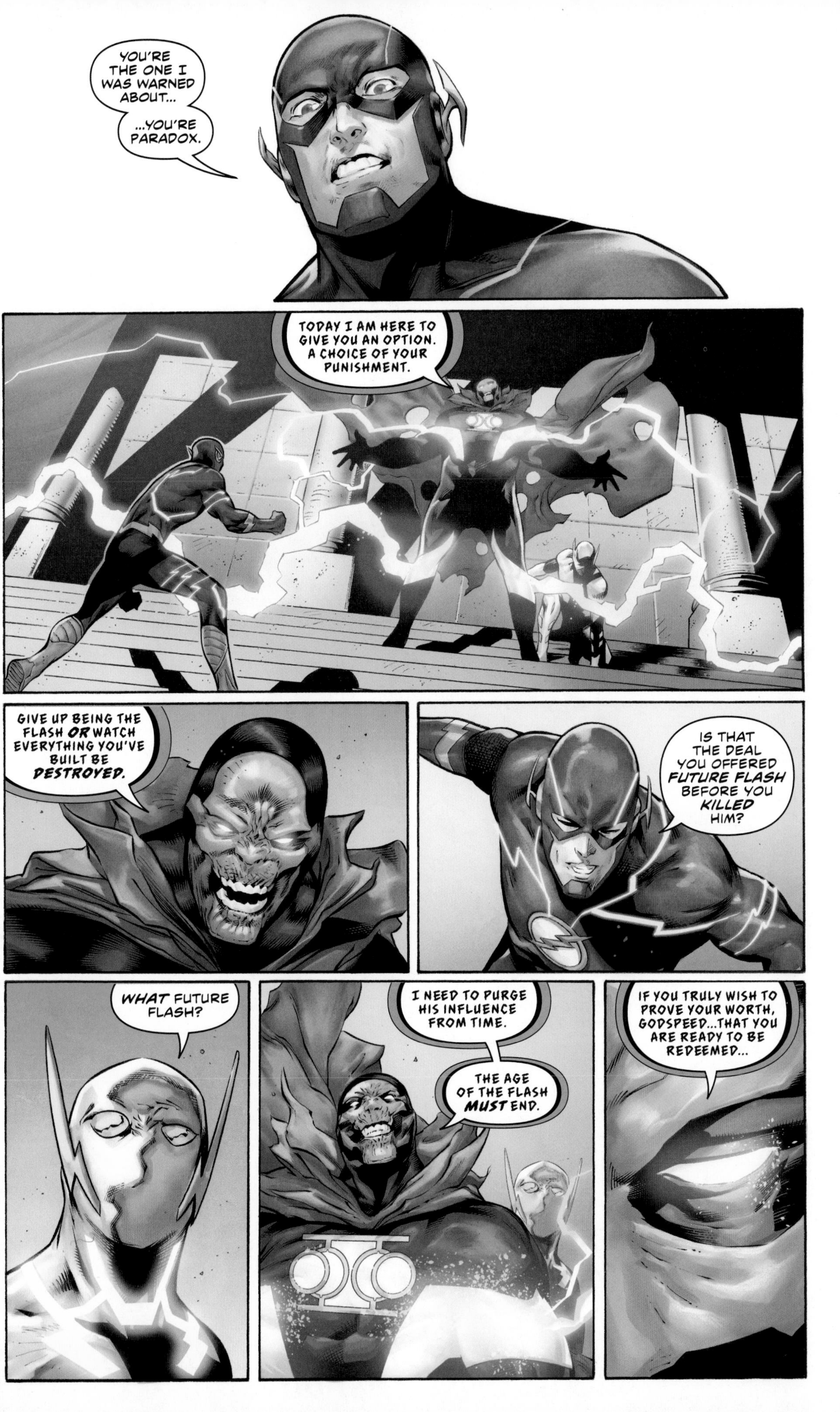

YOU'RE THE ONE I WAS WARNED ABOUT...
...YOU'RE PARADOX.
TODAY I AM HERE TO GIVE YOU AN OPTION. A CHOICE OF YOUR PUNISHMENT.
GIVE UP BEING THE FLASH OR WATCH EVERYTHING YOU'VE BUILT BE DESTROYED.
IS THAT THE DEAL YOU OFFERED FUTURE FLASH BEFORE YOU KILLED HIM?
WHAT FUTURE FLASH?
I NEED TO PURGE HIS INFLUENCE FROM TIME.
THE AGE OF THE FLASH MUST END.
IF YOU TRULY WISH TO PROVE YOUR WORTH, GODSPEED...THAT YOU ARE READY TO BE REDEEMED...

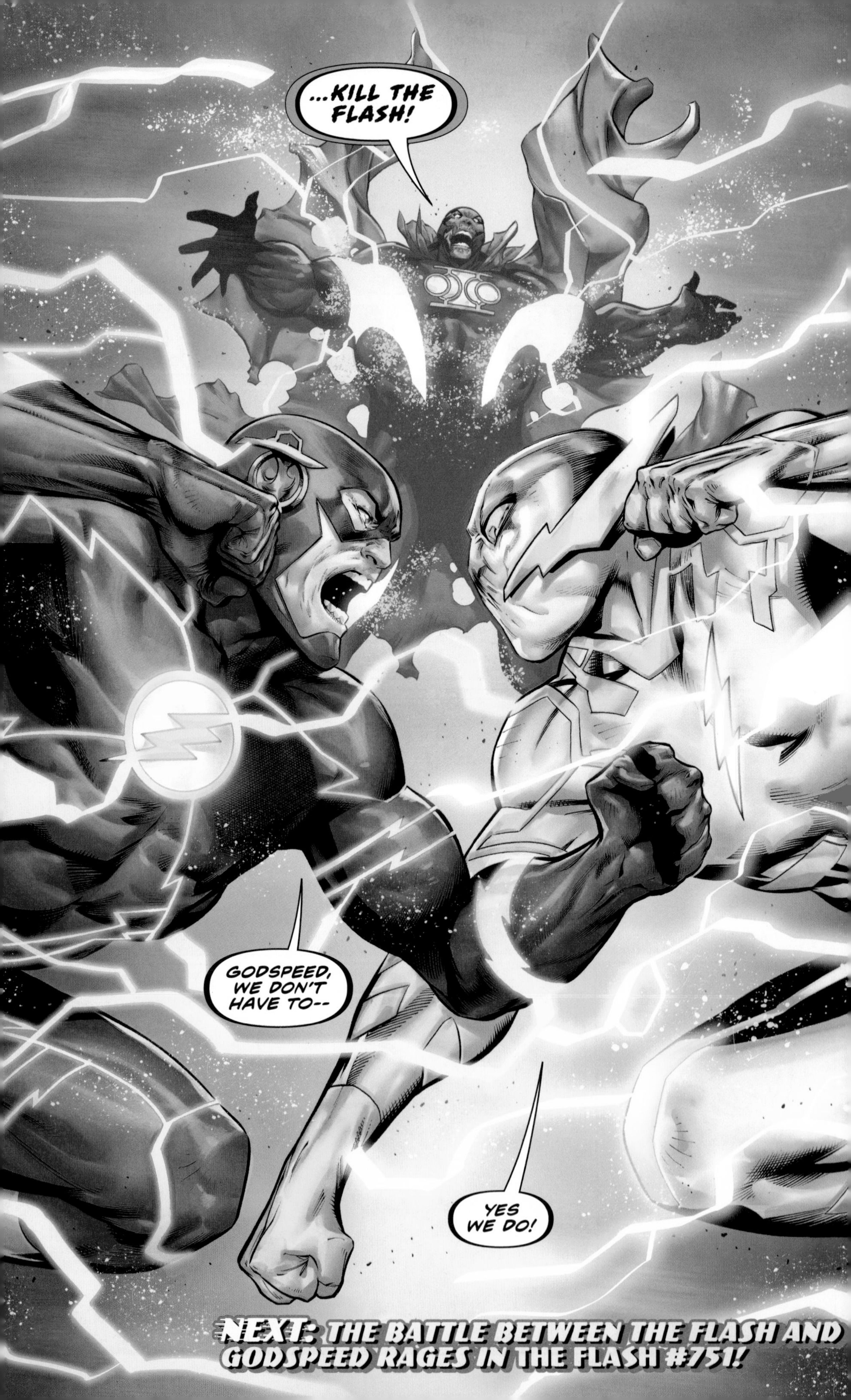
...KILL THE FLASH!
GODSPEED, WE DON'T HAVE TO--
YES WE DO!
NEXT: THE BATTLE BETWEEN THE FLASH AND GODSPEED RAGES IN THE FLASH #751!

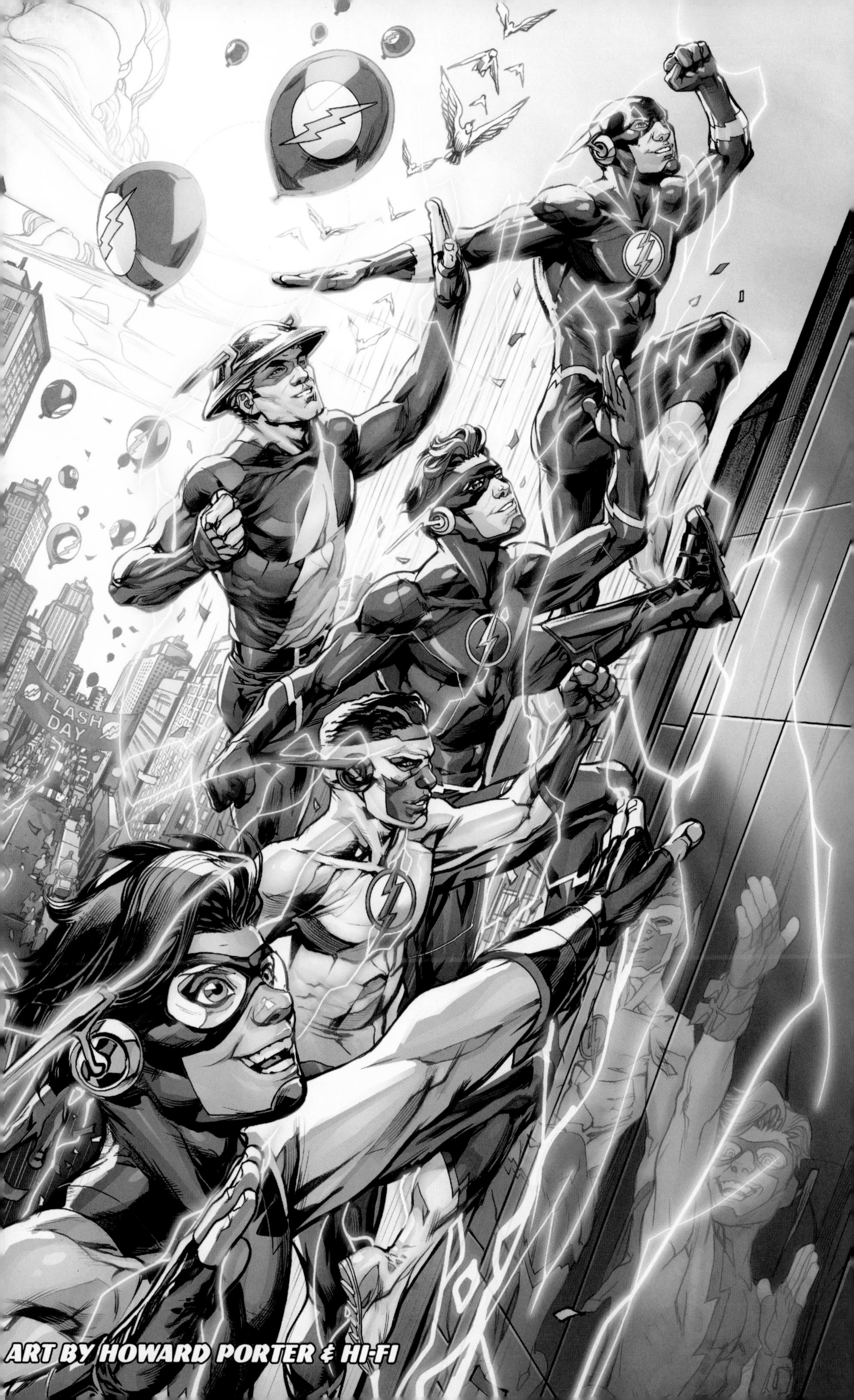
FLASH DAY

ART BY HOWARD PORTER & HI-FI

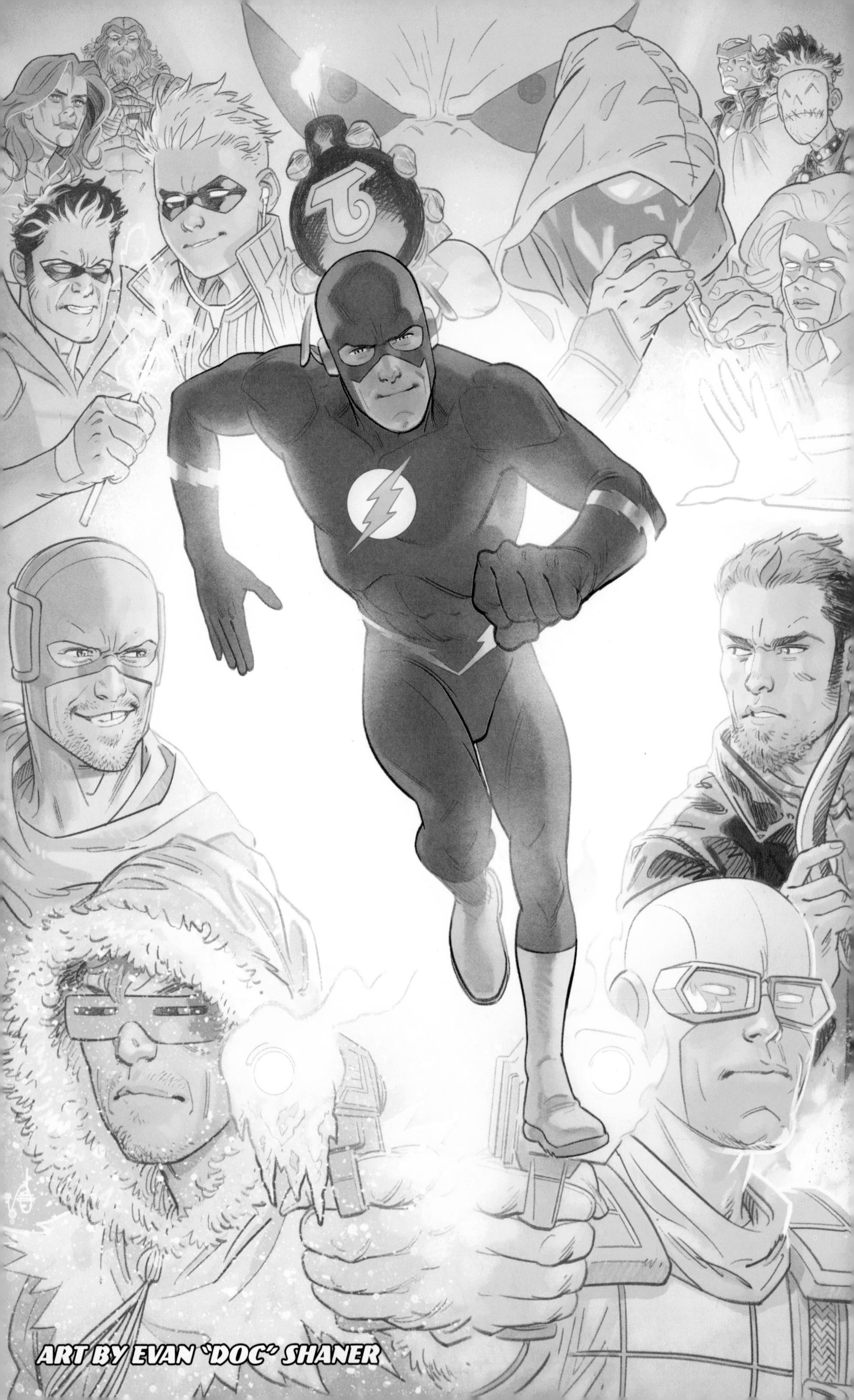

ART BY EVAN "DOC" SHANER

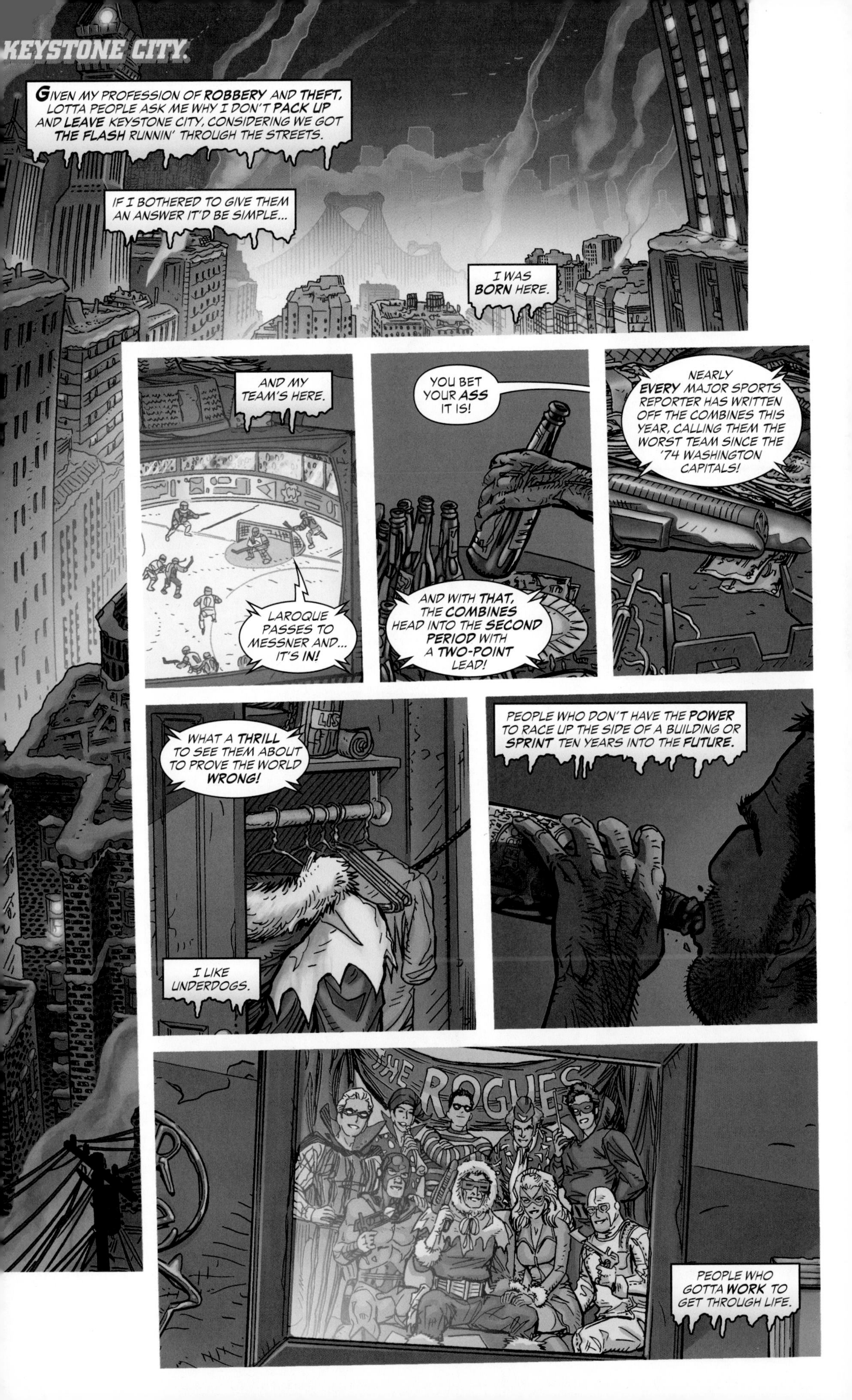
KEYSTONE CITY.
GIVEN MY PROFESSION OF ROBBERY AND THEFT, LOTTA PEOPLE ASK ME WHY I DON'T PACK UP AND LEAVE KEYSTONE CITY, CONSIDERING WE GOT THE FLASH RUNNIN' THROUGH THE STREETS.
IF I BOTHERED TO GIVE THEM AN ANSWER IT'D BE SIMPLE...
I WAS BORN HERE.
AND MY TEAM'S HERE.
LAROQUE PASSES TO MESSNER AND... IT'S IN!
YOU BET YOUR ASS IT IS!
AND WITH THAT, THE COMBINES HEAD INTO THE SECOND PERIOD WITH A TWO-POINT LEAD!
NEARLY EVERY MAJOR SPORTS REPORTER HAS WRITTEN OFF THE COMBINES THIS YEAR, CALLING THEM THE WORST TEAM SINCE THE '74 WASHINGTON CAPITALS!
WHAT A THRILL TO SEE THEM ABOUT TO PROVE THE WORLD WRONG!
I LIKE UNDERDOGS.
PEOPLE WHO DON'T HAVE THE POWER TO RACE UP THE SIDE OF A BUILDING OR SPRINT TEN YEARS INTO THE FUTURE.
THE ROGUES
PEOPLE WHO GOTTA WORK TO GET THROUGH LIFE.

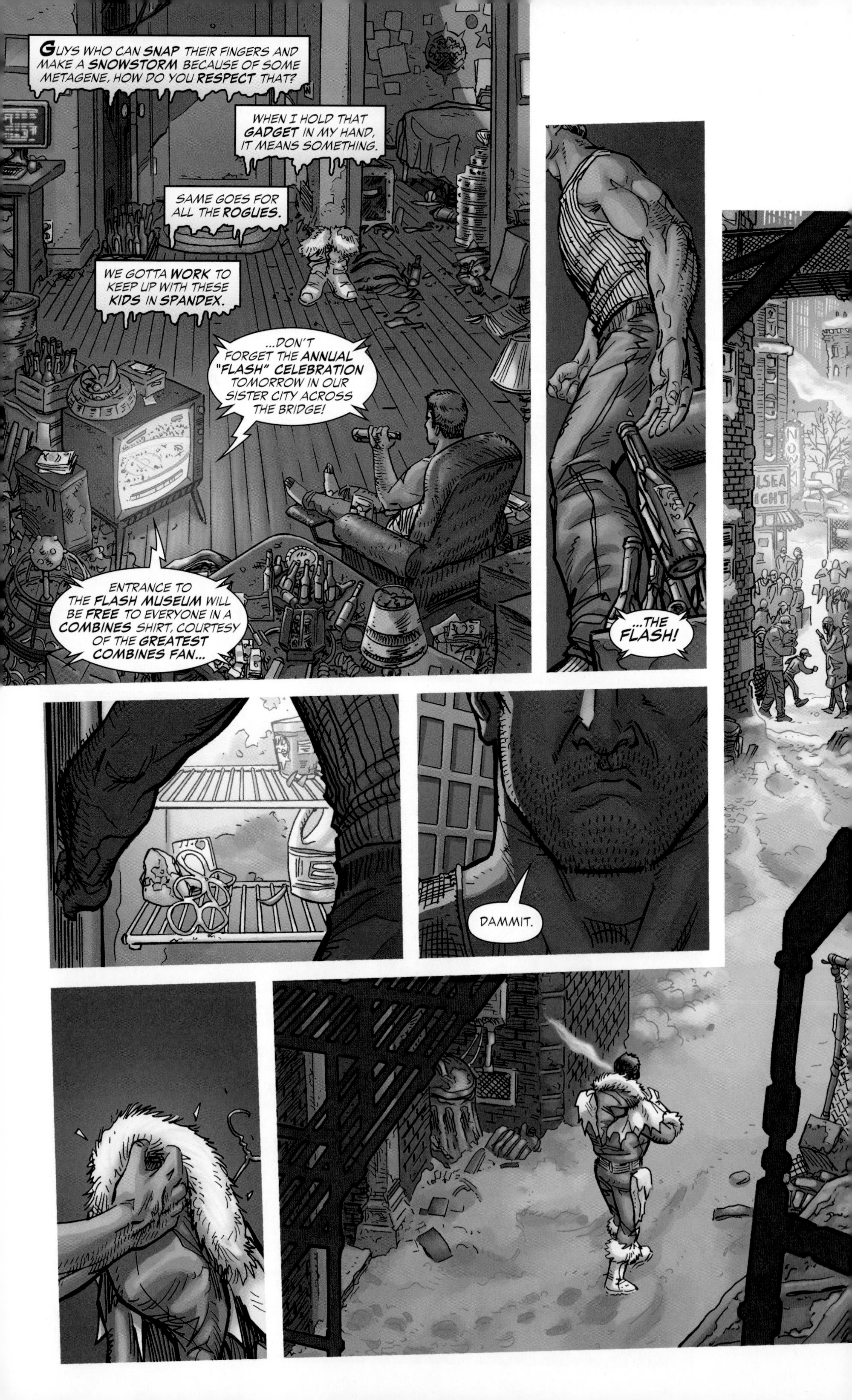
GUYS WHO CAN SNAP THEIR FINGERS AND MAKE A SNOWSTORM BECAUSE OF SOME METAGENE, HOW DO YOU RESPECT THAT?
WHEN I HOLD THAT GADGET IN MY HAND, IT MEANS SOMETHING.
SAME GOES FOR ALL THE ROGUES.
WE GOTTA WORK TO KEEP UP WITH THESE KIDS IN SPANDEX.
...DON'T FORGET THE ANNUAL "FLASH" CELEBRATION TOMORROW IN OUR SISTER CITY ACROSS THE BRIDGE!
ENTRANCE TO THE FLASH MUSEUM WILL BE FREE TO EVERYONE IN A COMBINES SHIRT, COURTESY OF THE GREATEST COMBINES FAN...
...THE FLASH!
DAMMIT.

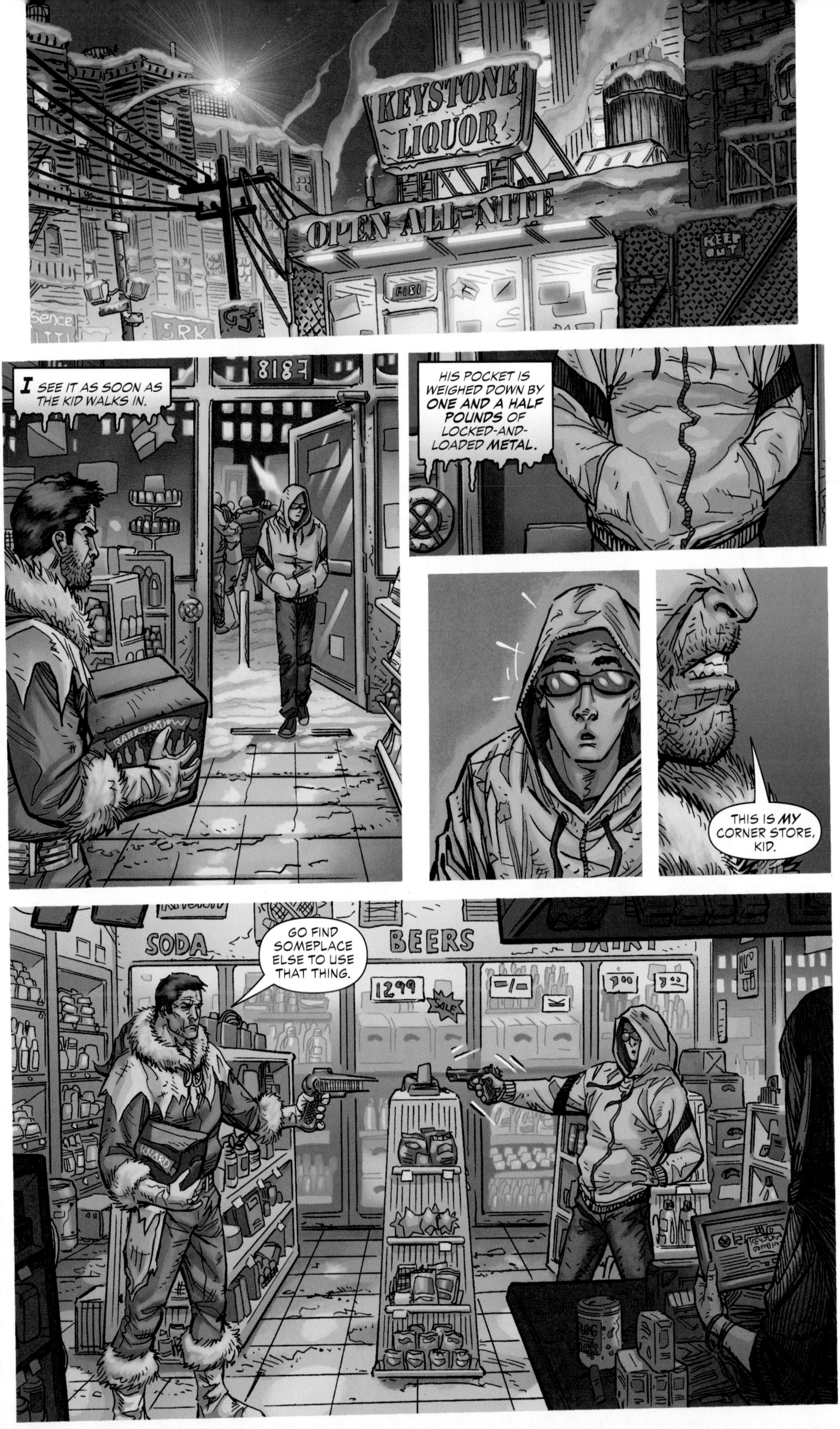
KEYSTONE LIQUOR
OPEN ALL-NITE
KEEP OUT
I SEE IT AS SOON AS THE KID WALKS IN.
HIS POCKET IS WEIGHED DOWN BY ONE AND A HALF POUNDS OF LOCKED-AND-LOADED METAL.
THIS IS MY CORNER STORE, KID.
SODA
BEERS
GO FIND SOMEPLACE ELSE TO USE THAT THING.

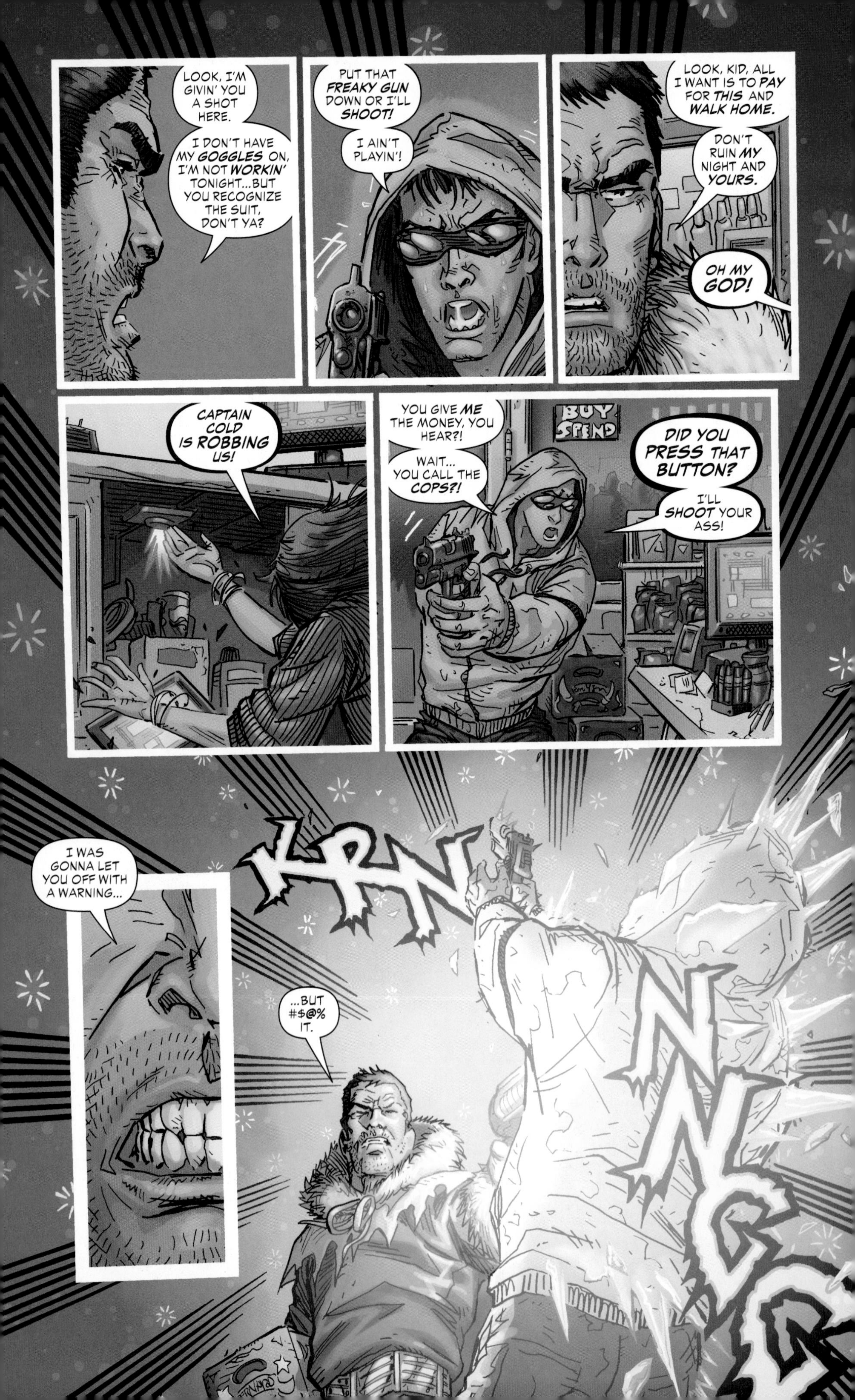

LOOK, I'M GIVIN' YOU A SHOT HERE.
I DON'T HAVE MY GOGGLES ON, I'M NOT WORKIN' TONIGHT...BUT YOU RECOGNIZE THE SUIT, DON'T YA?
PUT THAT FREAKY GUN DOWN OR I'LL SHOOT!
I AIN'T PLAYIN'!
LOOK, KID, ALL I WANT IS TO PAY FOR THIS AND WALK HOME.
DON'T RUIN MY NIGHT AND YOURS.
OH MY GOD!
CAPTAIN COLD IS ROBBING US!
BUY SPEND
YOU GIVE ME THE MONEY, YOU HEAR?!
WAIT... YOU CALL THE COPS?!
DID YOU PRESS THAT BUTTON?
I'LL SHOOT YOUR ASS!
I WAS GONNA LET YOU OFF WITH A WARNING...
KRNNNG
...BUT #$@% IT.

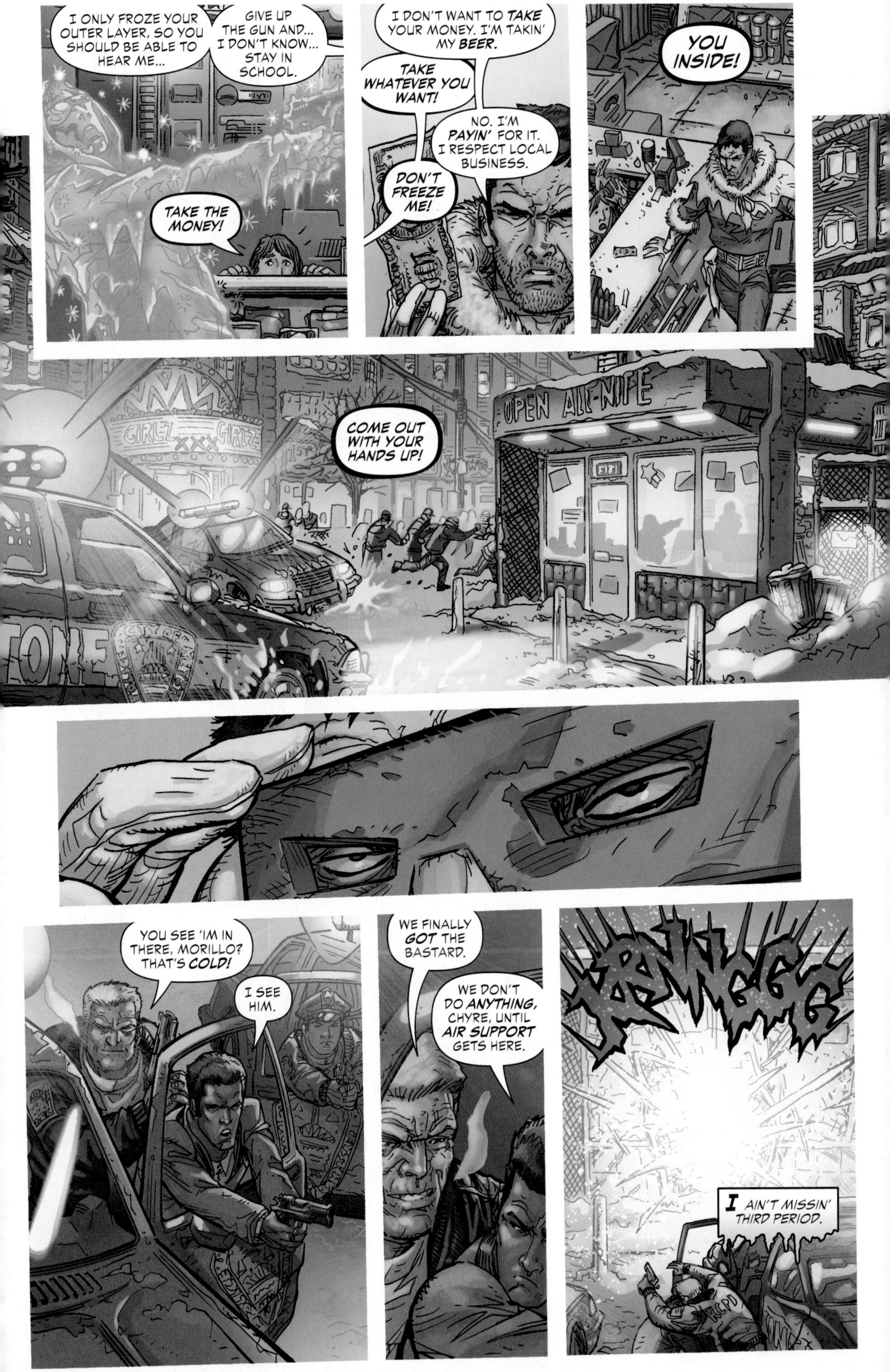
I ONLY FROZE YOUR OUTER LAYER, SO YOU SHOULD BE ABLE TO HEAR ME...
GIVE UP THE GUN AND... I DON'T KNOW... STAY IN SCHOOL.
TAKE THE MONEY!
I DON'T WANT TO TAKE YOUR MONEY. I'M TAKIN' MY BEER.
TAKE WHATEVER YOU WANT!
NO. I'M PAYIN' FOR IT. I RESPECT LOCAL BUSINESS.
DON'T FREEZE ME!
YOU INSIDE!
OPEN ALL-NITE
GIRLZ XXX GIRLZ
COME OUT WITH YOUR HANDS UP!
YOU SEE 'IM IN THERE, MORILLO? THAT'S COLD!
I SEE HIM.
WE FINALLY GOT THE BASTARD.
WE DON'T DO ANYTHING, CHYRE, UNTIL AIR SUPPORT GETS HERE.
I AIN'T MISSIN' THIRD PERIOD.

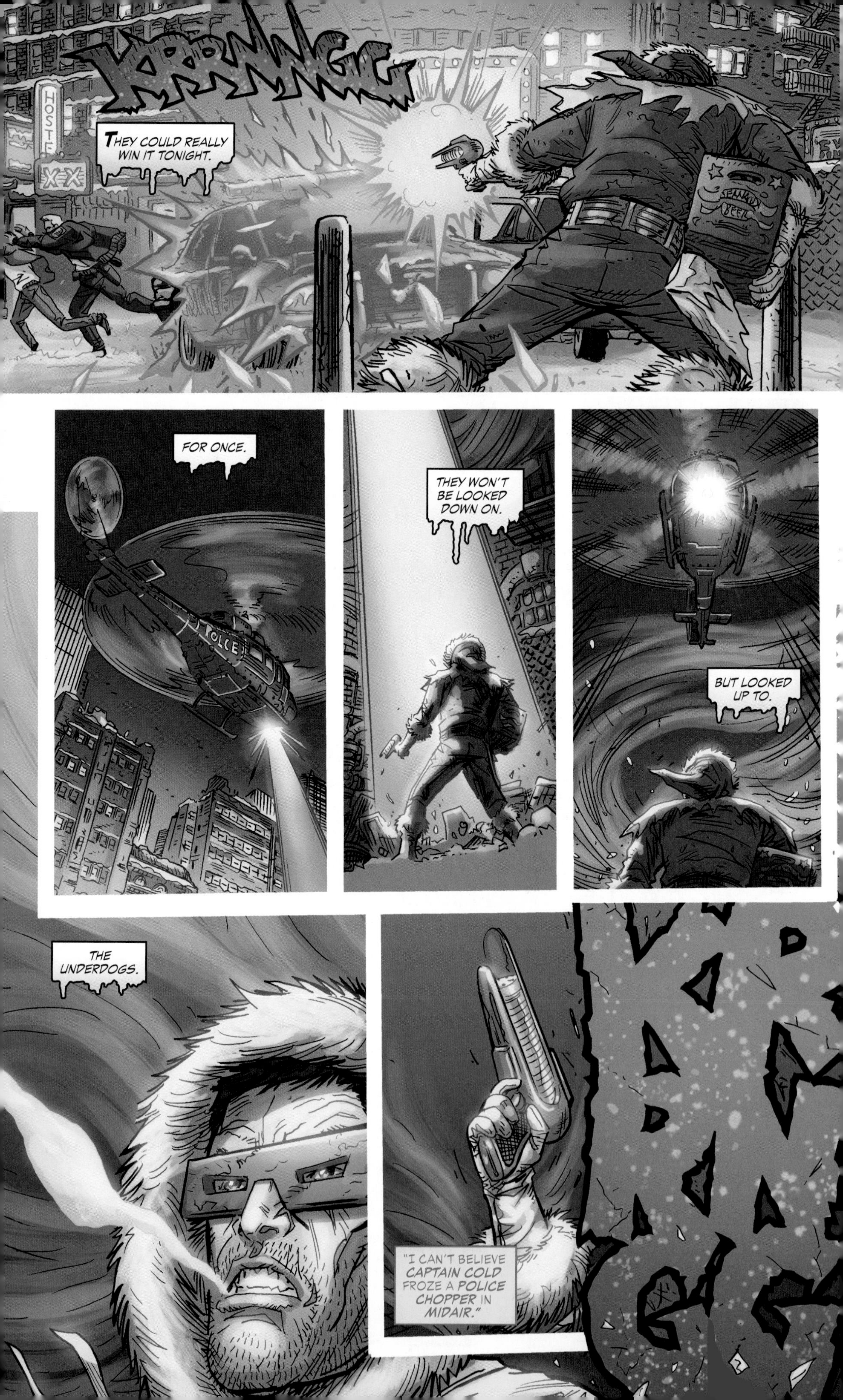
KRRNNGG
HOSTEL
XX
THEY COULD REALLY WIN IT TONIGHT.
FOR ONCE.
POLICE
THEY WON'T BE LOOKED DOWN ON.
BUT LOOKED UP TO.
THE UNDERDOGS.
"I CAN'T BELIEVE CAPTAIN COLD FROZE A POLICE CHOPPER IN MIDAIR."

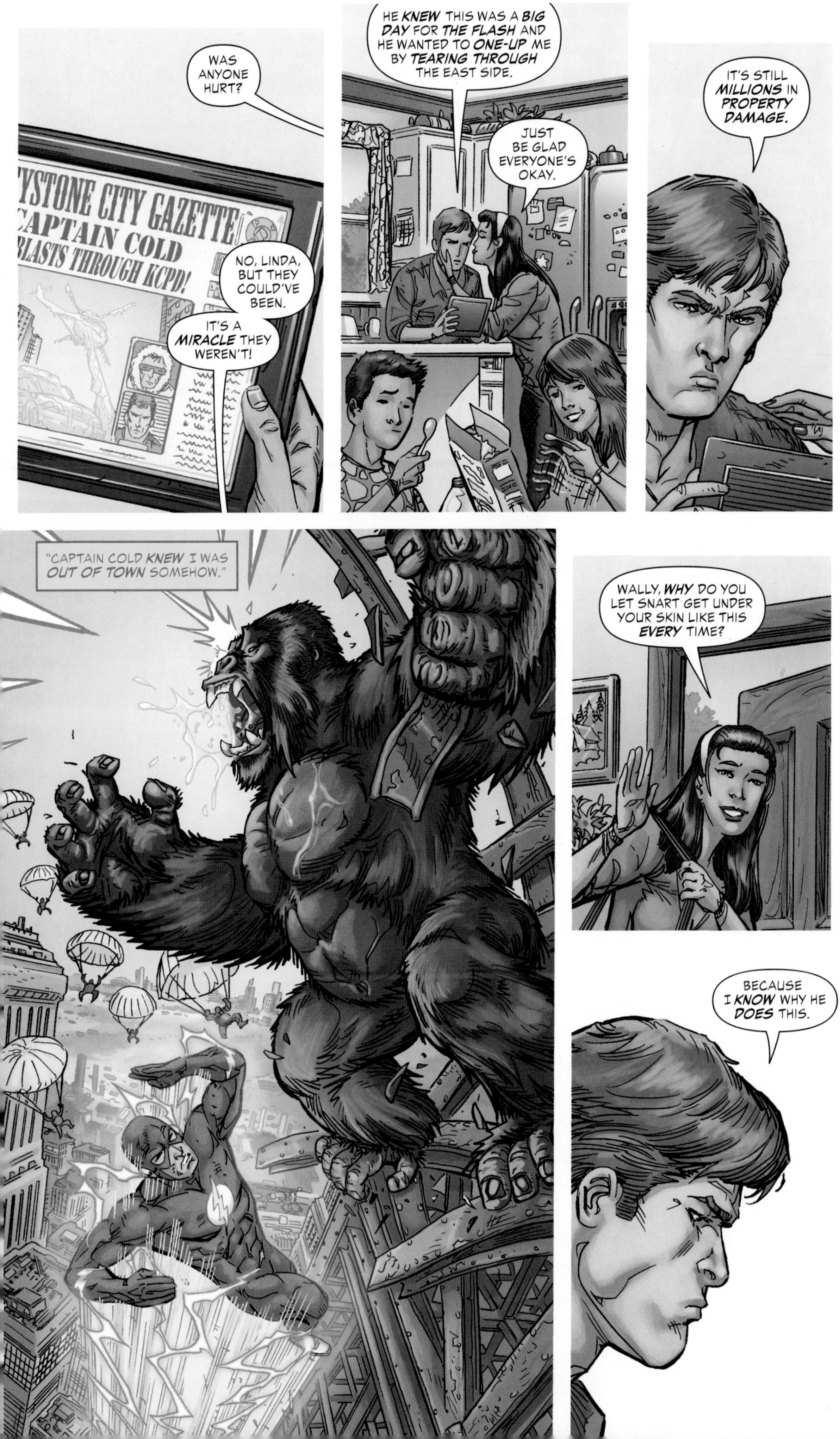
WAS ANYONE HURT?
YSTONE CITY GAZETTE
CAPTAIN COLD BLASTS THROUGH KCPD!
NO, LINDA, BUT THEY COULD'VE BEEN.
IT'S A MIRACLE THEY WEREN'T!
HE KNEW THIS WAS A BIG DAY FOR THE FLASH AND HE WANTED TO ONE-UP ME BY TEARING THROUGH THE EAST SIDE.
JUST BE GLAD EVERYONE'S OKAY.
IT'S STILL MILLIONS IN PROPERTY DAMAGE.
"CAPTAIN COLD KNEW I WAS OUT OF TOWN SOMEHOW."
WALLY, WHY DO YOU LET SNART GET UNDER YOUR SKIN LIKE THIS EVERY TIME?
BECAUSE I KNOW WHY HE DOES THIS.

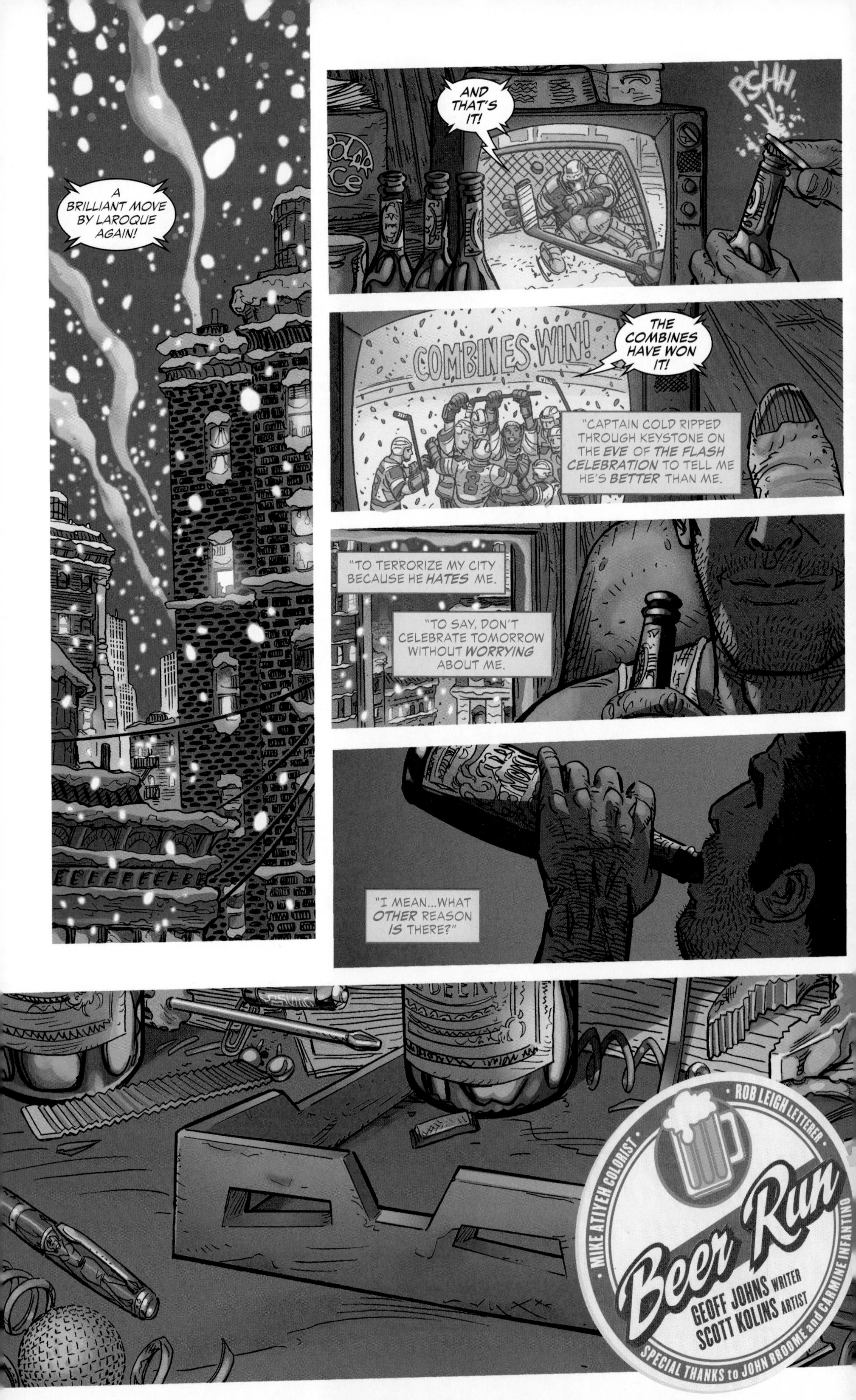
A BRILLIANT MOVE BY LAROQUE AGAIN!
AND THAT'S IT!
PSHH
THE COMBINES HAVE WON IT!
COMBINES WIN!
"CAPTAIN COLD RIPPED THROUGH KEYSTONE ON THE EVE OF THE FLASH CELEBRATION TO TELL ME HE'S BETTER THAN ME.
"TO TERRORIZE MY CITY BECAUSE HE HATES ME.
"TO SAY, DON'T CELEBRATE TOMORROW WITHOUT WORRYING ABOUT ME.
"I MEAN...WHAT OTHER REASON IS THERE?"
Beer Run
GEOFF JOHNS WRITER
SCOTT KOLINS ARTIST
MIKE ATIYEH COLORIST
ROB LEIGH LETTERER
SPECIAL THANKS to JOHN BROOME and CARMINE INFANTINO

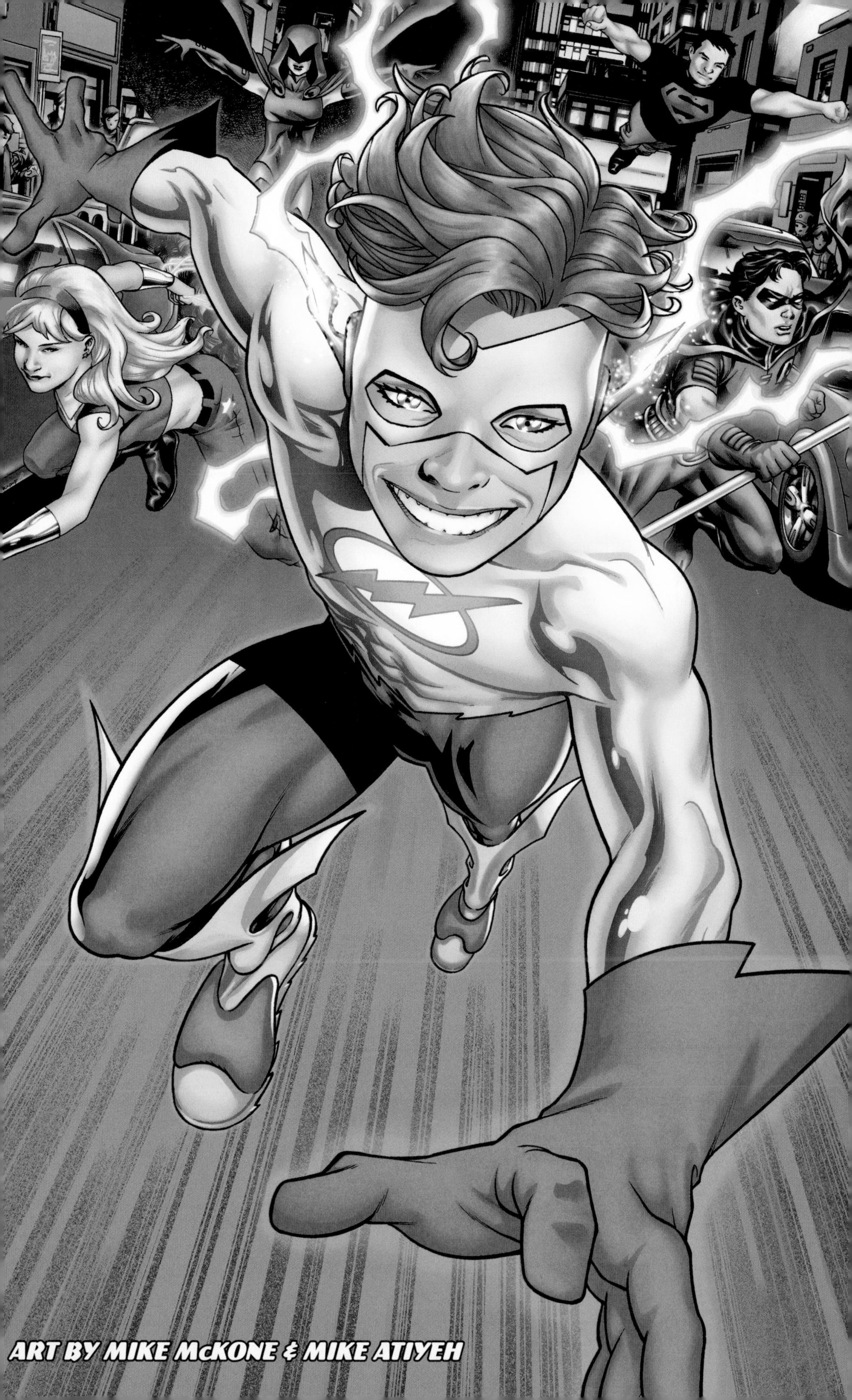

ART BY MIKE McKONE & MIKE ATIYEH

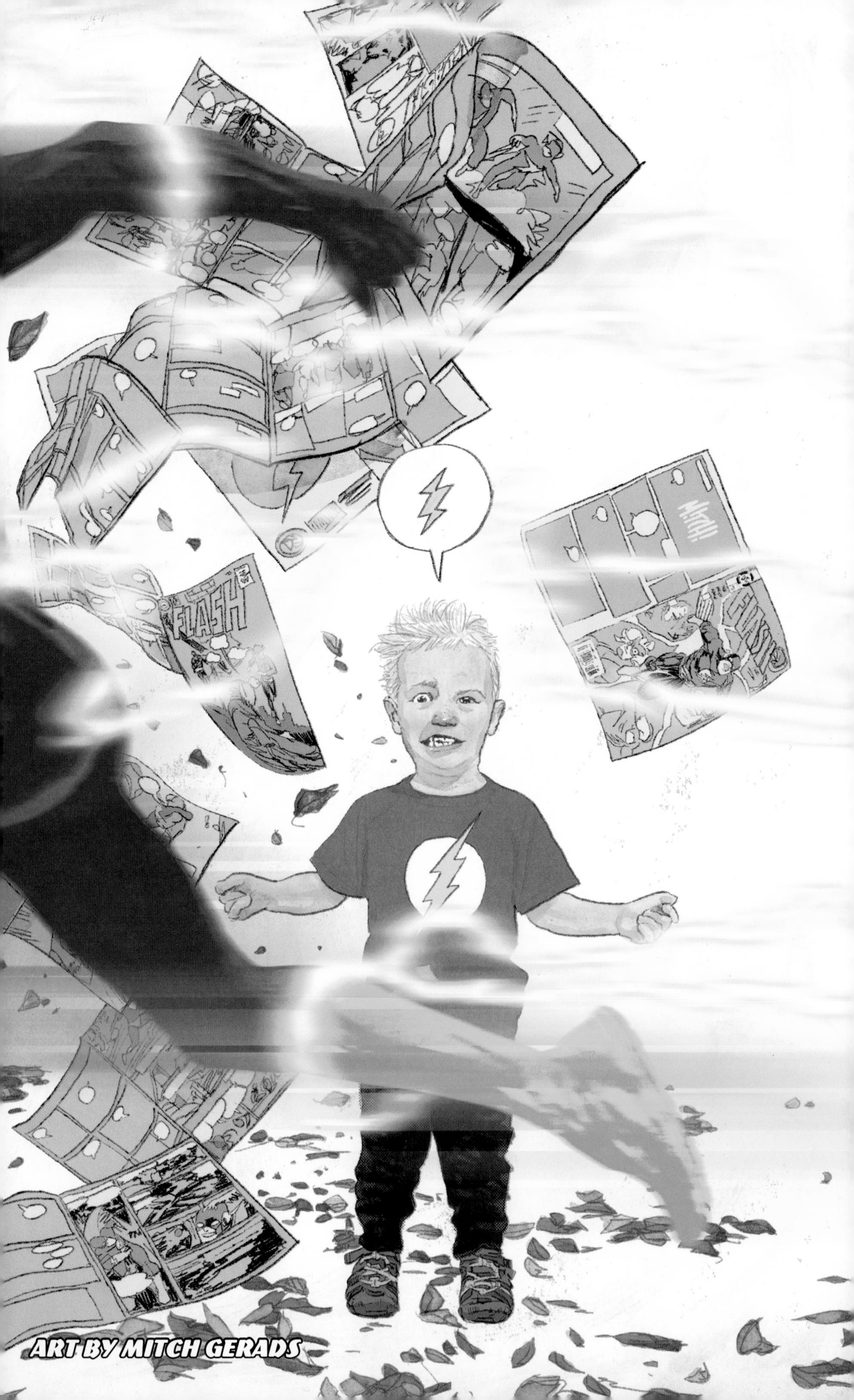
FLASH

ART BY MITCH GERADS

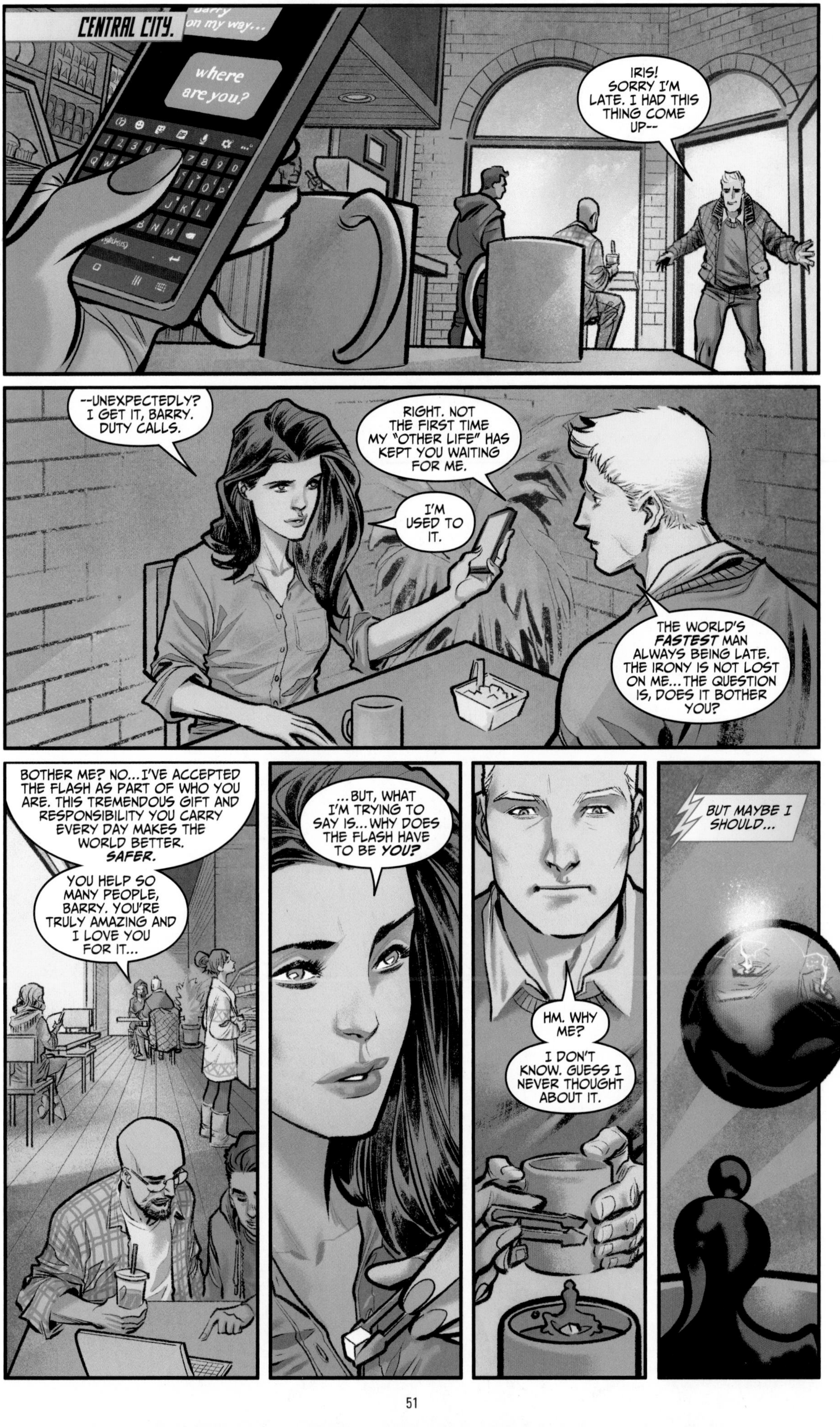
CENTRAL CITY.
Barry on my way...
where are you?
IRIS! SORRY I'M LATE. I HAD THIS THING COME UP--
--UNEXPECTEDLY? I GET IT, BARRY. DUTY CALLS.
RIGHT. NOT THE FIRST TIME MY "OTHER LIFE" HAS KEPT YOU WAITING FOR ME.
I'M USED TO IT.
THE WORLD'S FASTEST MAN ALWAYS BEING LATE. THE IRONY IS NOT LOST ON ME...THE QUESTION IS, DOES IT BOTHER YOU?
BOTHER ME? NO...I'VE ACCEPTED THE FLASH AS PART OF WHO YOU ARE. THIS TREMENDOUS GIFT AND RESPONSIBILITY YOU CARRY EVERY DAY MAKES THE WORLD BETTER. SAFER.
YOU HELP SO MANY PEOPLE, BARRY. YOU'RE TRULY AMAZING AND I LOVE YOU FOR IT...
...BUT, WHAT I'M TRYING TO SAY IS...WHY DOES THE FLASH HAVE TO BE YOU?
HM. WHY ME?
I DON'T KNOW. GUESS I NEVER THOUGHT ABOUT IT.
BUT MAYBE I SHOULD...

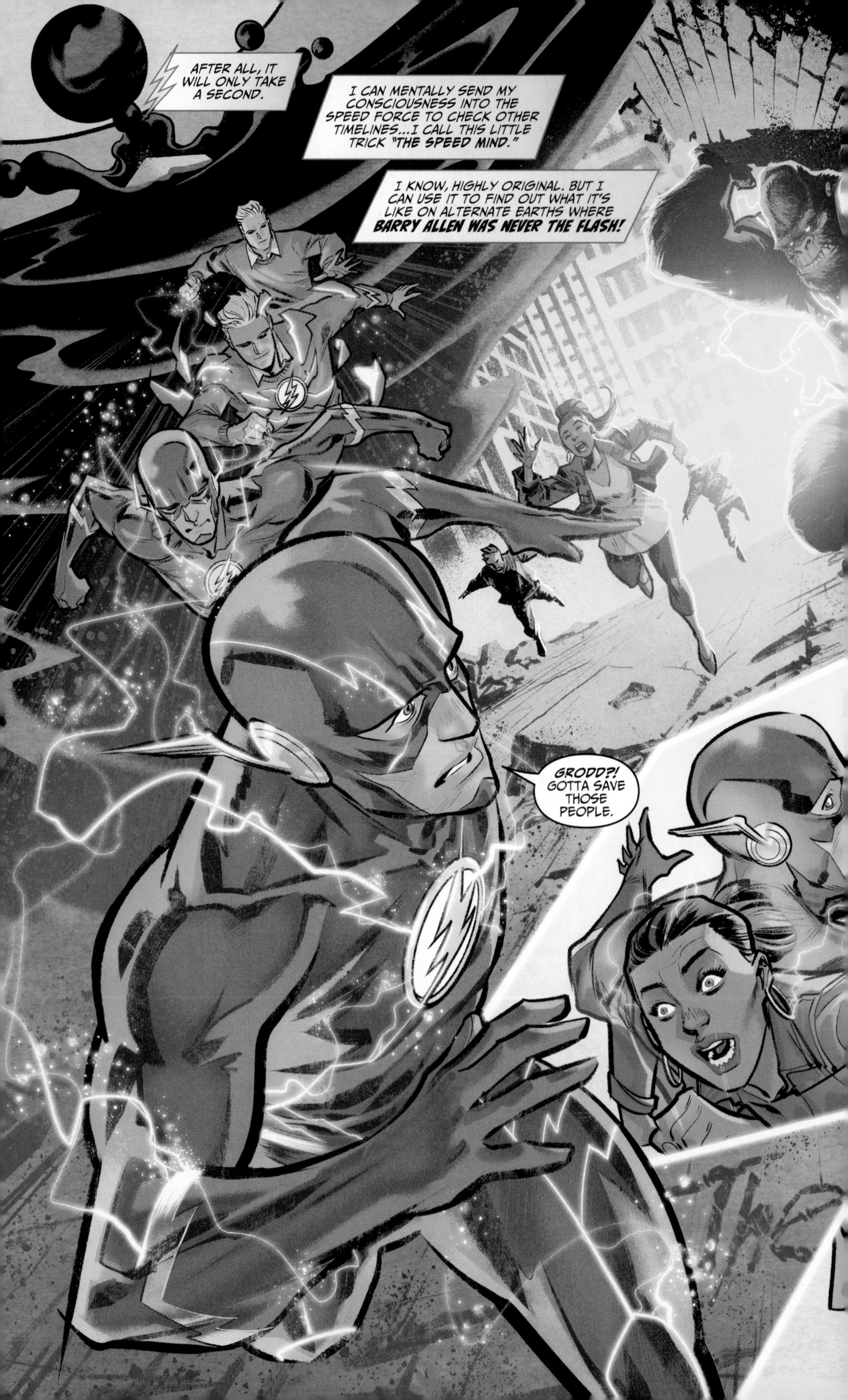
AFTER ALL, IT WILL ONLY TAKE A SECOND.
I CAN MENTALLY SEND MY CONSCIOUSNESS INTO THE SPEED FORCE TO CHECK OTHER TIMELINES...I CALL THIS LITTLE TRICK "THE SPEED MIND."
I KNOW, HIGHLY ORIGINAL. BUT I CAN USE IT TO FIND OUT WHAT IT'S LIKE ON ALTERNATE EARTHS WHERE BARRY ALLEN WAS NEVER THE FLASH!
GRODD?! GOTTA SAVE THOSE PEOPLE.

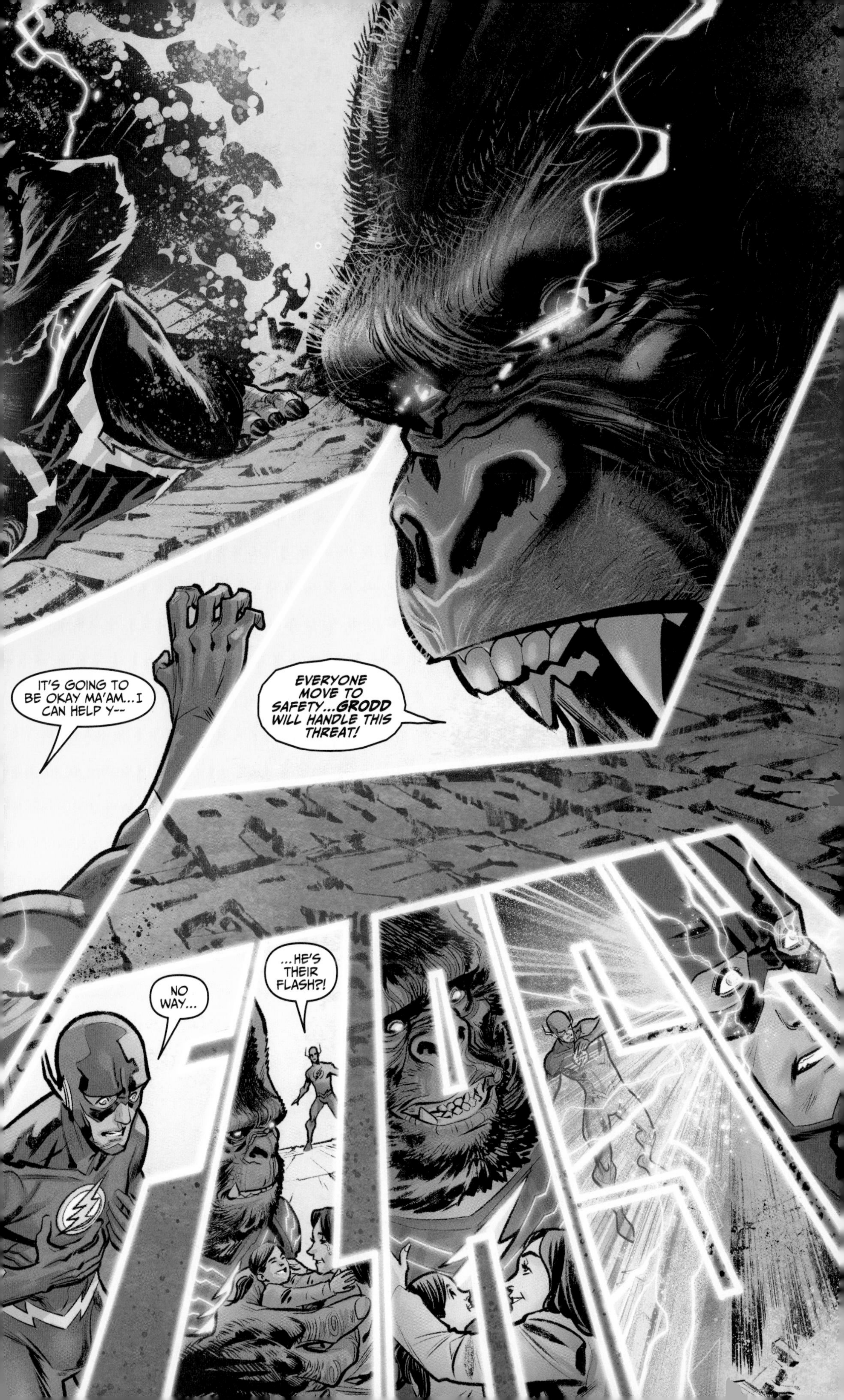
IT'S GOING TO BE OKAY MA'AM...I CAN HELP Y--
EVERYONE MOVE TO SAFETY...GRODD WILL HANDLE THIS THREAT!
NO WAY...
...HE'S THEIR FLASH?!

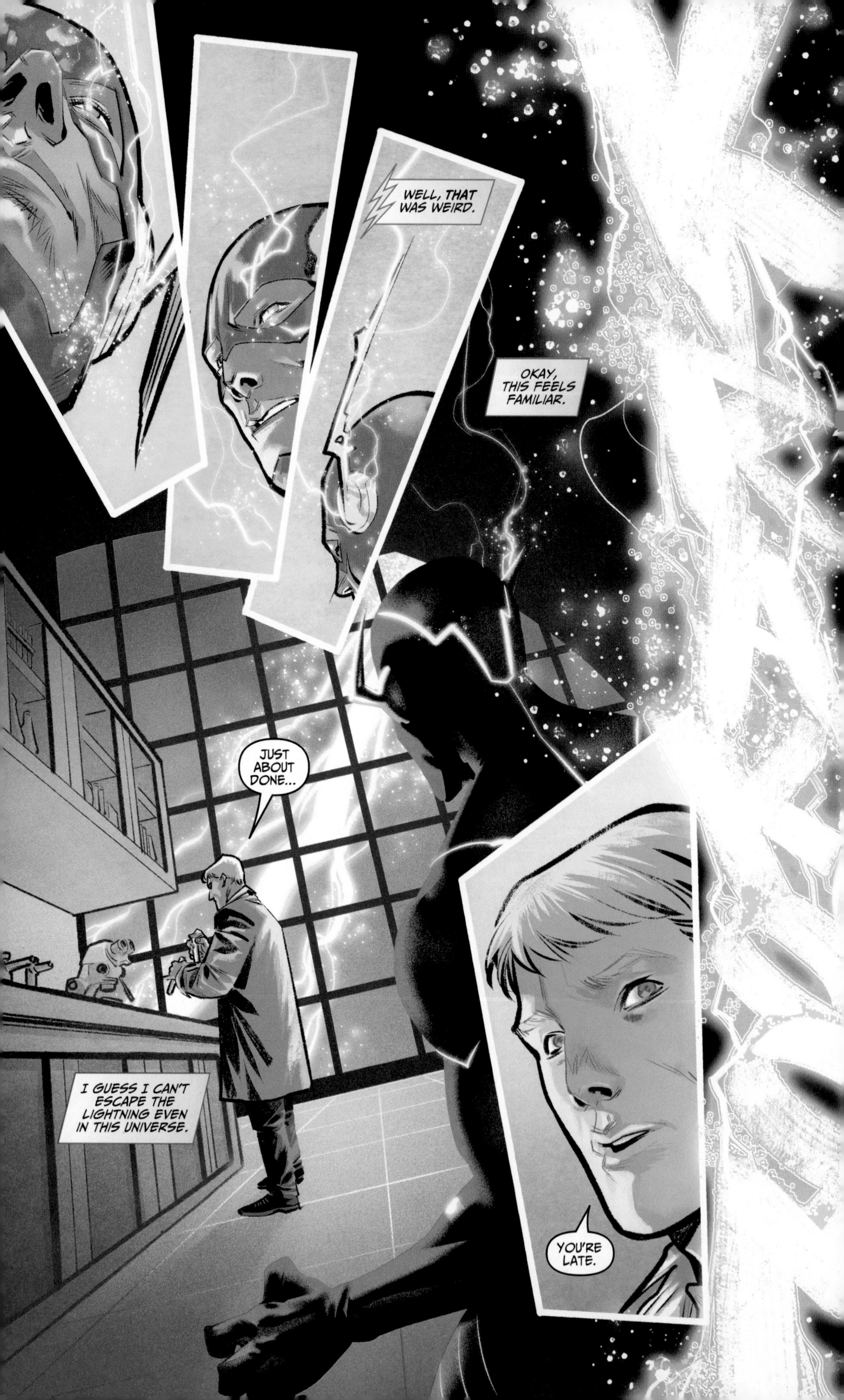
WELL, THAT WAS WEIRD.
OKAY, THIS FEELS FAMILIAR.
JUST ABOUT DONE...
I GUESS I CAN'T ESCAPE THE LIGHTNING EVEN IN THIS UNIVERSE.
YOU'RE LATE.

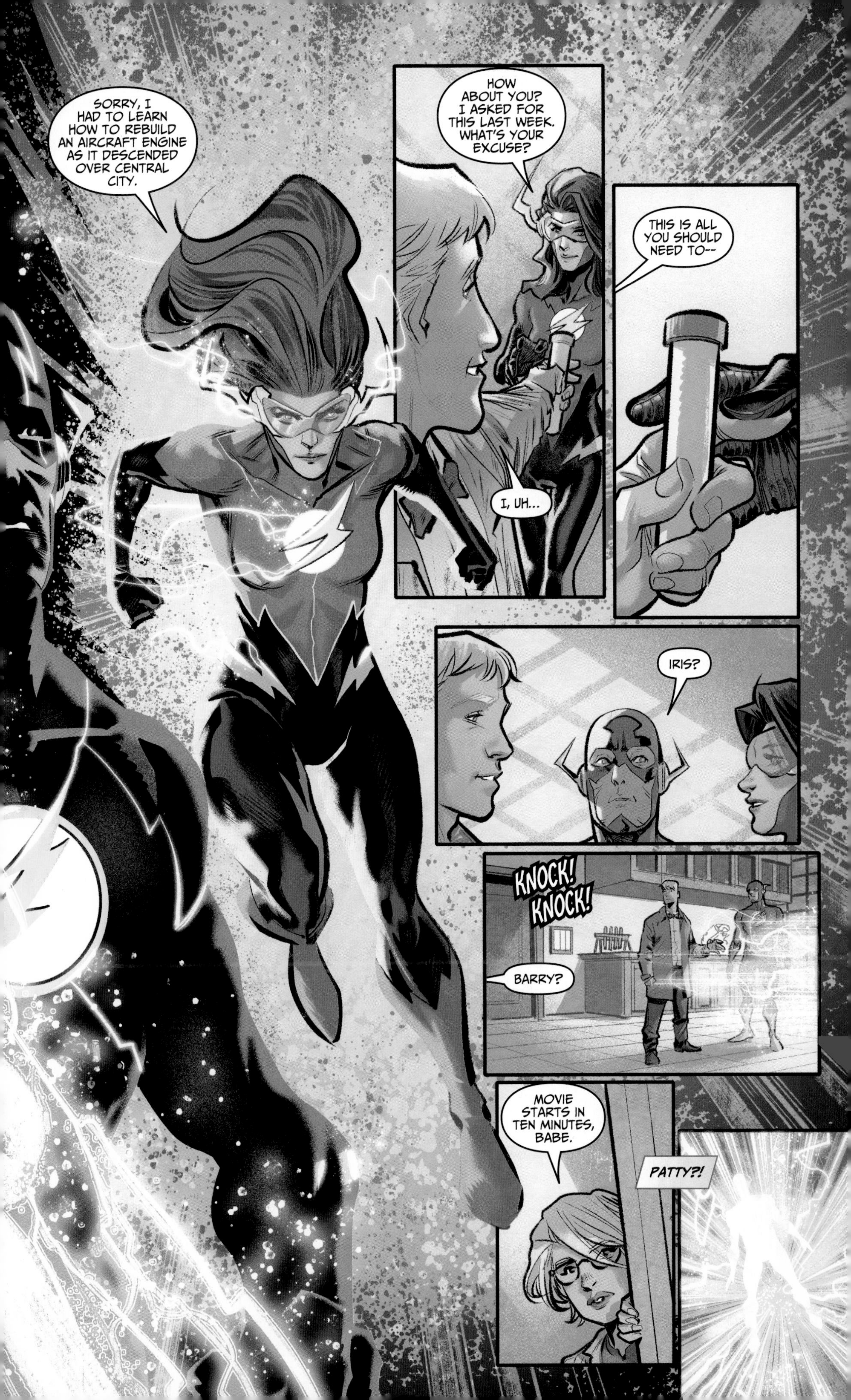
SORRY, I HAD TO LEARN HOW TO REBUILD AN AIRCRAFT ENGINE AS IT DESCENDED OVER CENTRAL CITY.
HOW ABOUT YOU? I ASKED FOR THIS LAST WEEK. WHAT'S YOUR EXCUSE?
I, UH...
THIS IS ALL YOU SHOULD NEED TO--
IRIS?
KNOCK! KNOCK!
BARRY?
MOVIE STARTS IN TEN MINUTES, BABE.
PATTY?!

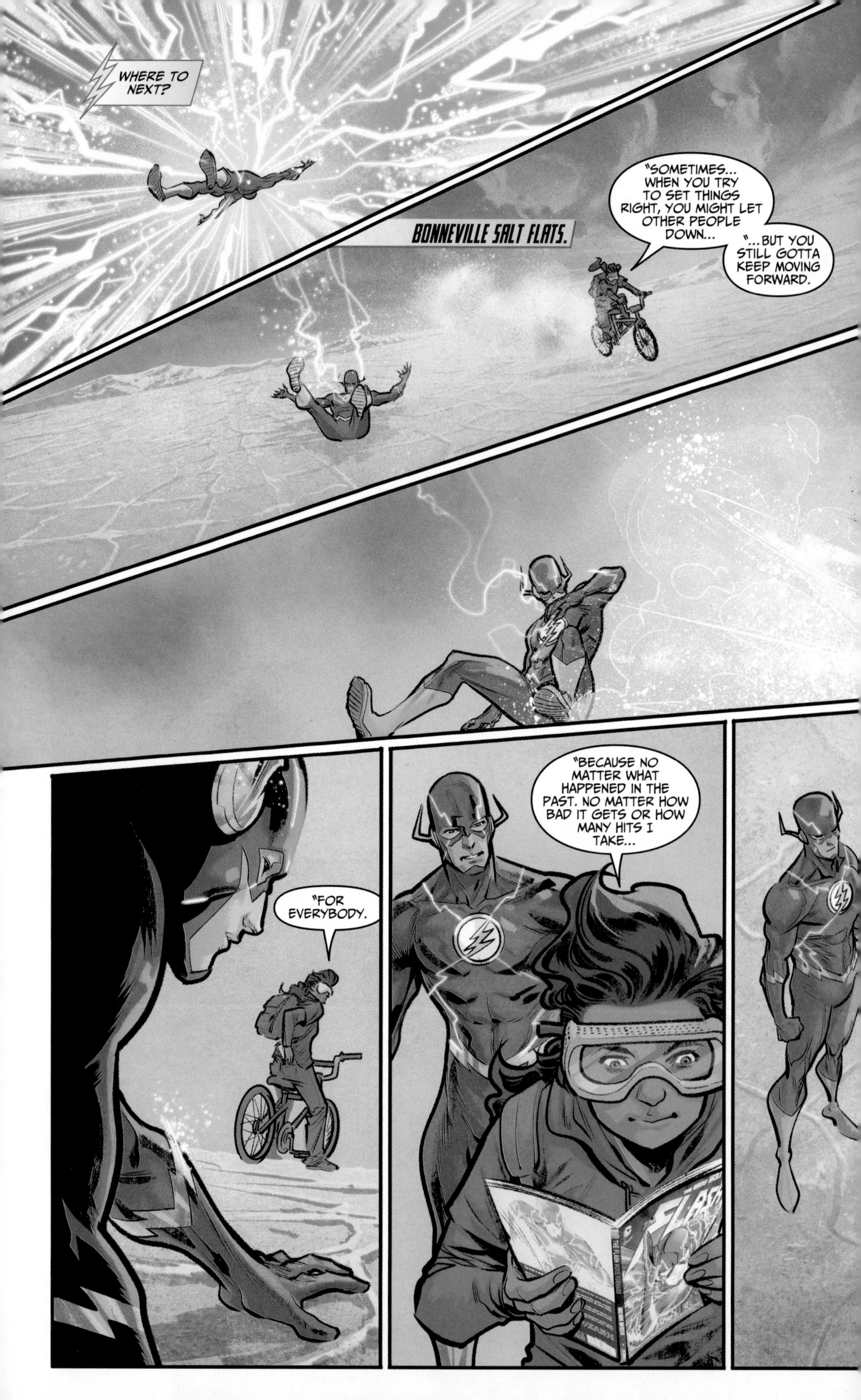
WHERE TO NEXT?
BONNEVILLE SALT FLATS.
"SOMETIMES... WHEN YOU TRY TO SET THINGS RIGHT, YOU MIGHT LET OTHER PEOPLE DOWN...
"...BUT YOU STILL GOTTA KEEP MOVING FORWARD.
"FOR EVERYBODY.
"BECAUSE NO MATTER WHAT HAPPENED IN THE PAST. NO MATTER HOW BAD IT GETS OR HOW MANY HITS I TAKE...

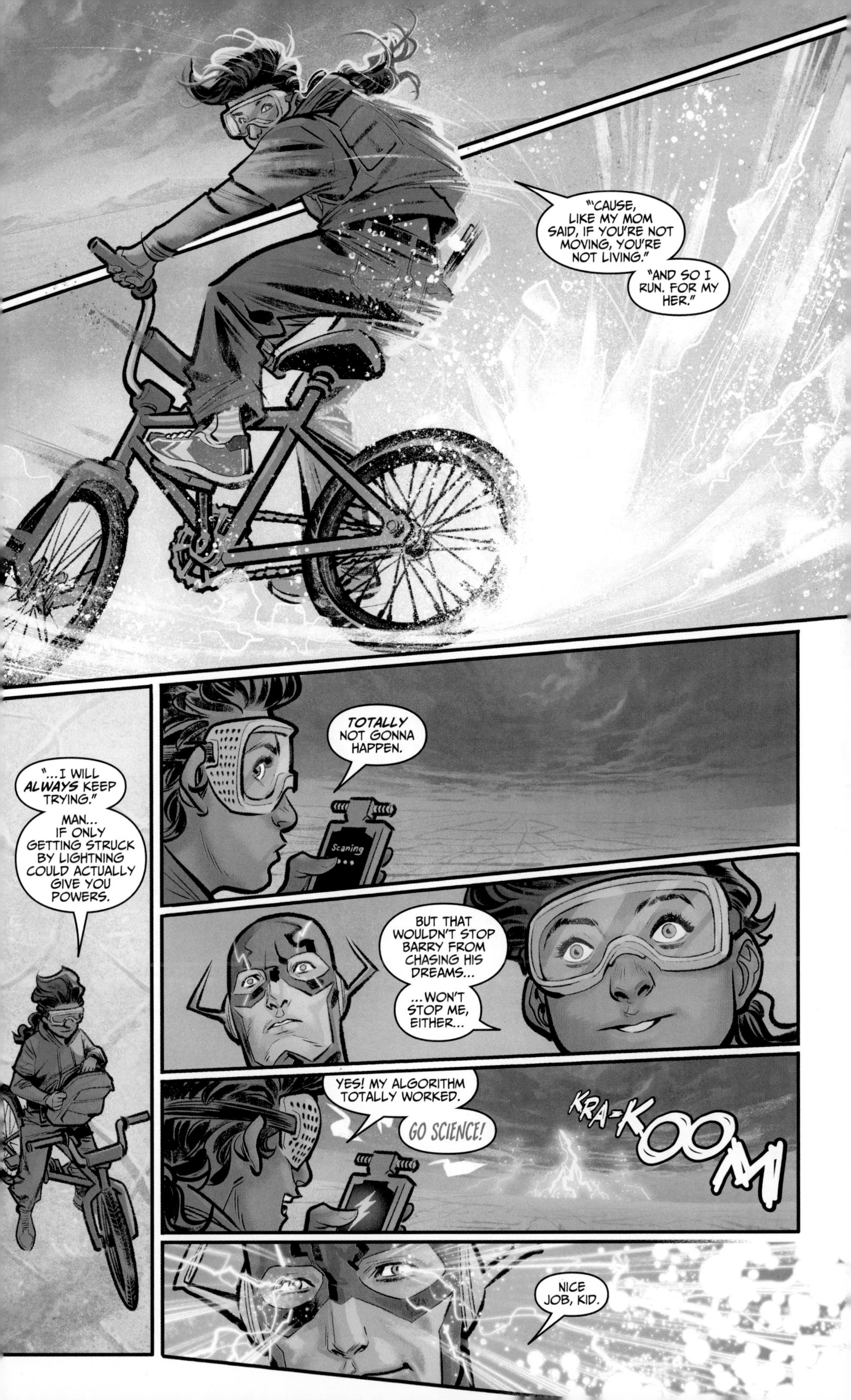

"'CAUSE, LIKE MY MOM SAID, IF YOU'RE NOT MOVING, YOU'RE NOT LIVING."
"AND SO I RUN. FOR MY HER."
"...I WILL *ALWAYS* KEEP TRYING."
MAN... IF ONLY GETTING STRUCK BY LIGHTNING COULD ACTUALLY GIVE YOU POWERS.
TOTALLY NOT GONNA HAPPEN.
Scaning
BUT THAT WOULDN'T STOP BARRY FROM CHASING HIS DREAMS...
...WON'T STOP ME, EITHER...
YES! MY ALGORITHM TOTALLY WORKED.
GO SCIENCE!
KRA-KOOOM
NICE JOB, KID.

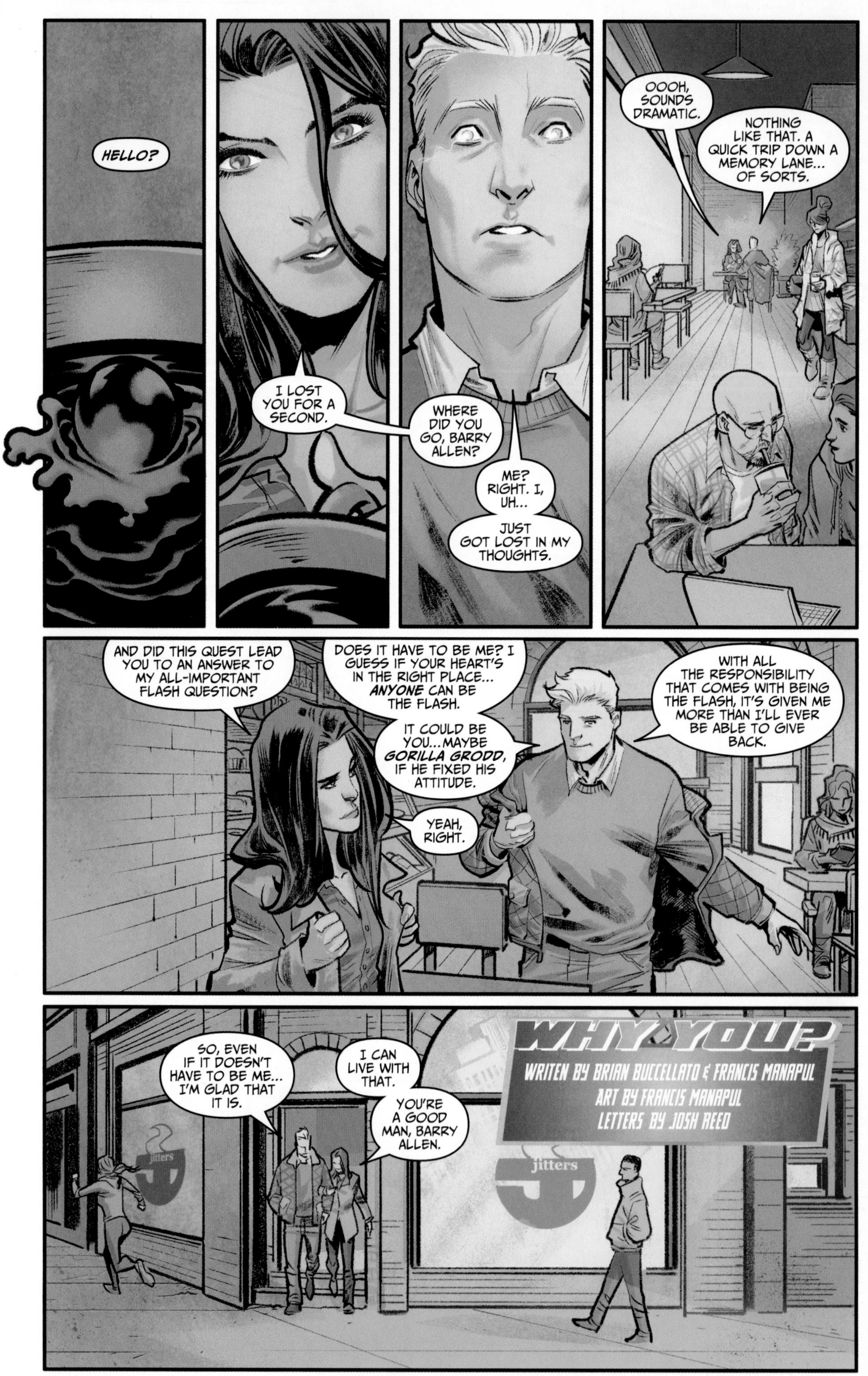
HELLO?
I LOST YOU FOR A SECOND.
WHERE DID YOU GO, BARRY ALLEN?
ME? RIGHT. I, UH...
JUST GOT LOST IN MY THOUGHTS.
OOOH, SOUNDS DRAMATIC.
NOTHING LIKE THAT. A QUICK TRIP DOWN A MEMORY LANE... OF SORTS.
AND DID THIS QUEST LEAD YOU TO AN ANSWER TO MY ALL-IMPORTANT FLASH QUESTION?
DOES IT HAVE TO BE ME? I GUESS IF YOUR HEART'S IN THE RIGHT PLACE... ANYONE CAN BE THE FLASH.
IT COULD BE YOU...MAYBE GORILLA GRODD, IF HE FIXED HIS ATTITUDE.
YEAH, RIGHT.
WITH ALL THE RESPONSIBILITY THAT COMES WITH BEING THE FLASH, IT'S GIVEN ME MORE THAN I'LL EVER BE ABLE TO GIVE BACK.
SO, EVEN IF IT DOESN'T HAVE TO BE ME... I'M GLAD THAT IT IS.
I CAN LIVE WITH THAT.
YOU'RE A GOOD MAN, BARRY ALLEN.
WHY YOU?
WRITEN BY BRIAN BUCCELLATO & FRANCIS MANAPUL
ART BY FRANCIS MANAPUL
LETTERS BY JOSH REED
jitters
jitters

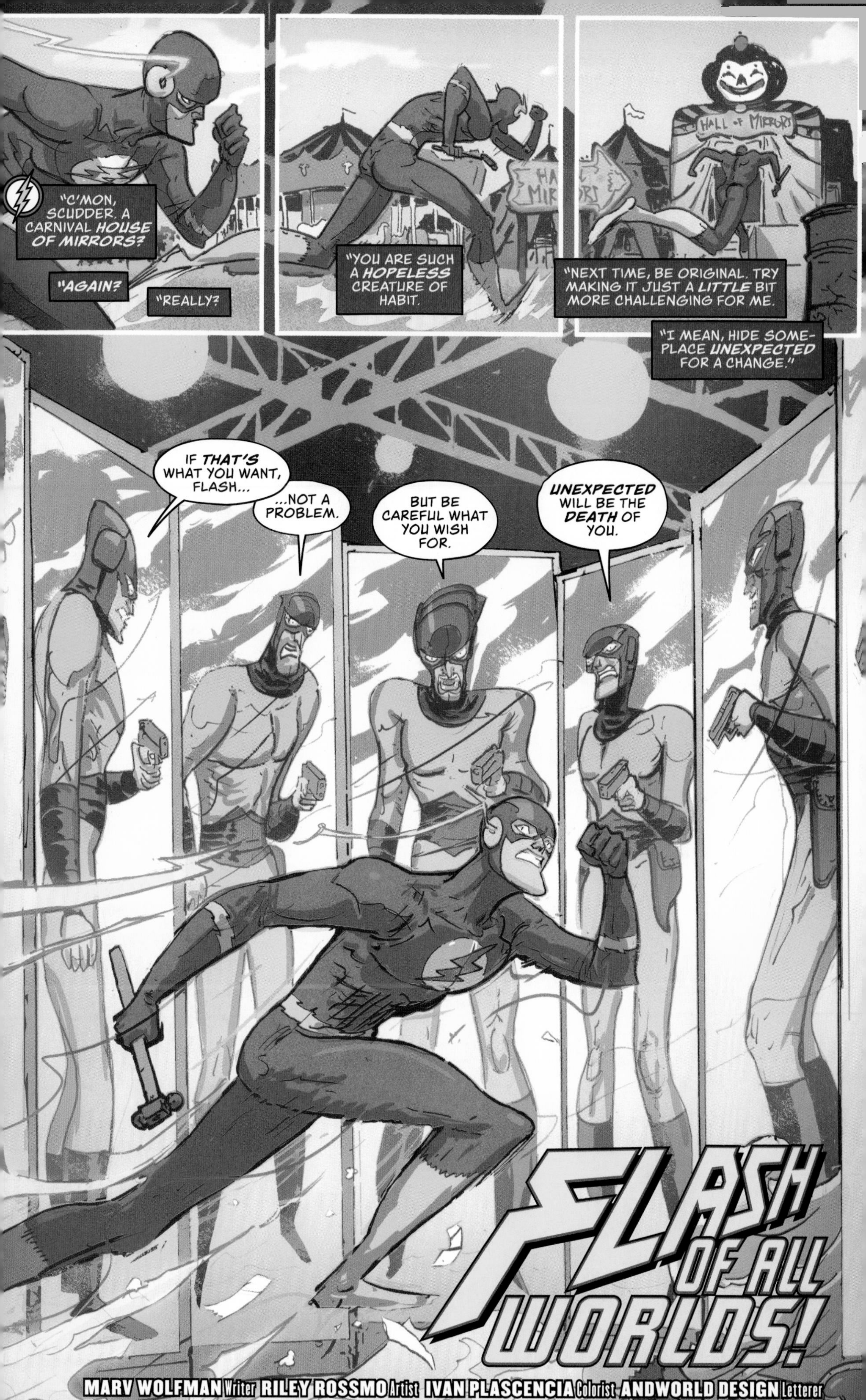
"C'MON, SCUDDER. A CARNIVAL HOUSE OF MIRRORS?
"AGAIN?
"REALLY?
"YOU ARE SUCH A HOPELESS CREATURE OF HABIT.
HALL OF MIRRORS
"NEXT TIME, BE ORIGINAL. TRY MAKING IT JUST A LITTLE BIT MORE CHALLENGING FOR ME.
"I MEAN, HIDE SOME-PLACE UNEXPECTED FOR A CHANGE."
IF THAT'S WHAT YOU WANT, FLASH...
...NOT A PROBLEM.
BUT BE CAREFUL WHAT YOU WISH FOR.
UNEXPECTED WILL BE THE DEATH OF YOU.
FLASH OF ALL WORLDS!

MARV WOLFMAN Writer RILEY ROSSMO Artist IVAN PLASCENCIA Colorist ANDWORLD DESIGN Letterer

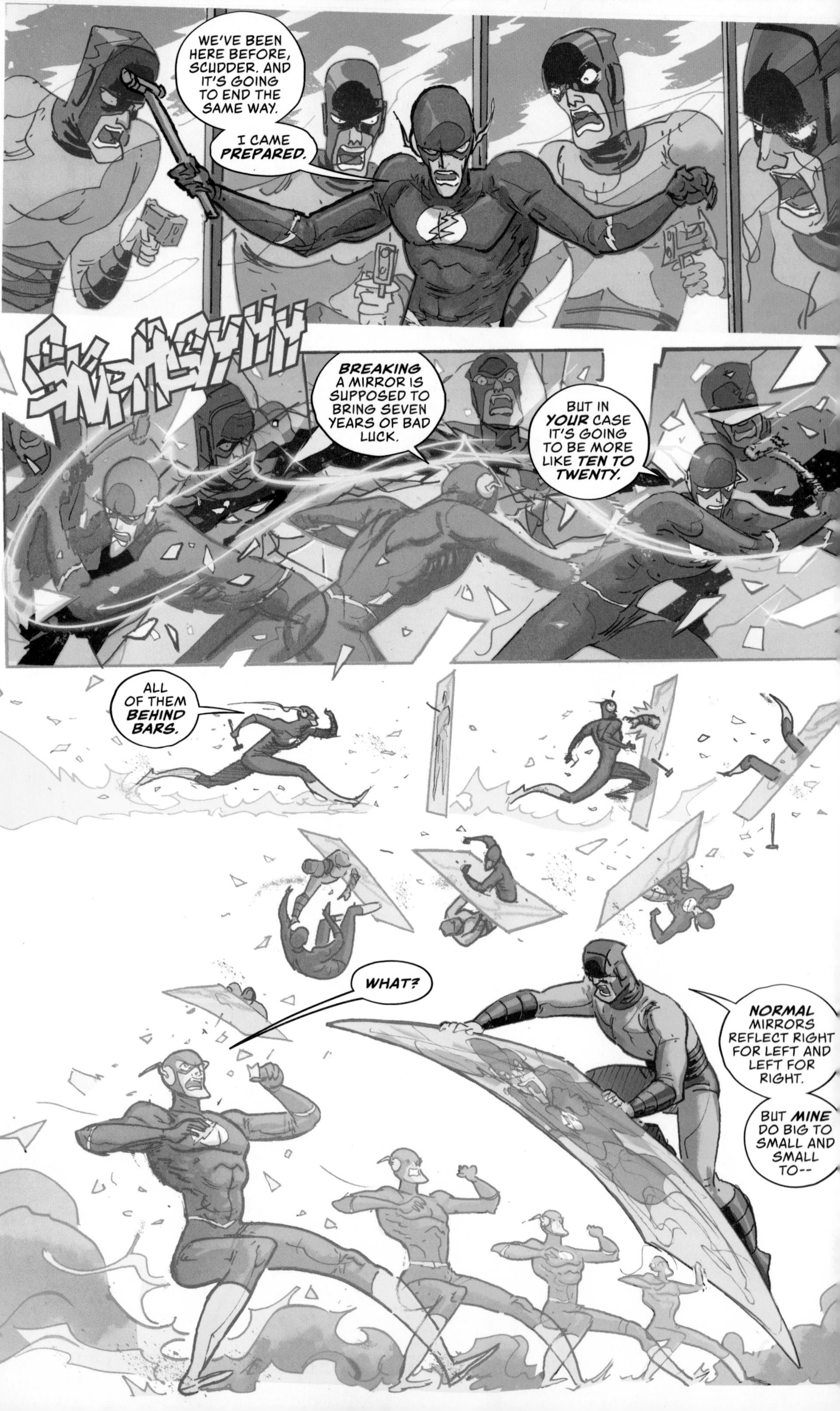
WE'VE BEEN HERE BEFORE, SCUDDER. AND IT'S GOING TO END THE SAME WAY.
I CAME PREPARED.
BREAKING A MIRROR IS SUPPOSED TO BRING SEVEN YEARS OF BAD LUCK.
BUT IN YOUR CASE IT'S GOING TO BE MORE LIKE TEN TO TWENTY.
ALL OF THEM BEHIND BARS.
WHAT?
NORMAL MIRRORS REFLECT RIGHT FOR LEFT AND LEFT FOR RIGHT.
BUT MINE DO BIG TO SMALL AND SMALL TO--

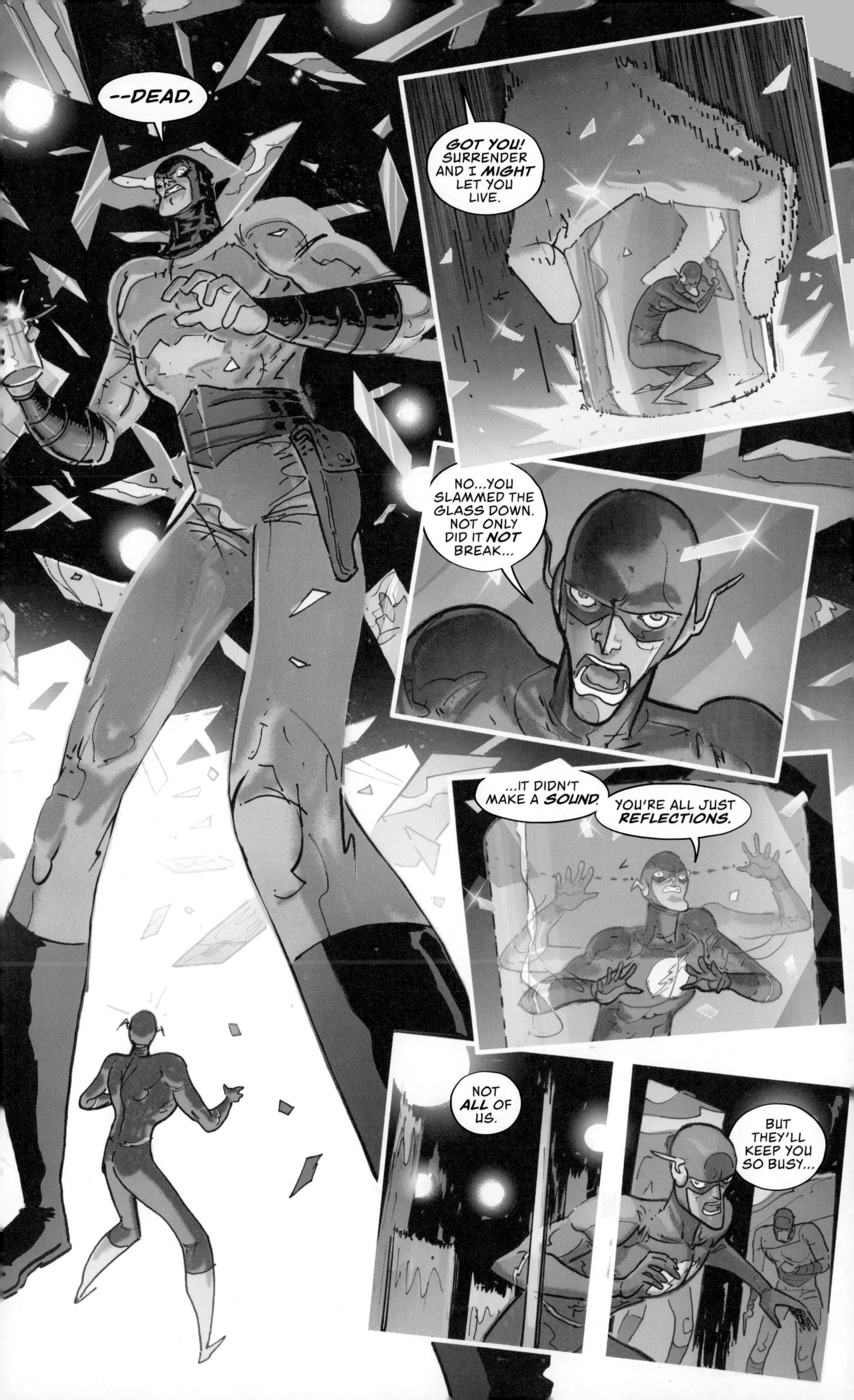
--DEAD.
GOT YOU! SURRENDER AND I MIGHT LET YOU LIVE.
NO...YOU SLAMMED THE GLASS DOWN. NOT ONLY DID IT NOT BREAK...
...IT DIDN'T MAKE A SOUND.
YOU'RE ALL JUST REFLECTIONS.
NOT ALL OF US.
BUT THEY'LL KEEP YOU SO BUSY...

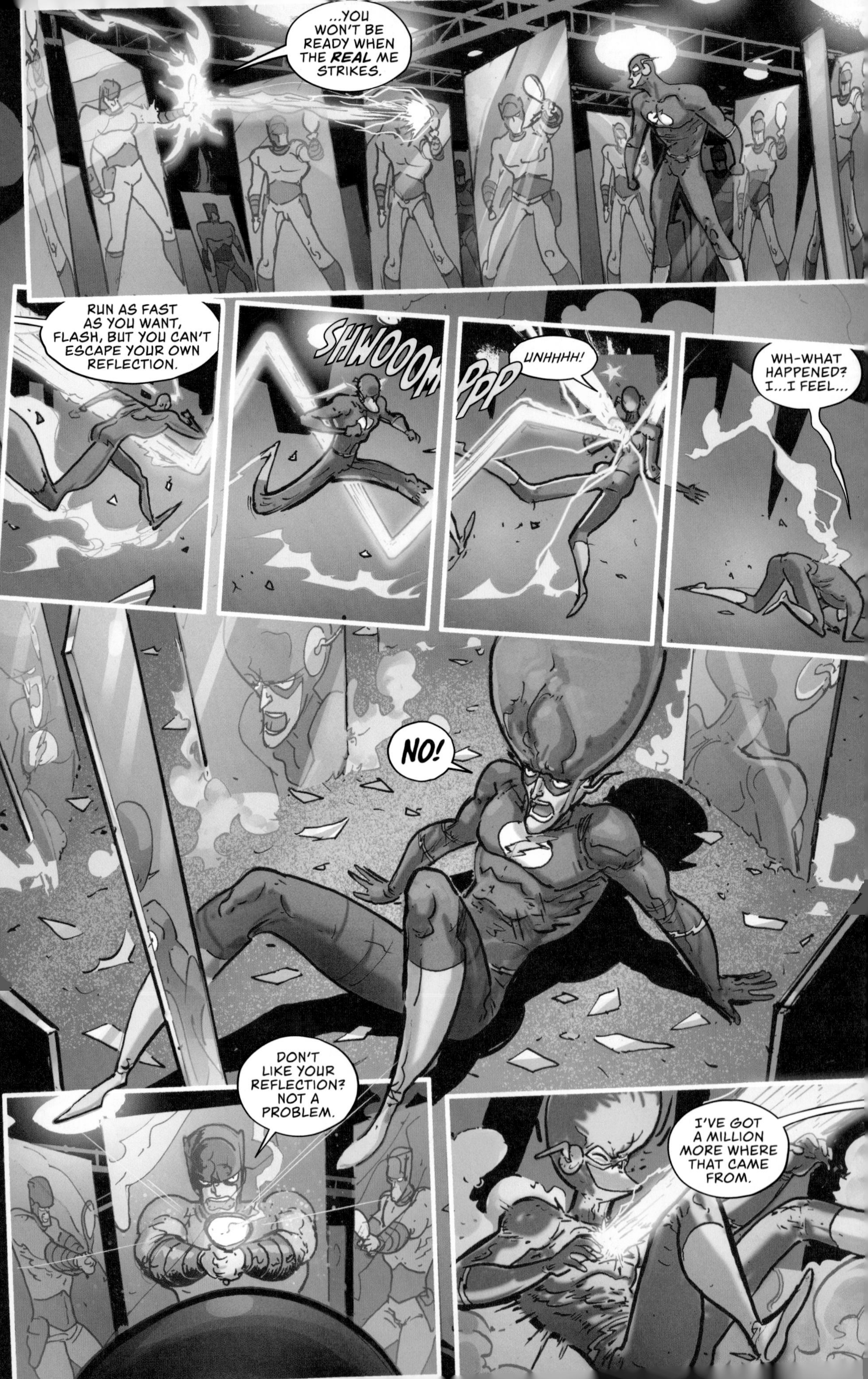

...YOU WON'T BE READY WHEN THE ***REAL*** ME STRIKES.
RUN AS FAST AS YOU WANT, FLASH, BUT YOU CAN'T ESCAPE YOUR OWN REFLECTION.
SHWOOOMPPP
UNHHHH!
WH-WHAT HAPPENED? I...I FEEL...
NO!
DON'T LIKE YOUR REFLECTION? NOT A PROBLEM.
I'VE GOT A MILLION MORE WHERE THAT CAME FROM.

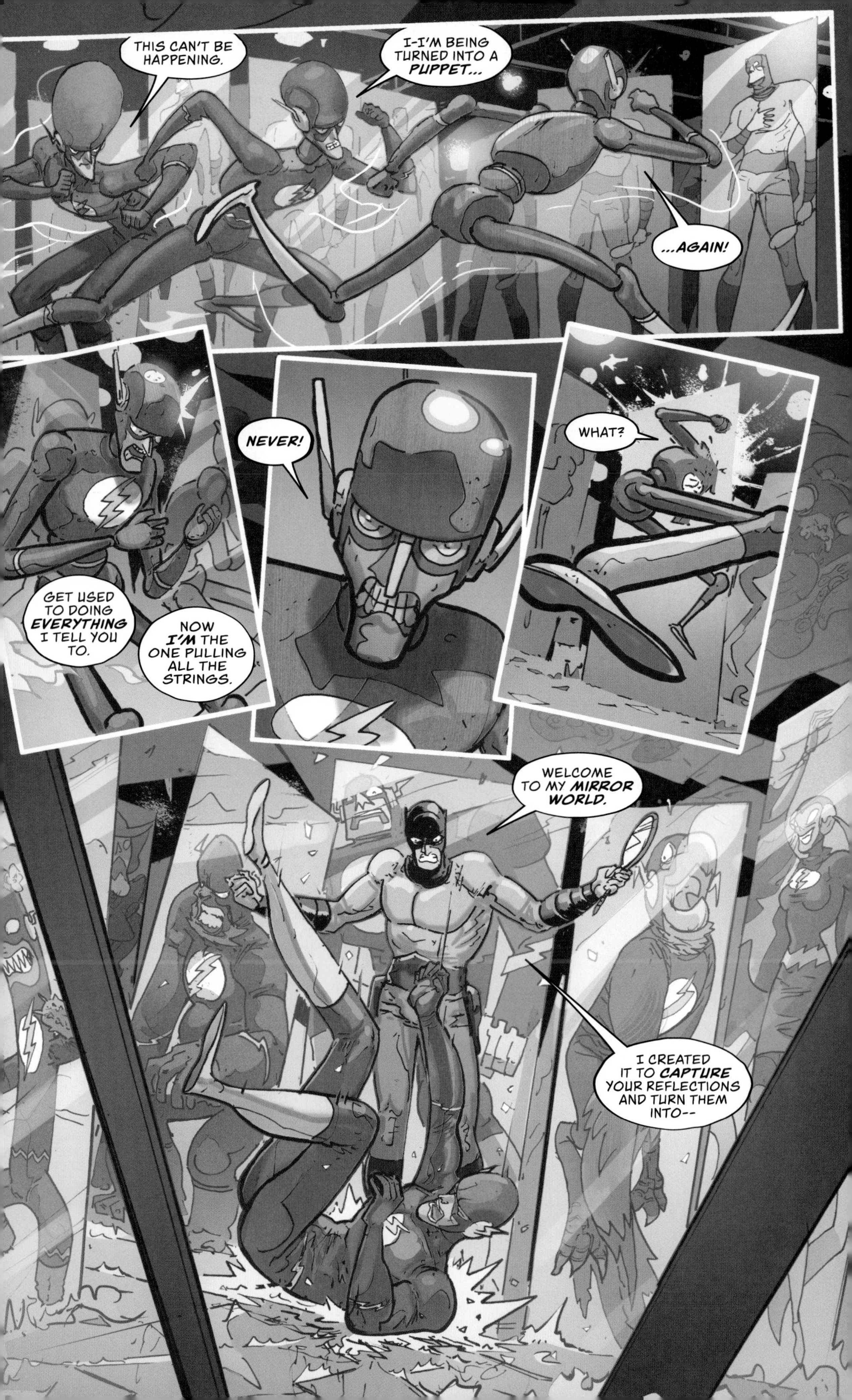
THIS CAN'T BE HAPPENING.
I-I'M BEING TURNED INTO A PUPPET...
...AGAIN!
GET USED TO DOING EVERYTHING I TELL YOU TO.
NOW I'M THE ONE PULLING ALL THE STRINGS.
NEVER!
WHAT?
WELCOME TO MY MIRROR WORLD.
I CREATED IT TO CAPTURE YOUR REFLECTIONS AND TURN THEM INTO--

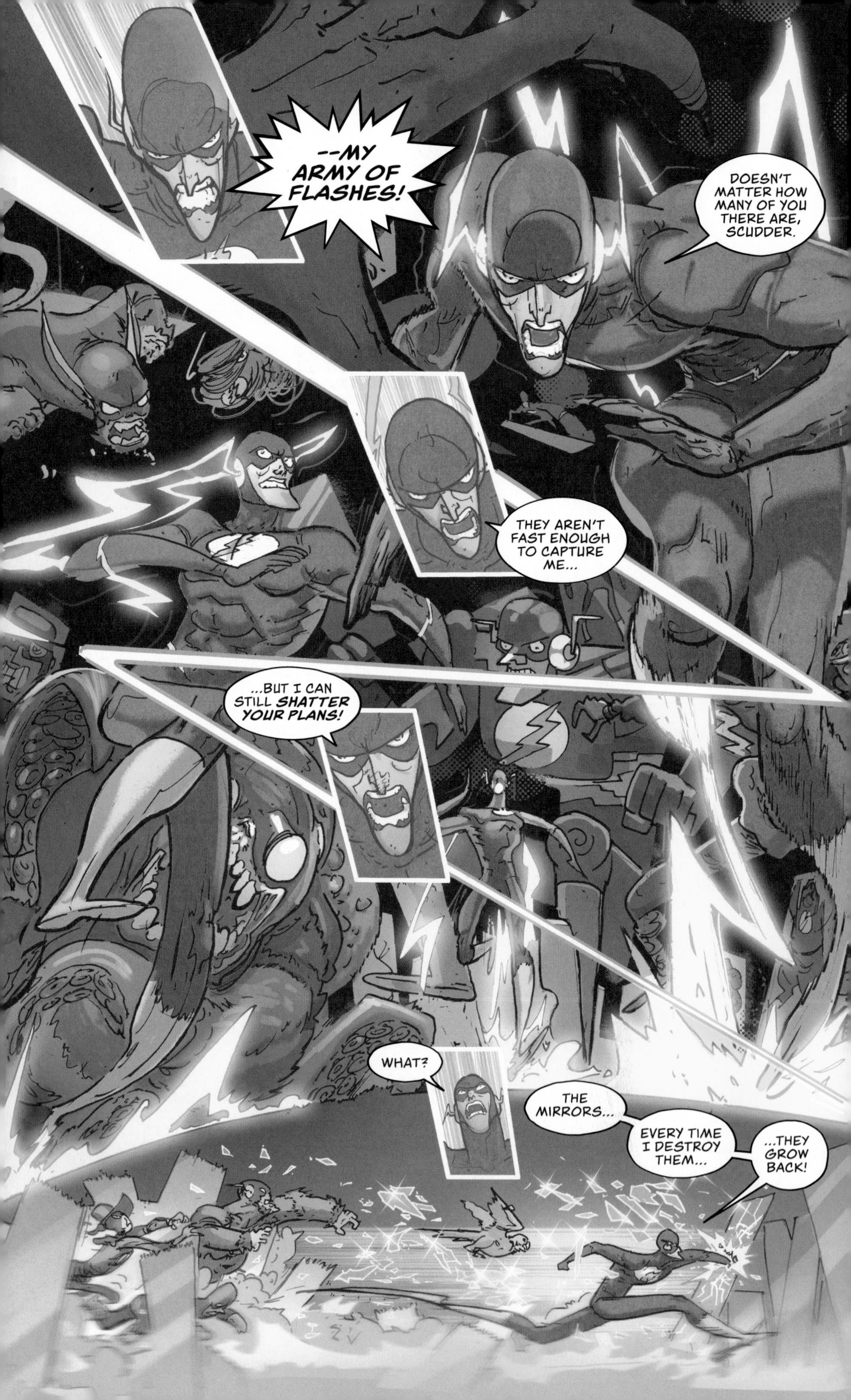
--MY ARMY OF FLASHES!
DOESN'T MATTER HOW MANY OF YOU THERE ARE, SCUDDER.
THEY AREN'T FAST ENOUGH TO CAPTURE ME...
...BUT I CAN STILL SHATTER YOUR PLANS!
WHAT?
THE MIRRORS...
EVERY TIME I DESTROY THEM...
...THEY GROW BACK!

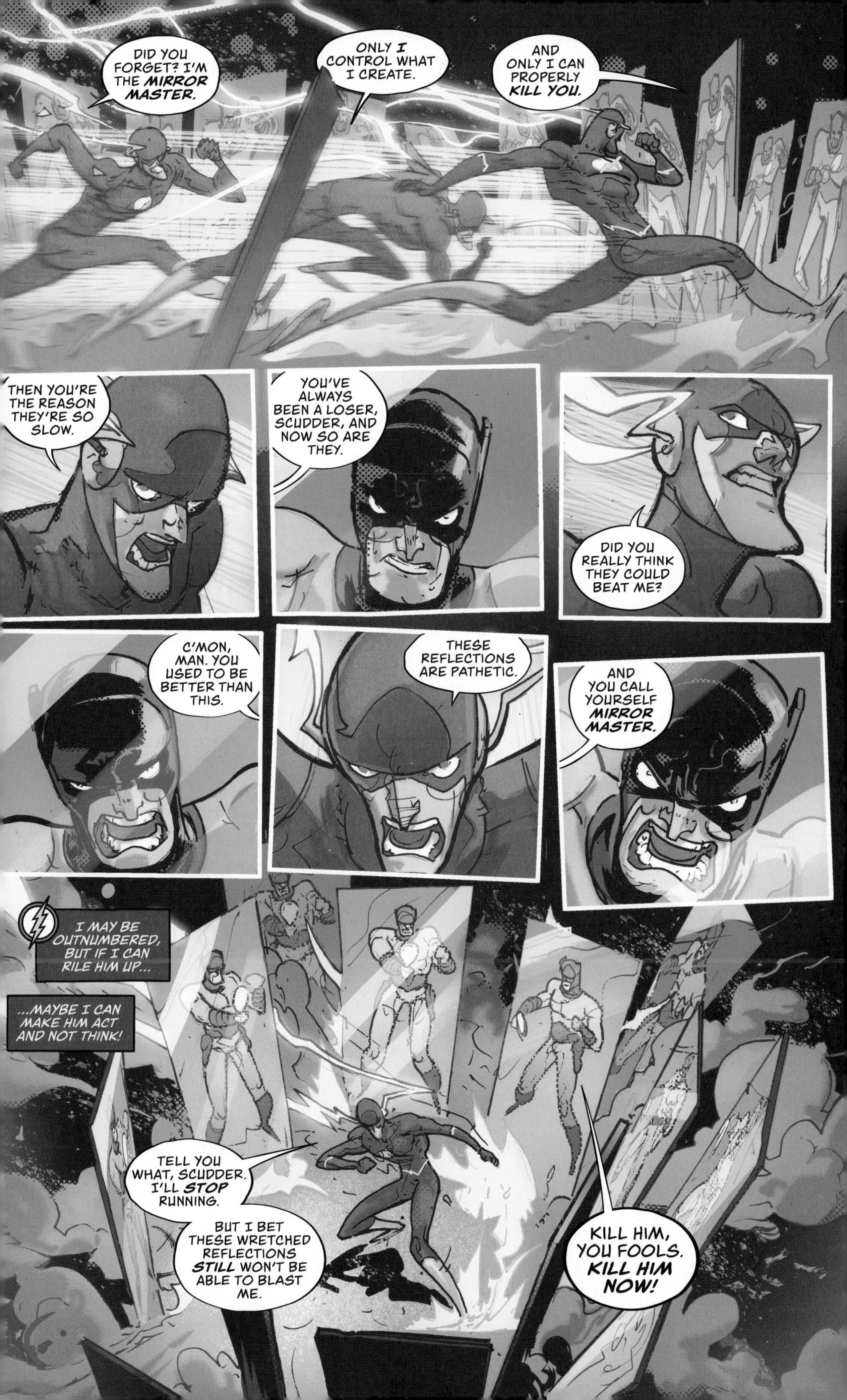
DID YOU FORGET? I'M THE MIRROR MASTER.
ONLY I CONTROL WHAT I CREATE.
AND ONLY I CAN PROPERLY KILL YOU.
THEN YOU'RE THE REASON THEY'RE SO SLOW.
YOU'VE ALWAYS BEEN A LOSER, SCUDDER, AND NOW SO ARE THEY.
DID YOU REALLY THINK THEY COULD BEAT ME?
C'MON, MAN. YOU USED TO BE BETTER THAN THIS.
THESE REFLECTIONS ARE PATHETIC.
AND YOU CALL YOURSELF MIRROR MASTER.
I MAY BE OUTNUMBERED, BUT IF I CAN RILE HIM UP...
...MAYBE I CAN MAKE HIM ACT AND NOT THINK!
TELL YOU WHAT, SCUDDER. I'LL STOP RUNNING.
BUT I BET THESE WRETCHED REFLECTIONS STILL WON'T BE ABLE TO BLAST ME.
KILL HIM, YOU FOOLS. KILL HIM NOW!

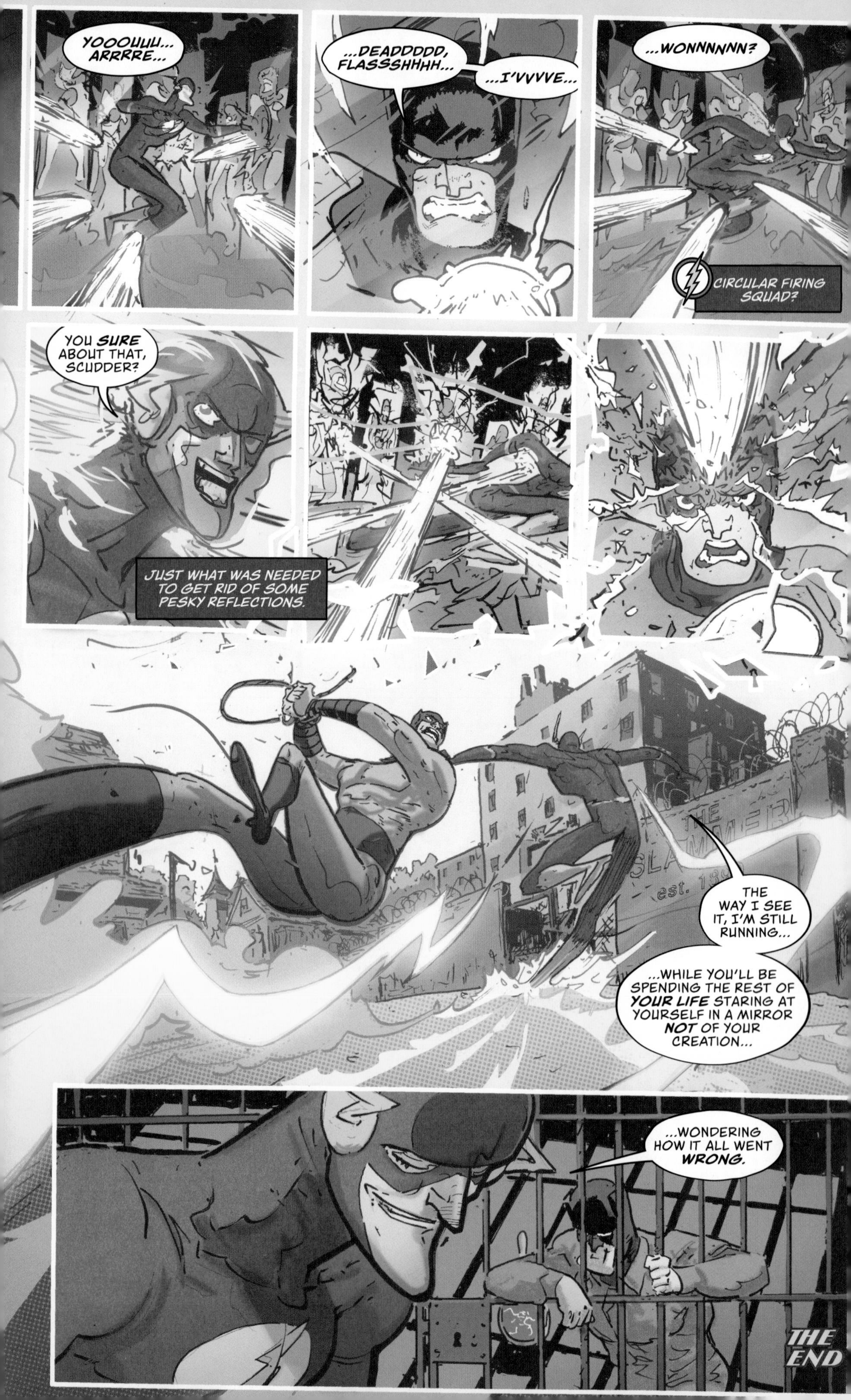
YOOOUUU... ARRRRE...
...DEADDDDD, FLASSSHHHH...
...I'VVVVE...
...WONNNNNN?
CIRCULAR FIRING SQUAD?
YOU SURE ABOUT THAT, SCUDDER?
JUST WHAT WAS NEEDED TO GET RID OF SOME PESKY REFLECTIONS.
THE WAY I SEE IT, I'M STILL RUNNING...
...WHILE YOU'LL BE SPENDING THE REST OF YOUR LIFE STARING AT YOURSELF IN A MIRROR NOT OF YOUR CREATION...
...WONDERING HOW IT ALL WENT WRONG.
THE END

"At the Starting Line..."

JOSHUA WILLIAMSON writer
DAVID MARQUEZ artist
ALEJANDRO SANCHEZ colors
STEVE WANDS letters

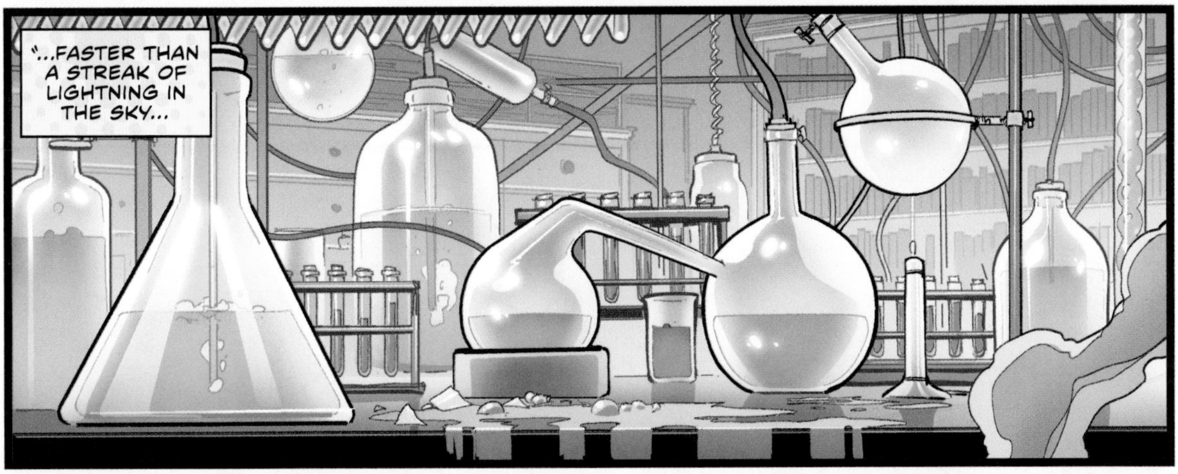

"...FASTER THAN A STREAK OF LIGHTNING IN THE SKY...

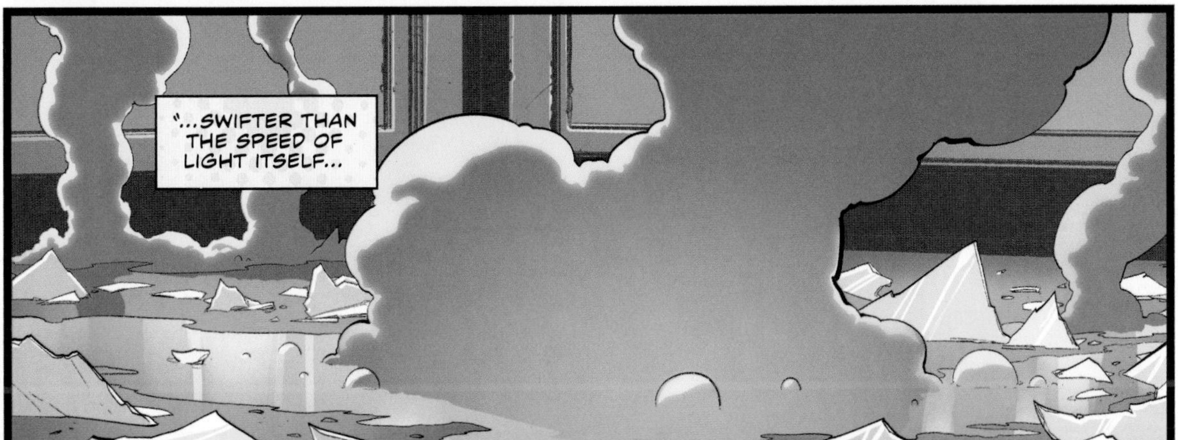

"...SWIFTER THAN THE SPEED OF LIGHT ITSELF...

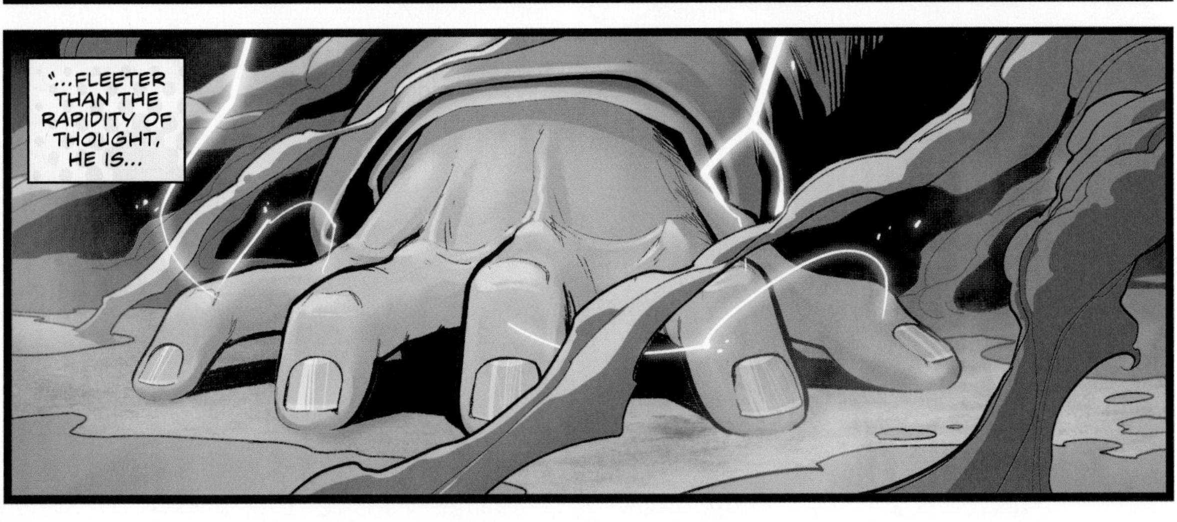

"...FLEETER THAN THE RAPIDITY OF THOUGHT, HE IS...

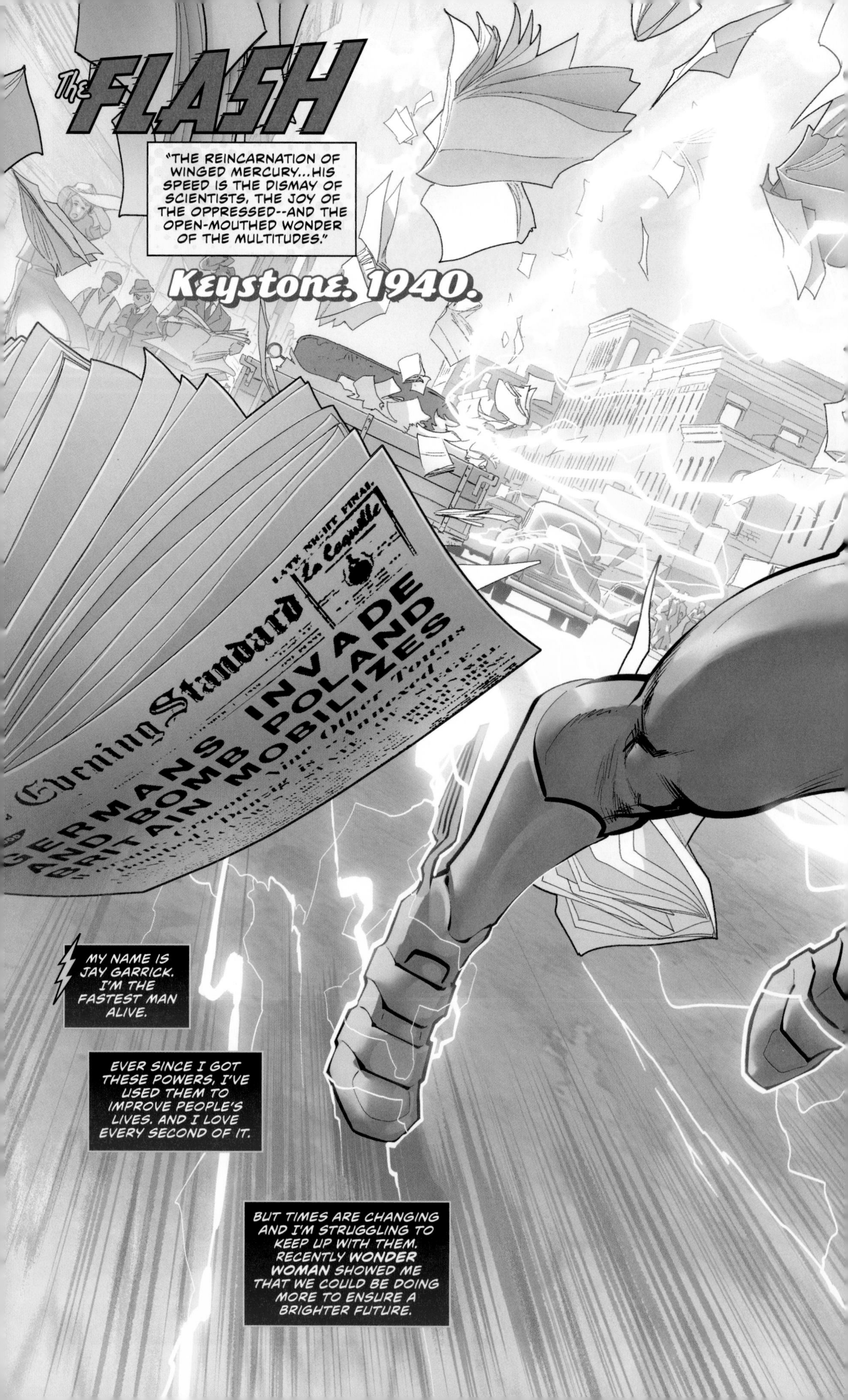

The FLASH
"THE REINCARNATION OF WINGED MERCURY...HIS SPEED IS THE DISMAY OF SCIENTISTS, THE JOY OF THE OPPRESSED--AND THE OPEN-MOUTHED WONDER OF THE MULTITUDES."
Keystone. 1940.
Evening Standard
GERMANS INVADE
AND BOMB POLAND
BRITAIN MOBILIZES
MY NAME IS JAY GARRICK. I'M THE FASTEST MAN ALIVE.
EVER SINCE I GOT THESE POWERS, I'VE USED THEM TO IMPROVE PEOPLE'S LIVES. AND I LOVE EVERY SECOND OF IT.
BUT TIMES ARE CHANGING AND I'M STRUGGLING TO KEEP UP WITH THEM. RECENTLY WONDER WOMAN SHOWED ME THAT WE COULD BE DOING MORE TO ENSURE A BRIGHTER FUTURE.

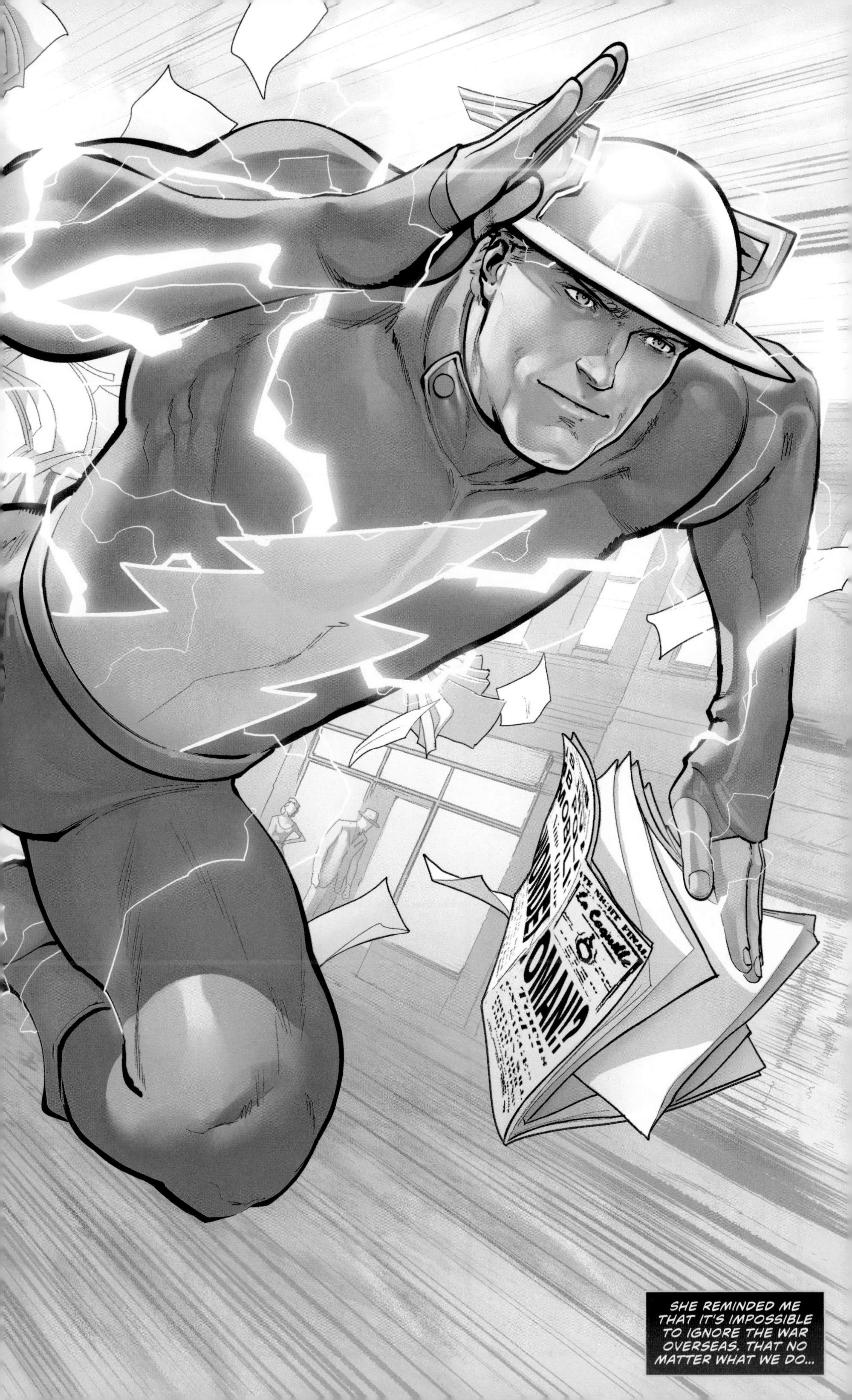
SHE REMINDED ME THAT IT'S IMPOSSIBLE TO IGNORE THE WAR OVERSEAS. THAT NO MATTER WHAT WE DO...

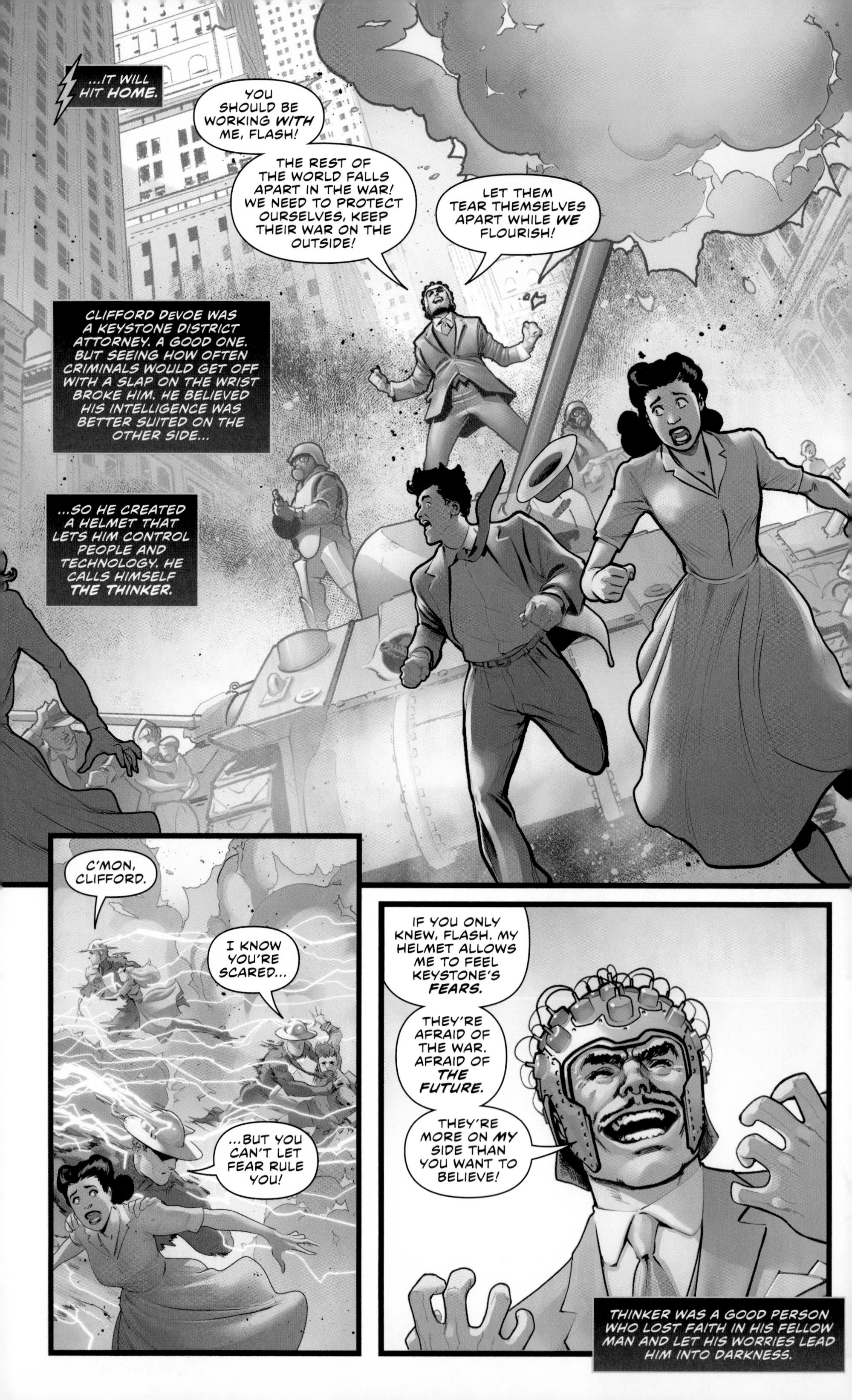

...IT WILL HIT **HOME.**
YOU SHOULD BE WORKING **WITH** ME, FLASH!
THE REST OF THE WORLD FALLS APART IN THE WAR! WE NEED TO PROTECT OURSELVES, KEEP THEIR WAR ON THE OUTSIDE!
LET THEM TEAR THEMSELVES APART WHILE **WE** FLOURISH!
CLIFFORD DEVOE WAS A KEYSTONE DISTRICT ATTORNEY. A GOOD ONE. BUT SEEING HOW OFTEN CRIMINALS WOULD GET OFF WITH A SLAP ON THE WRIST BROKE HIM. HE BELIEVED HIS INTELLIGENCE WAS BETTER SUITED ON THE OTHER SIDE...
...SO HE CREATED A HELMET THAT LETS HIM CONTROL PEOPLE AND TECHNOLOGY. HE CALLS HIMSELF **THE THINKER.**
C'MON, CLIFFORD.
I KNOW YOU'RE SCARED...
...BUT YOU CAN'T LET FEAR RULE YOU!
IF YOU ONLY KNEW, FLASH. MY HELMET ALLOWS ME TO FEEL KEYSTONE'S **FEARS.**
THEY'RE AFRAID OF THE WAR. AFRAID OF **THE FUTURE.**
THEY'RE MORE ON **MY** SIDE THAN YOU WANT TO BELIEVE!
THINKER WAS A GOOD PERSON WHO LOST FAITH IN HIS FELLOW MAN AND LET HIS WORRIES LEAD HIM INTO DARKNESS.

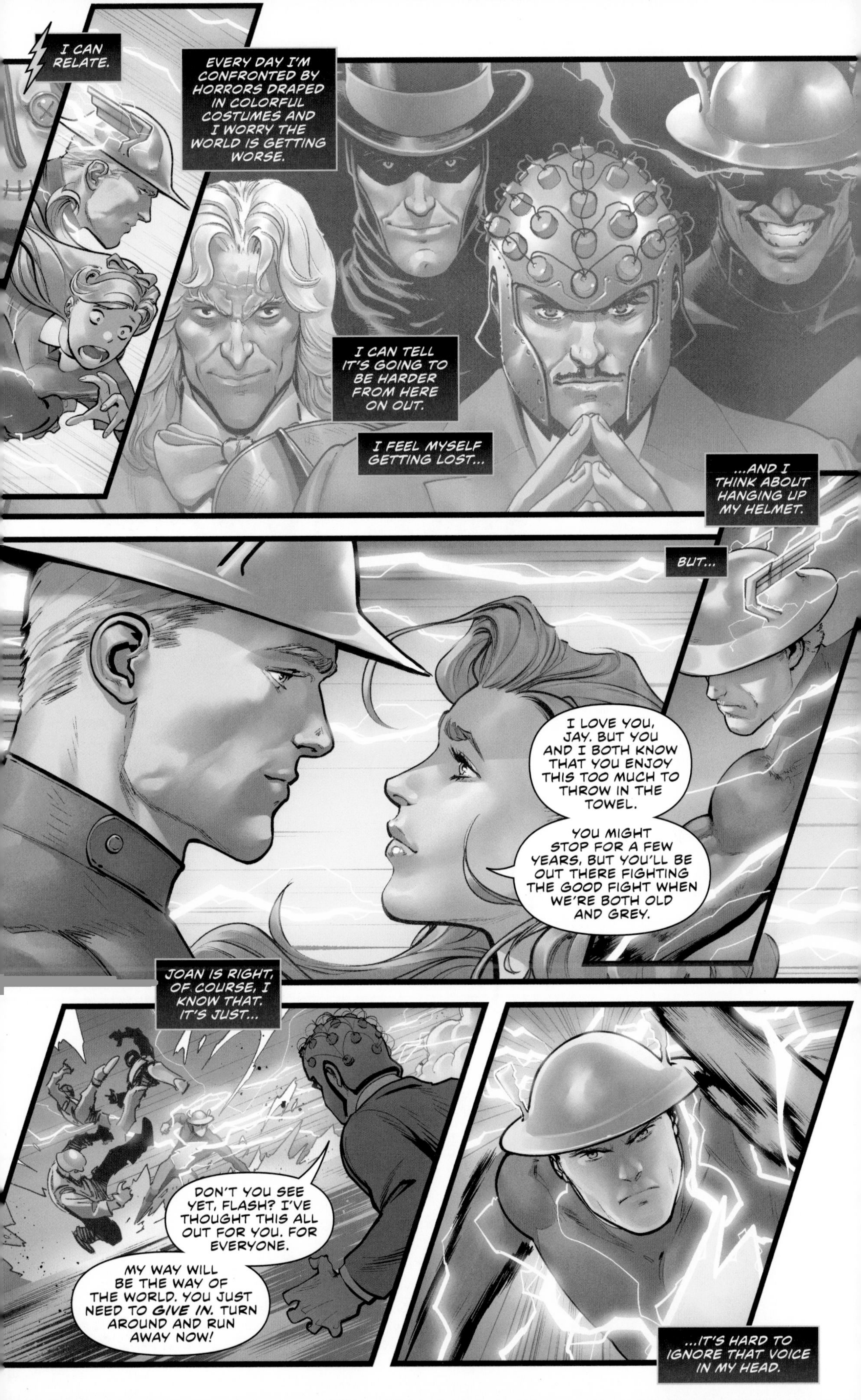
I CAN RELATE.
EVERY DAY I'M CONFRONTED BY HORRORS DRAPED IN COLORFUL COSTUMES AND I WORRY THE WORLD IS GETTING WORSE.
I CAN TELL IT'S GOING TO BE HARDER FROM HERE ON OUT.
I FEEL MYSELF GETTING LOST...
...AND I THINK ABOUT HANGING UP MY HELMET.
BUT...
I LOVE YOU, JAY. BUT YOU AND I BOTH KNOW THAT YOU ENJOY THIS TOO MUCH TO THROW IN THE TOWEL.
YOU MIGHT STOP FOR A FEW YEARS, BUT YOU'LL BE OUT THERE FIGHTING THE GOOD FIGHT WHEN WE'RE BOTH OLD AND GREY.
JOAN IS RIGHT, OF COURSE, I KNOW THAT. IT'S JUST...
DON'T YOU SEE YET, FLASH? I'VE THOUGHT THIS ALL OUT FOR YOU. FOR EVERYONE.
MY WAY WILL BE THE WAY OF THE WORLD. YOU JUST NEED TO GIVE IN. TURN AROUND AND RUN AWAY NOW!
...IT'S HARD TO IGNORE THAT VOICE IN MY HEAD.

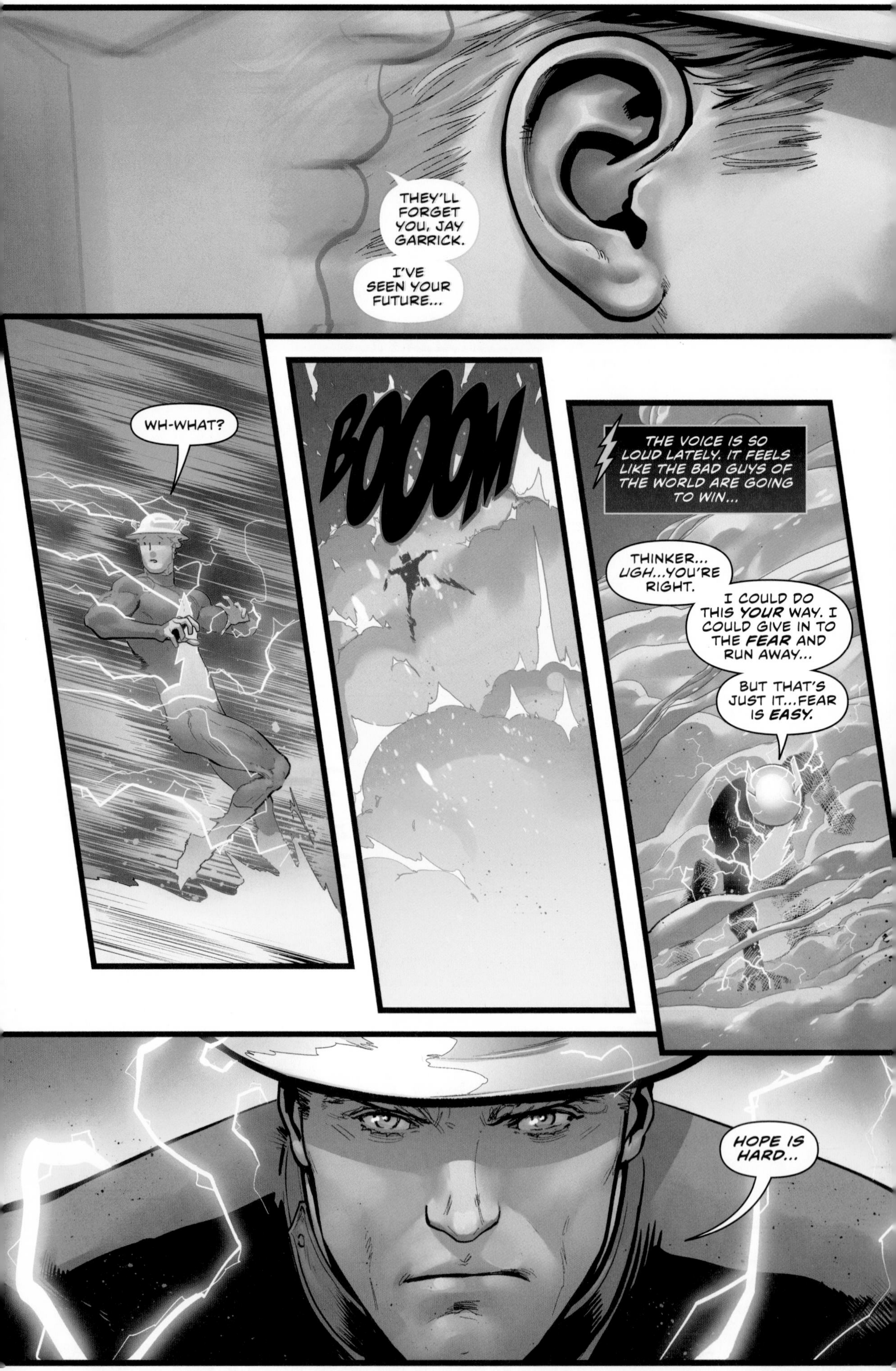
THEY'LL FORGET YOU, JAY GARRICK.
I'VE SEEN YOUR FUTURE...
WH-WHAT?
BOOOM
THE VOICE IS SO LOUD LATELY. IT FEELS LIKE THE BAD GUYS OF THE WORLD ARE GOING TO WIN...
THINKER... UGH...YOU'RE RIGHT.
I COULD DO THIS YOUR WAY. I COULD GIVE IN TO THE FEAR AND RUN AWAY...
BUT THAT'S JUST IT...FEAR IS EASY.
HOPE IS HARD...

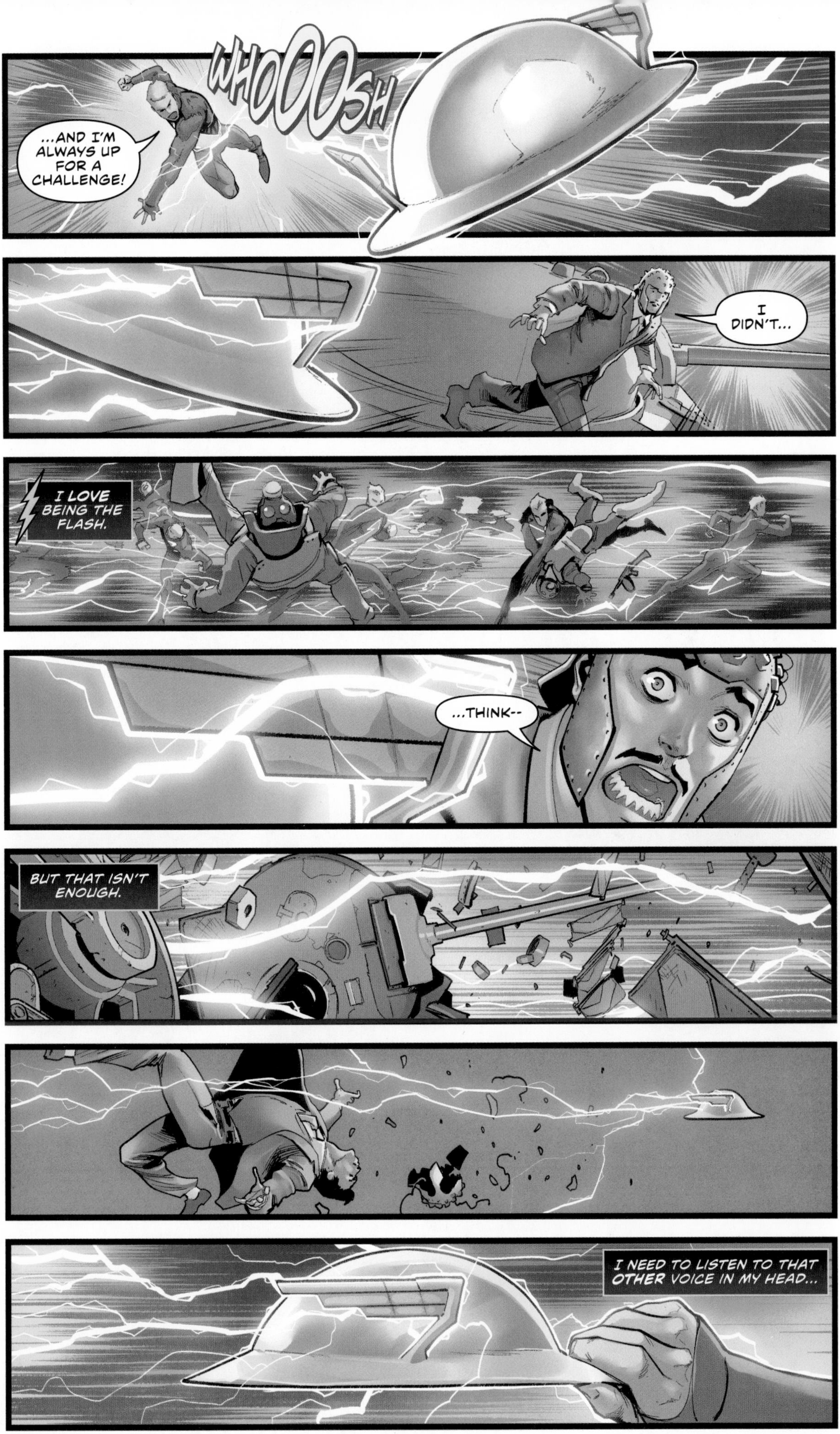
WHOOOOSH
...AND I'M ALWAYS UP FOR A CHALLENGE!
I DIDN'T...
I LOVE BEING THE FLASH.
...THINK--
BUT THAT ISN'T ENOUGH.
I NEED TO LISTEN TO THAT OTHER VOICE IN MY HEAD...

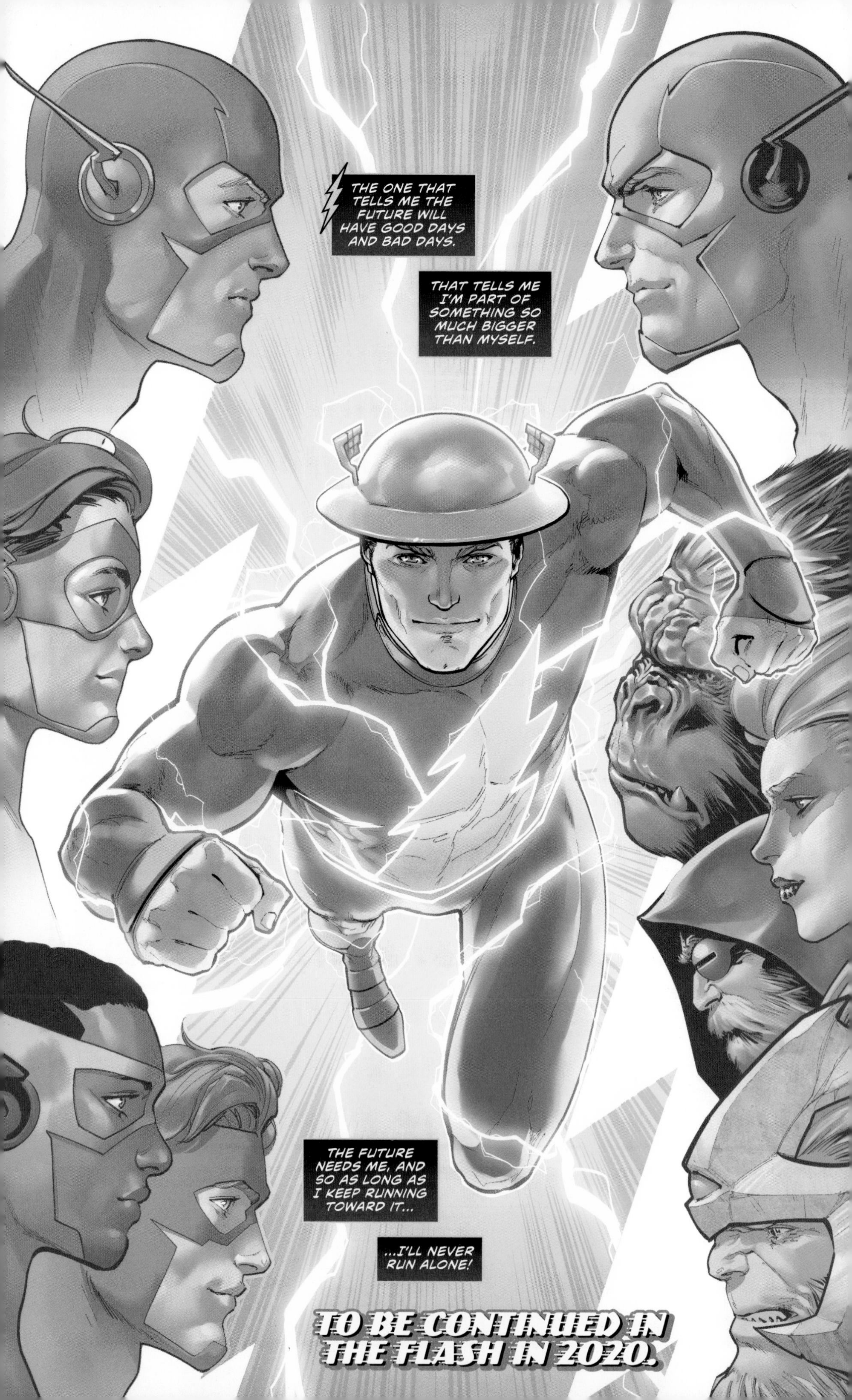
THE ONE THAT TELLS ME THE FUTURE WILL HAVE GOOD DAYS AND BAD DAYS.
THAT TELLS ME I'M PART OF SOMETHING SO MUCH BIGGER THAN MYSELF.
THE FUTURE NEEDS ME, AND SO AS LONG AS I KEEP RUNNING TOWARD IT...
...I'LL NEVER RUN ALONE!
TO BE CONTINUED IN THE FLASH IN 2020.

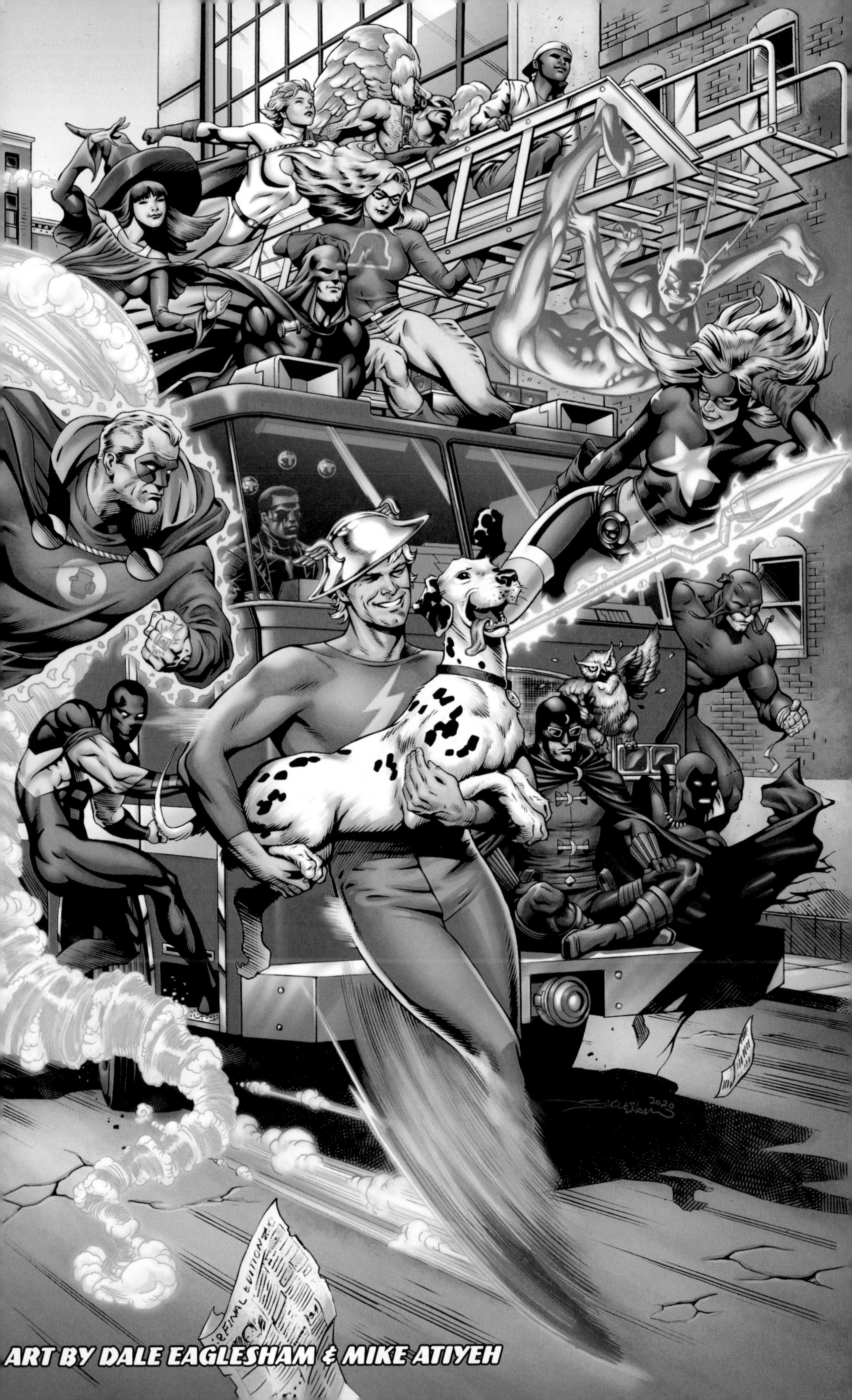
FINAL EDITION
EAGLESHAM 2020

ART BY DALE EAGLESHAM & MIKE ATIYEH

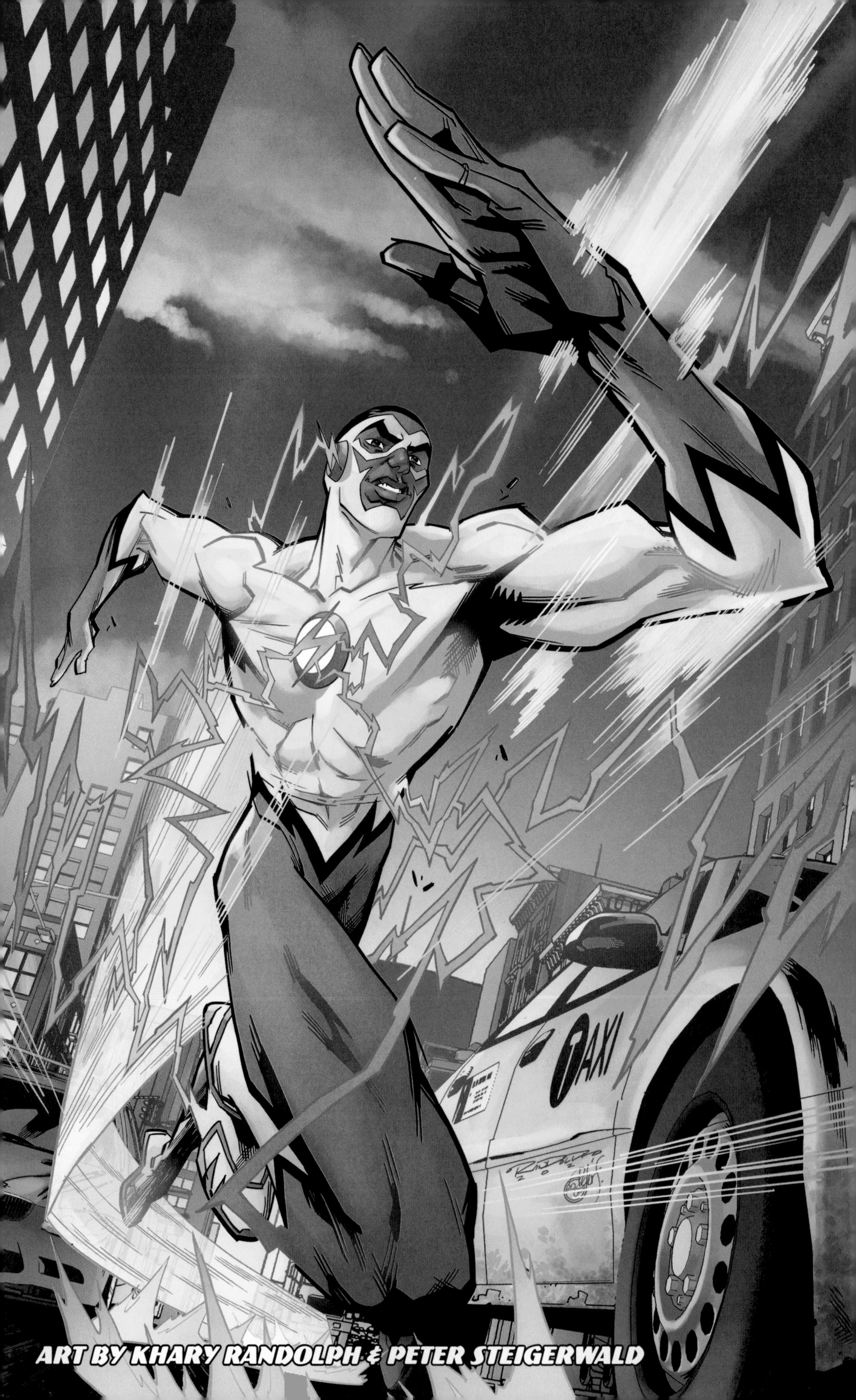
TAXI

ART BY KHARY RANDOLPH & PETER STEIGERWALD

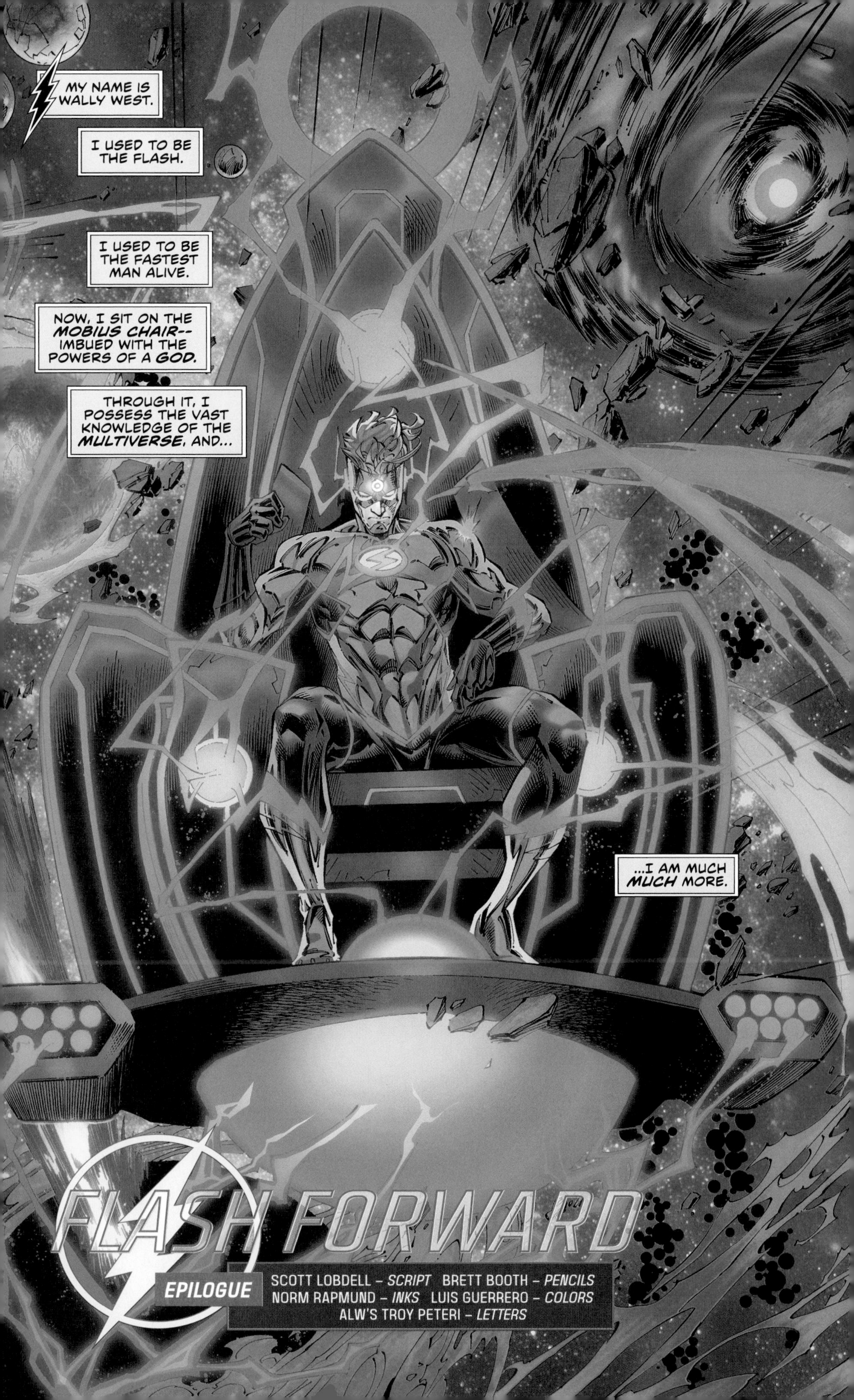
MY NAME IS WALLY WEST.
I USED TO BE THE FLASH.
I USED TO BE THE FASTEST MAN ALIVE.
NOW, I SIT ON THE MOBIUS CHAIR--IMBUED WITH THE POWERS OF A GOD.
THROUGH IT, I POSSESS THE VAST KNOWLEDGE OF THE MULTIVERSE, AND...
...I AM MUCH MUCH MORE.
FLASH FORWARD
EPILOGUE
SCOTT LOBDELL – SCRIPT BRETT BOOTH – PENCILS
NORM RAPMUND – INKS LUIS GUERRERO – COLORS
ALW'S TROY PETERI – LETTERS

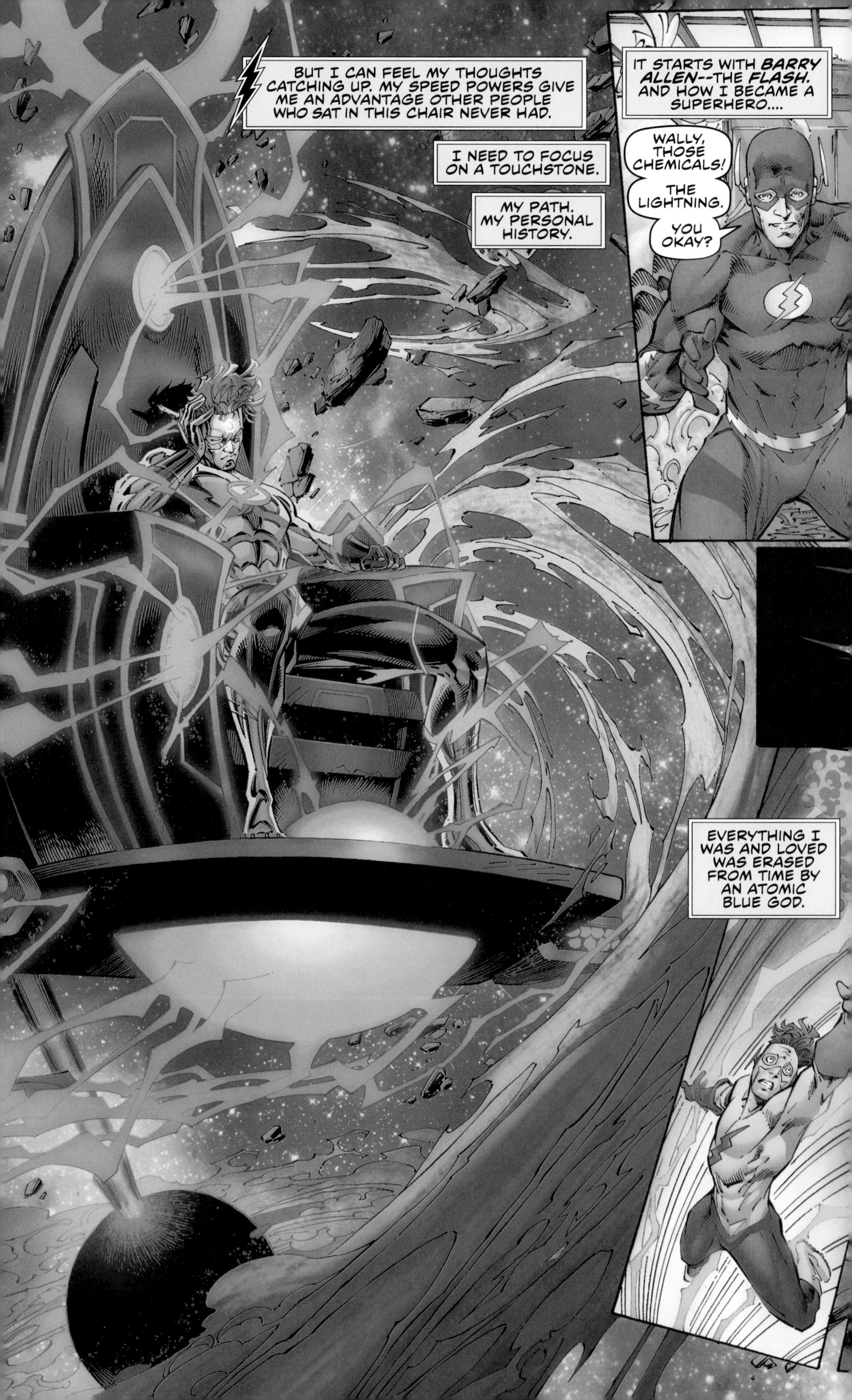
BUT I CAN FEEL MY THOUGHTS CATCHING UP. MY SPEED POWERS GIVE ME AN ADVANTAGE OTHER PEOPLE WHO SAT IN THIS CHAIR NEVER HAD.
I NEED TO FOCUS ON A TOUCHSTONE.
MY PATH. MY PERSONAL HISTORY.
IT STARTS WITH *BARRY ALLEN*--THE *FLASH.* AND HOW I BECAME A SUPERHERO....
WALLY, THOSE CHEMICALS!
THE LIGHTNING.
YOU OKAY?
EVERYTHING I WAS AND LOVED WAS ERASED FROM TIME BY AN ATOMIC BLUE GOD.

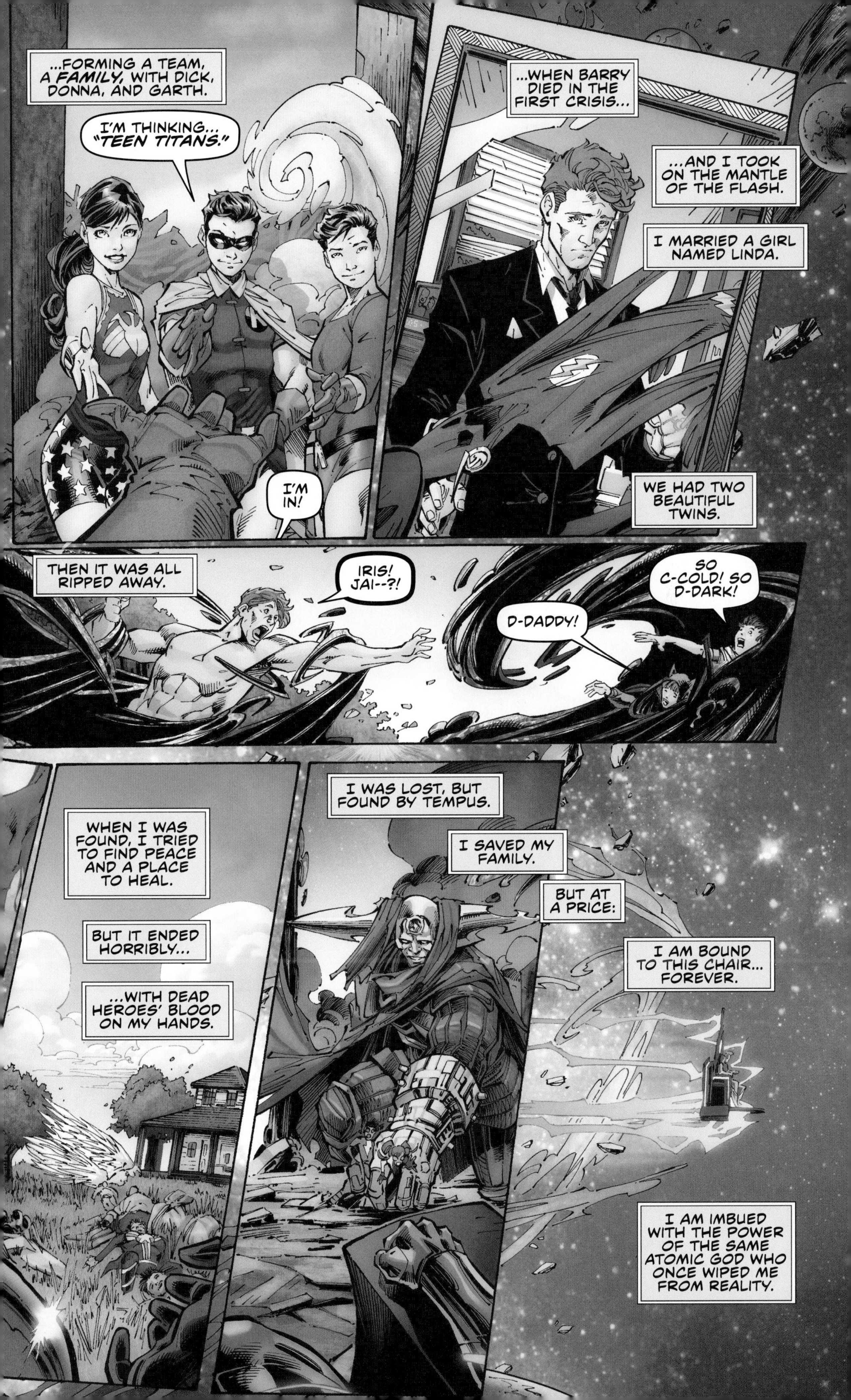

...FORMING A TEAM, A *FAMILY,* WITH DICK, DONNA, AND GARTH.
I'M THINKING... *"TEEN TITANS."*
I'M IN!
...WHEN BARRY DIED IN THE FIRST CRISIS...
...AND I TOOK ON THE MANTLE OF THE FLASH.
I MARRIED A GIRL NAMED LINDA.
WE HAD TWO BEAUTIFUL TWINS.
THEN IT WAS ALL RIPPED AWAY.
IRIS! JAI--?!
SO C-COLD! SO D-DARK!
D-DADDY!
WHEN I WAS FOUND, I TRIED TO FIND PEACE AND A PLACE TO HEAL.
BUT IT ENDED HORRIBLY...
...WITH DEAD HEROES' BLOOD ON MY HANDS.
I WAS LOST, BUT FOUND BY TEMPUS.
I SAVED MY FAMILY.
BUT AT A PRICE:
I AM BOUND TO THIS CHAIR... FOREVER.
I AM IMBUED WITH THE POWER OF THE SAME ATOMIC GOD WHO ONCE WIPED ME FROM REALITY.

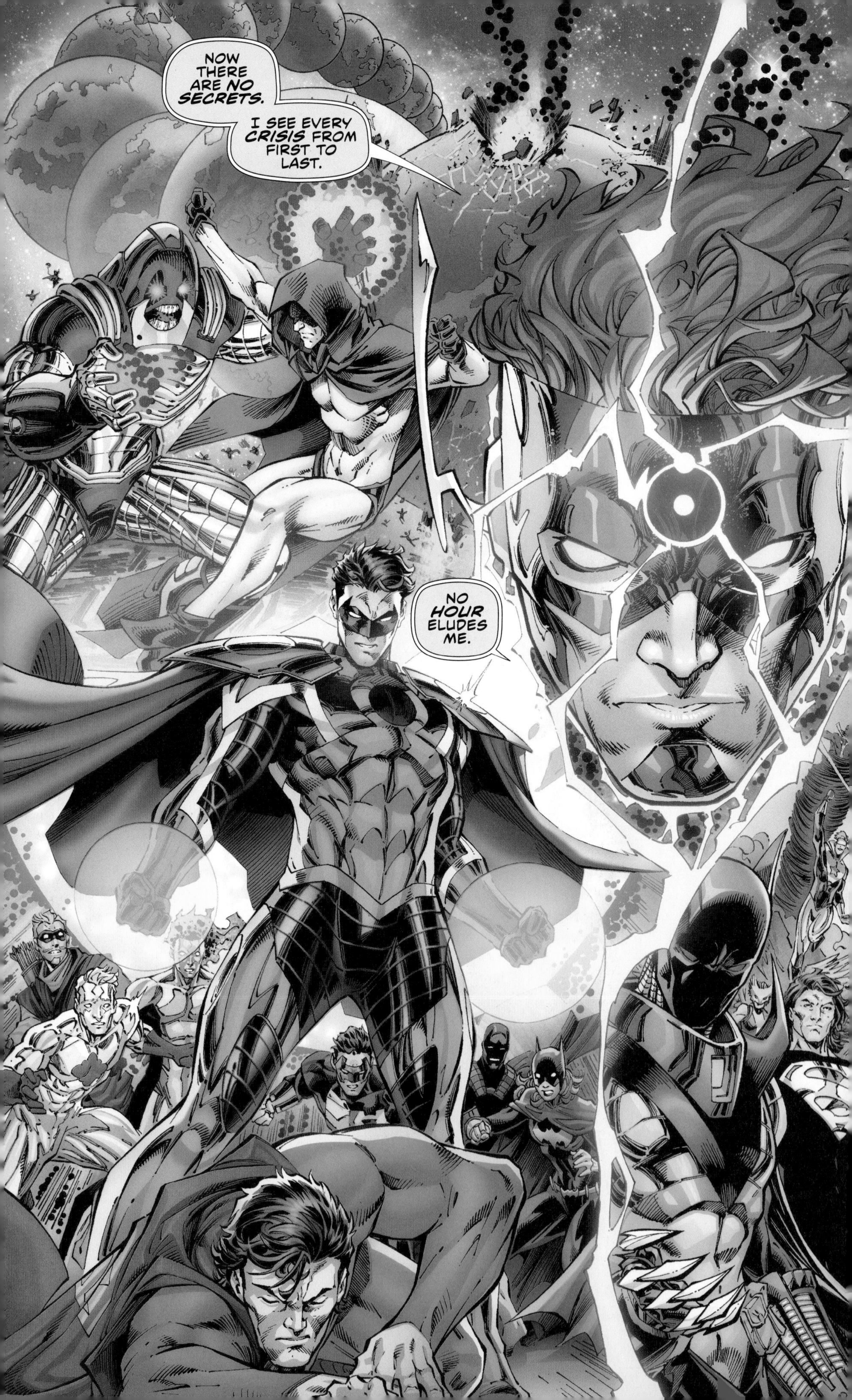
NOW THERE ARE NO SECRETS.
I SEE EVERY CRISIS FROM FIRST TO LAST.
NO HOUR ELUDES ME.

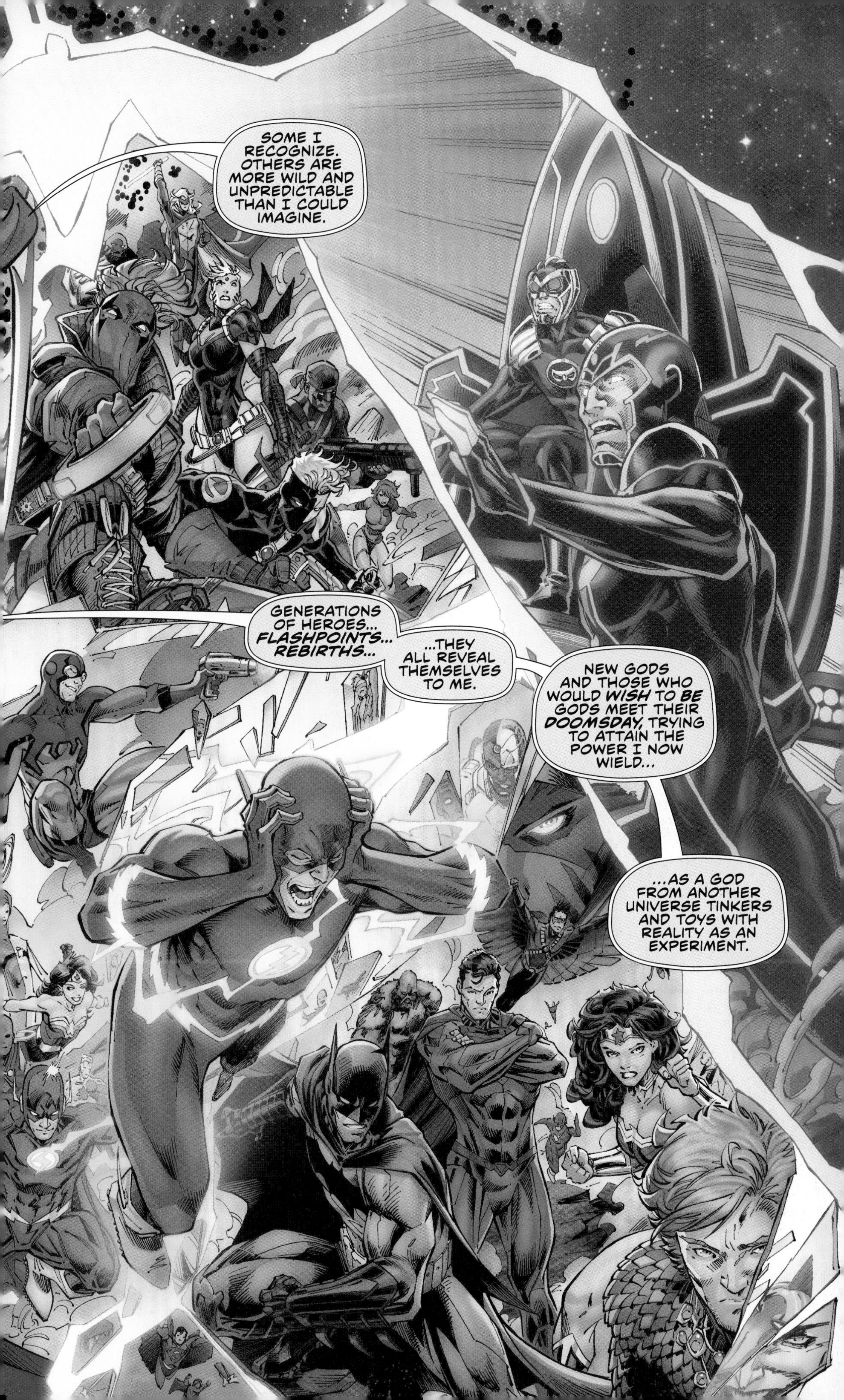
SOME I RECOGNIZE. OTHERS ARE MORE WILD AND UNPREDICTABLE THAN I COULD IMAGINE.
GENERATIONS OF HEROES... FLASHPOINTS... REBIRTHS...
...THEY ALL REVEAL THEMSELVES TO ME.
NEW GODS AND THOSE WHO WOULD WISH TO BE GODS MEET THEIR DOOMSDAY, TRYING TO ATTAIN THE POWER I NOW WIELD...
...AS A GOD FROM ANOTHER UNIVERSE TINKERS AND TOYS WITH REALITY AS AN EXPERIMENT.

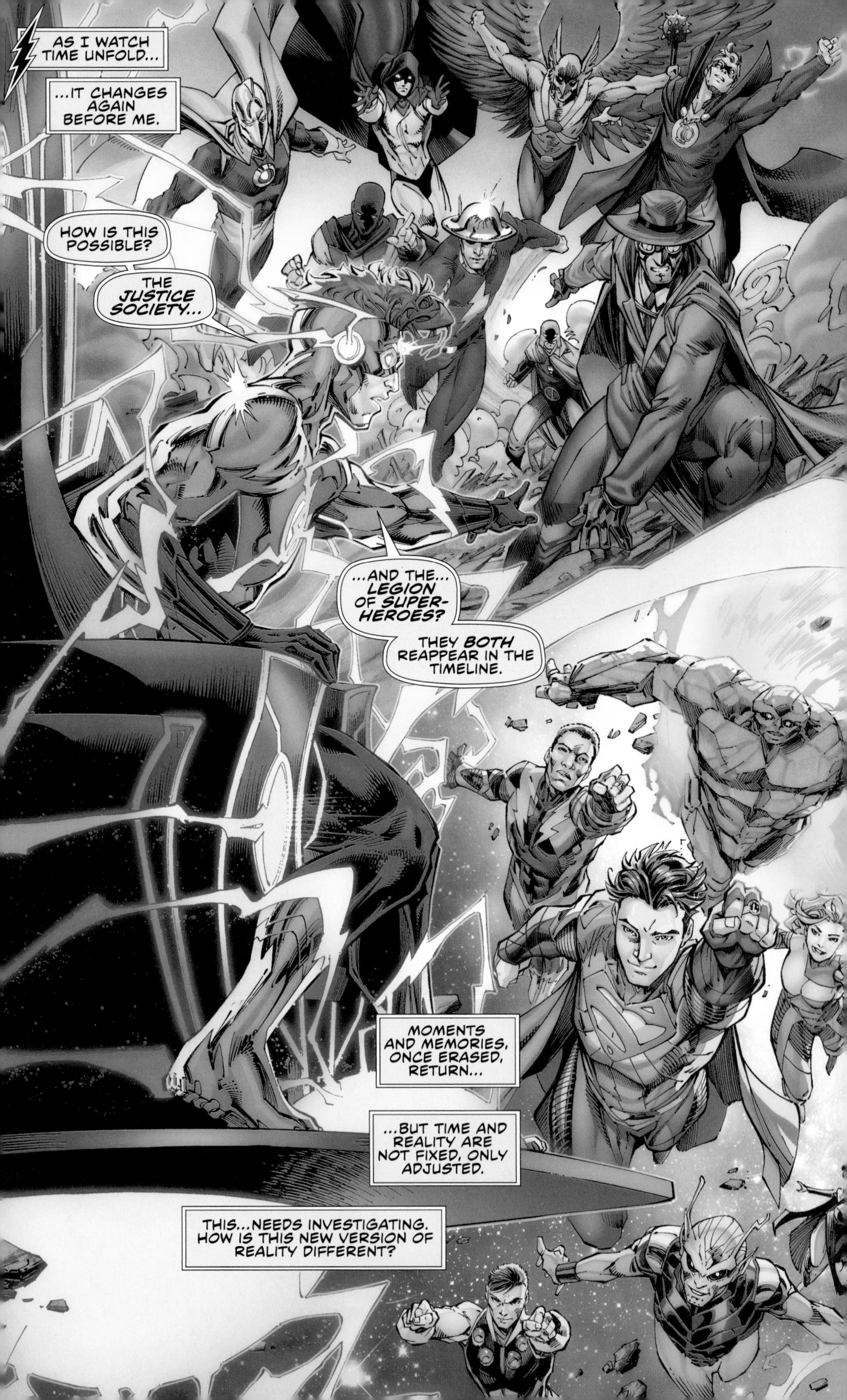

AS I WATCH TIME UNFOLD...
...IT CHANGES AGAIN BEFORE ME.
HOW IS THIS POSSIBLE?
THE *JUSTICE SOCIETY*...
...AND THE... *LEGION* OF *SUPER-HEROES*?
THEY *BOTH* REAPPEAR IN THE TIMELINE.
MOMENTS AND MEMORIES, ONCE ERASED, RETURN...
...BUT TIME AND REALITY ARE NOT FIXED, ONLY ADJUSTED.
THIS...NEEDS INVESTIGATING. HOW IS THIS NEW VERSION OF REALITY DIFFERENT?

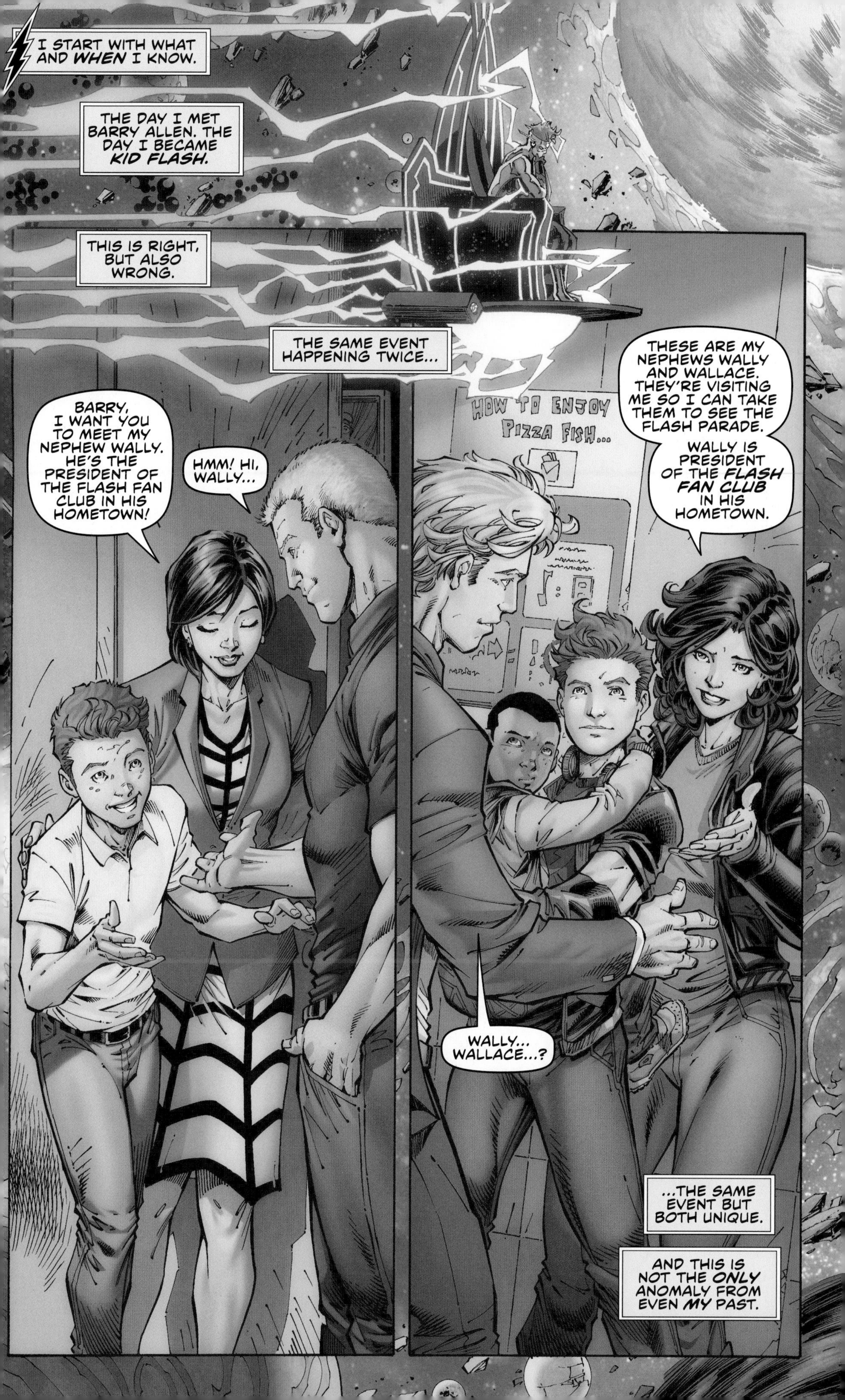
I START WITH WHAT AND WHEN I KNOW.
THE DAY I MET BARRY ALLEN. THE DAY I BECAME KID FLASH.
THIS IS RIGHT, BUT ALSO WRONG.
THE SAME EVENT HAPPENING TWICE...
BARRY, I WANT YOU TO MEET MY NEPHEW WALLY. HE'S THE PRESIDENT OF THE FLASH FAN CLUB IN HIS HOMETOWN!
HMM! HI, WALLY...
HOW TO ENJOY PIZZA FISH...
THESE ARE MY NEPHEWS WALLY AND WALLACE. THEY'RE VISITING ME SO I CAN TAKE THEM TO SEE THE FLASH PARADE.
WALLY IS PRESIDENT OF THE FLASH FAN CLUB IN HIS HOMETOWN.
WALLY... WALLACE...?
...THE SAME EVENT BUT BOTH UNIQUE.
AND THIS IS NOT THE ONLY ANOMALY FROM EVEN MY PAST.

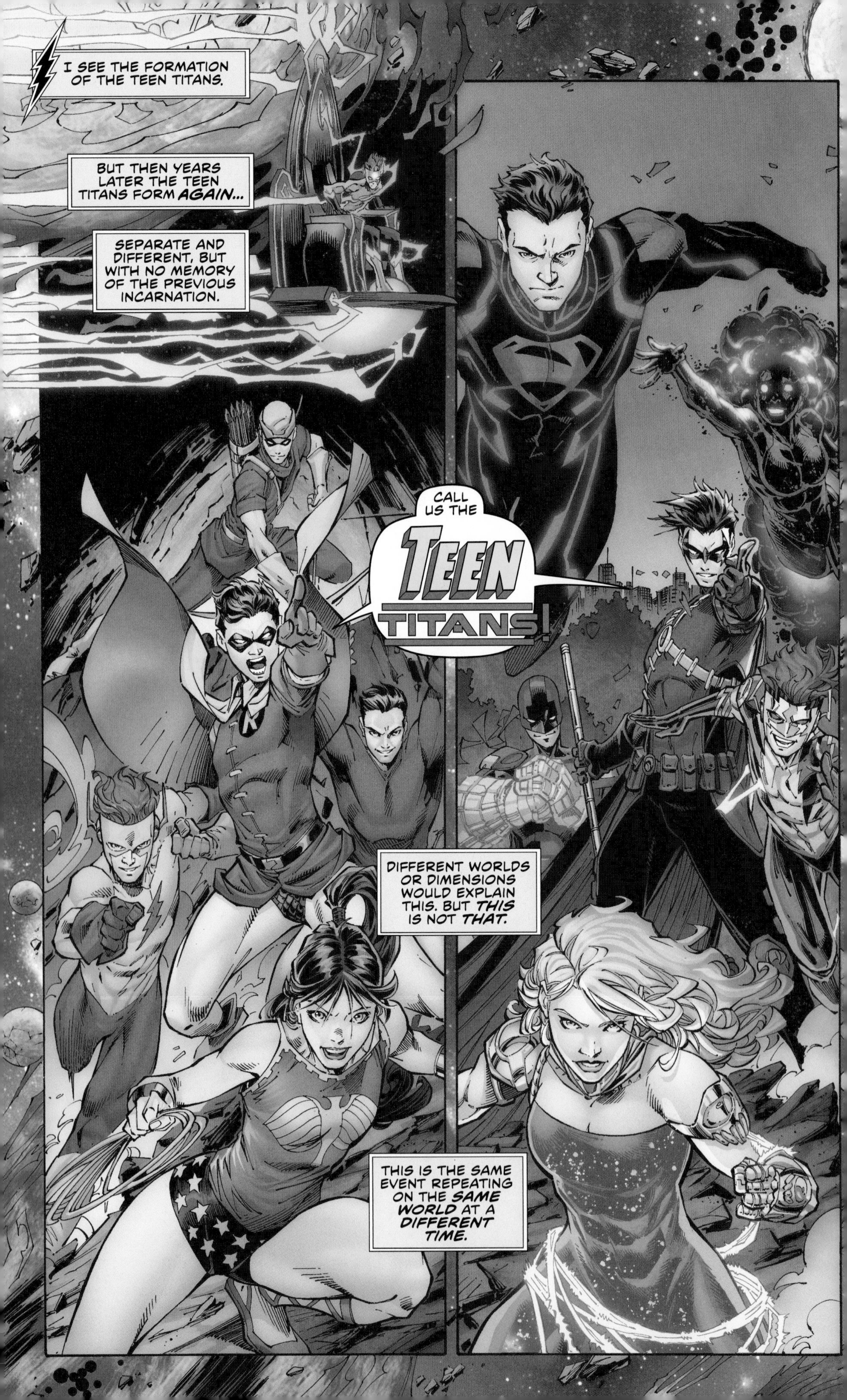

I SEE THE FORMATION OF THE TEEN TITANS.
BUT THEN YEARS LATER THE TEEN TITANS FORM AGAIN...
SEPARATE AND DIFFERENT, BUT WITH NO MEMORY OF THE PREVIOUS INCARNATION.
CALL US THE TEEN TITANS!
DIFFERENT WORLDS OR DIMENSIONS WOULD EXPLAIN THIS. BUT THIS IS NOT THAT.
THIS IS THE SAME EVENT REPEATING ON THE SAME WORLD AT A DIFFERENT TIME.

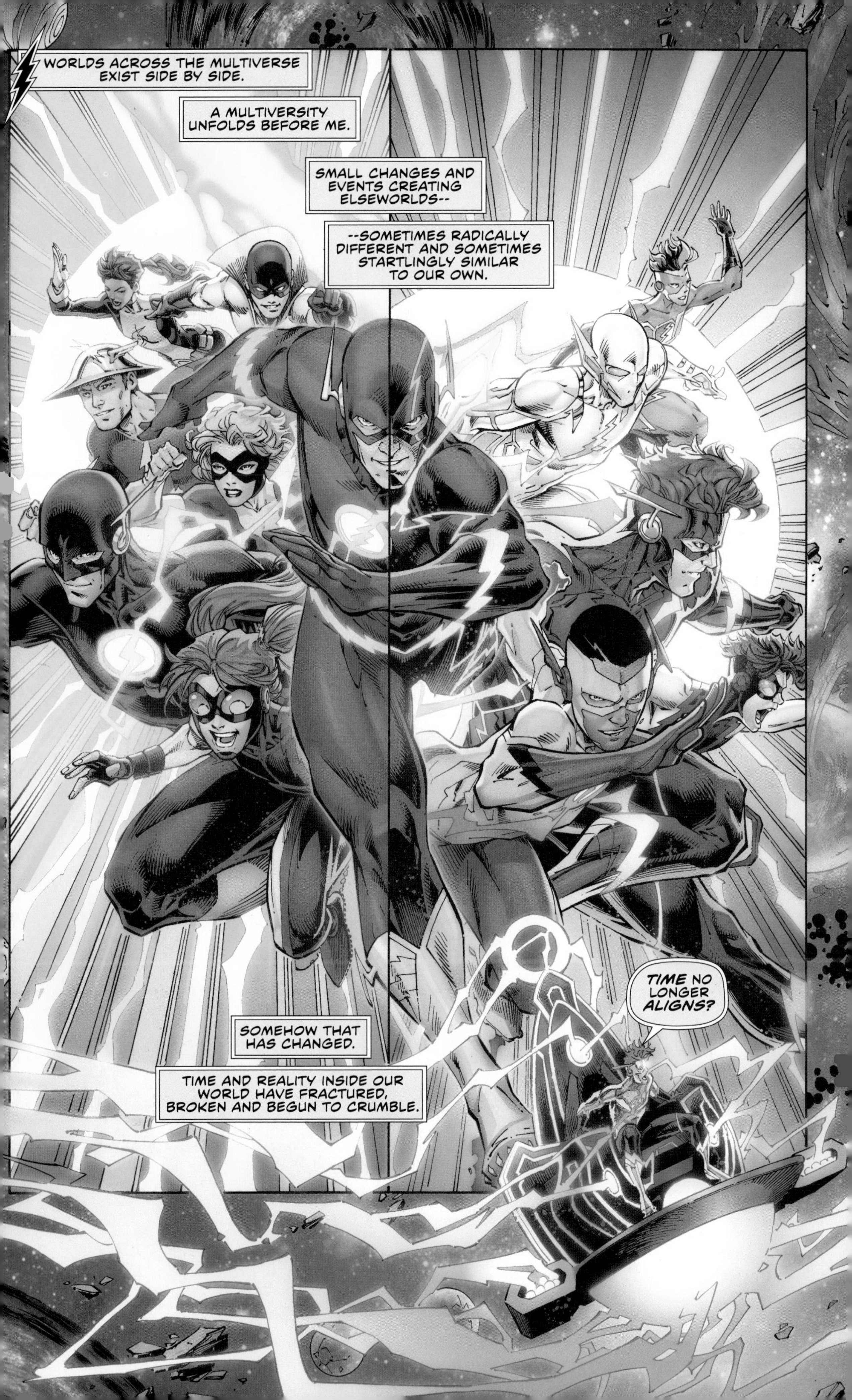
WORLDS ACROSS THE MULTIVERSE EXIST SIDE BY SIDE.
A MULTIVERSITY UNFOLDS BEFORE ME.
SMALL CHANGES AND EVENTS CREATING ELSEWORLDS--
--SOMETIMES RADICALLY DIFFERENT AND SOMETIMES STARTLINGLY SIMILAR TO OUR OWN.
SOMEHOW THAT HAS CHANGED.
TIME AND REALITY INSIDE OUR WORLD HAVE FRACTURED, BROKEN AND BEGUN TO CRUMBLE.
TIME NO LONGER ALIGNS?

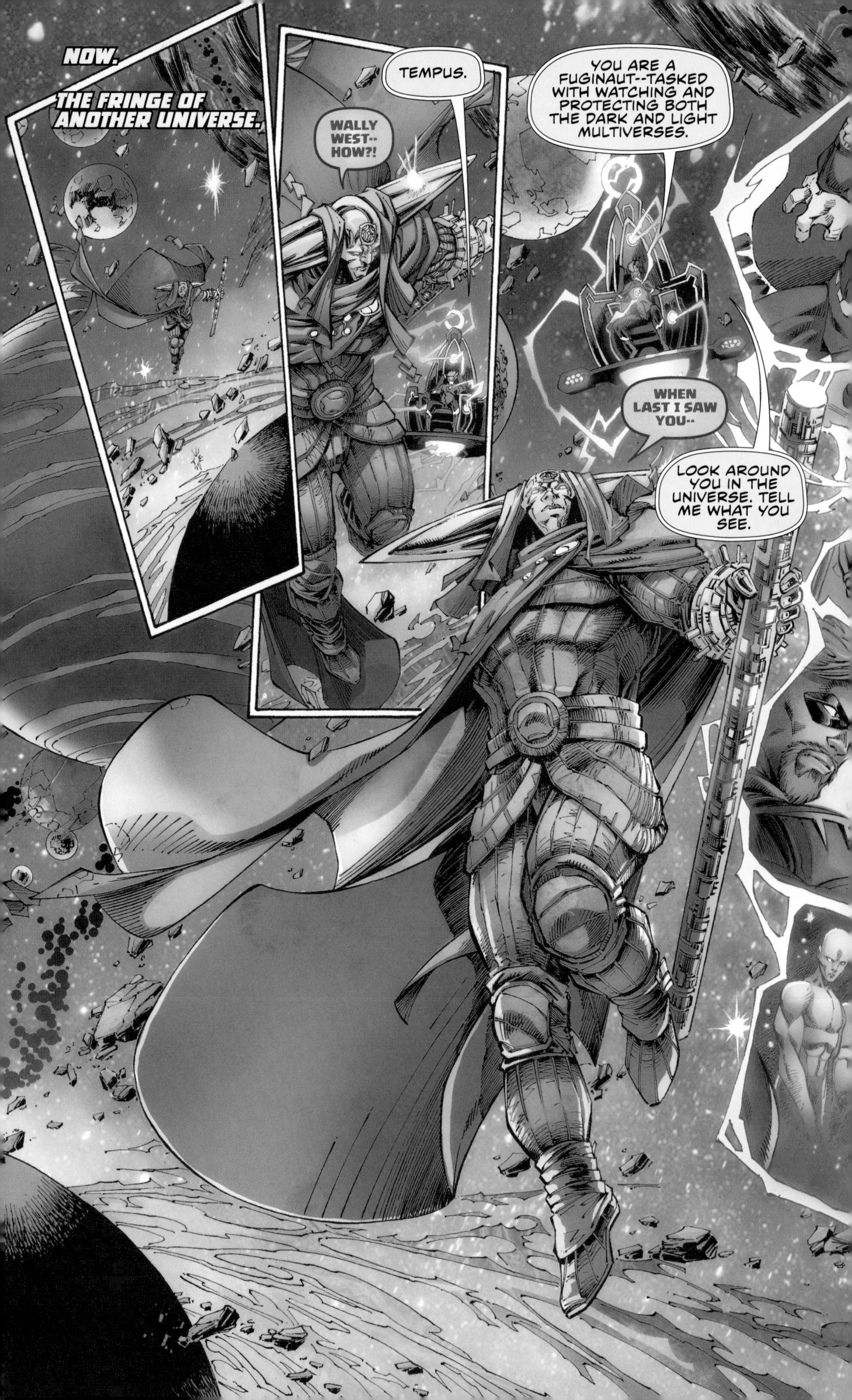
NOW.
THE FRINGE OF ANOTHER UNIVERSE.
TEMPUS.
WALLY WEST-- HOW?!
YOU ARE A FUGINAUT--TASKED WITH WATCHING AND PROTECTING BOTH THE DARK AND LIGHT MULTIVERSES.
WHEN LAST I SAW YOU--
LOOK AROUND YOU IN THE UNIVERSE. TELL ME WHAT YOU SEE.

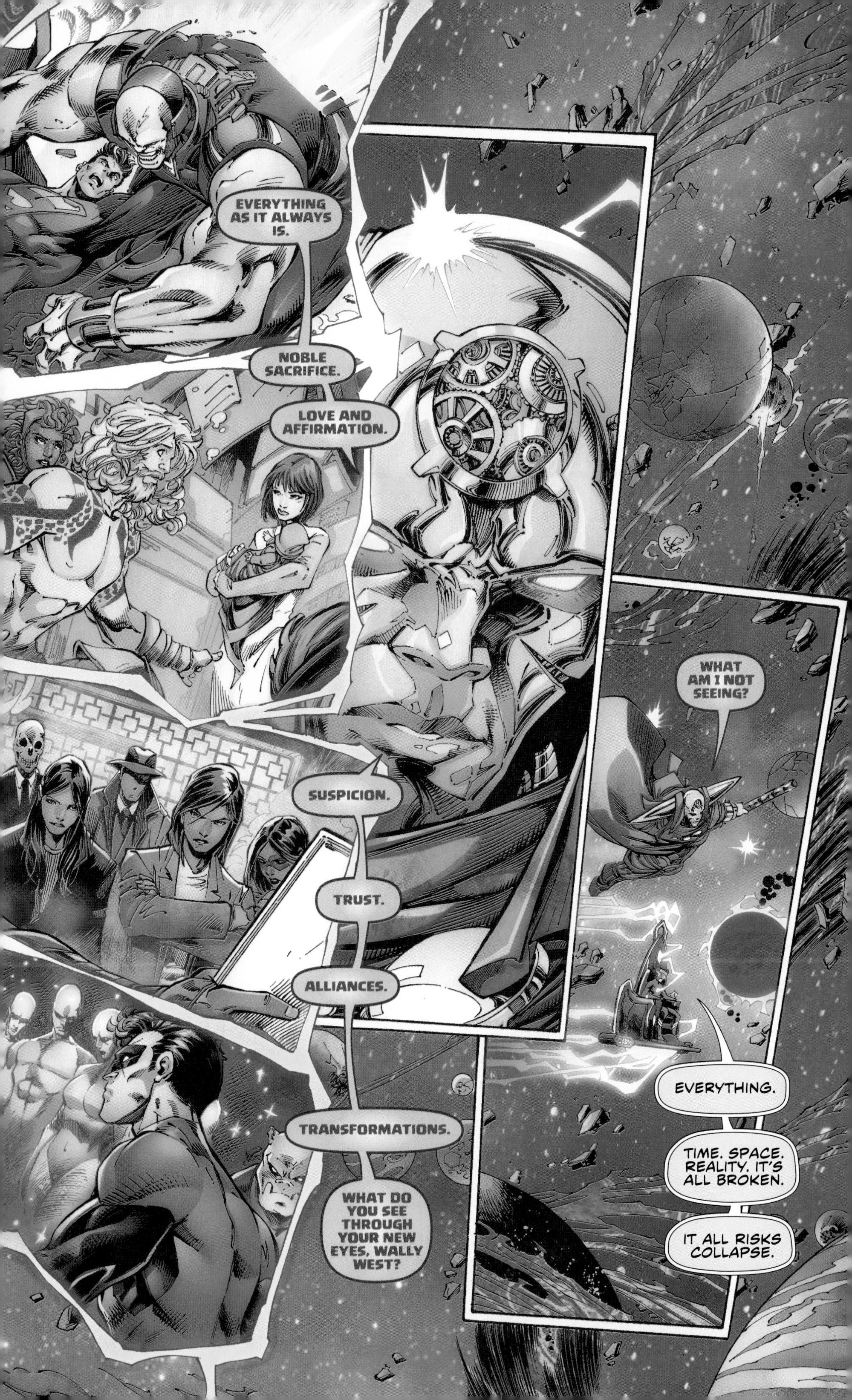
EVERYTHING AS IT ALWAYS IS.
NOBLE SACRIFICE.
LOVE AND AFFIRMATION.
SUSPICION.
TRUST.
ALLIANCES.
TRANSFORMATIONS.
WHAT DO YOU SEE THROUGH YOUR NEW EYES, WALLY WEST?
WHAT AM I NOT SEEING?
EVERYTHING.
TIME. SPACE. REALITY. IT'S ALL BROKEN.
IT ALL RISKS COLLAPSE.

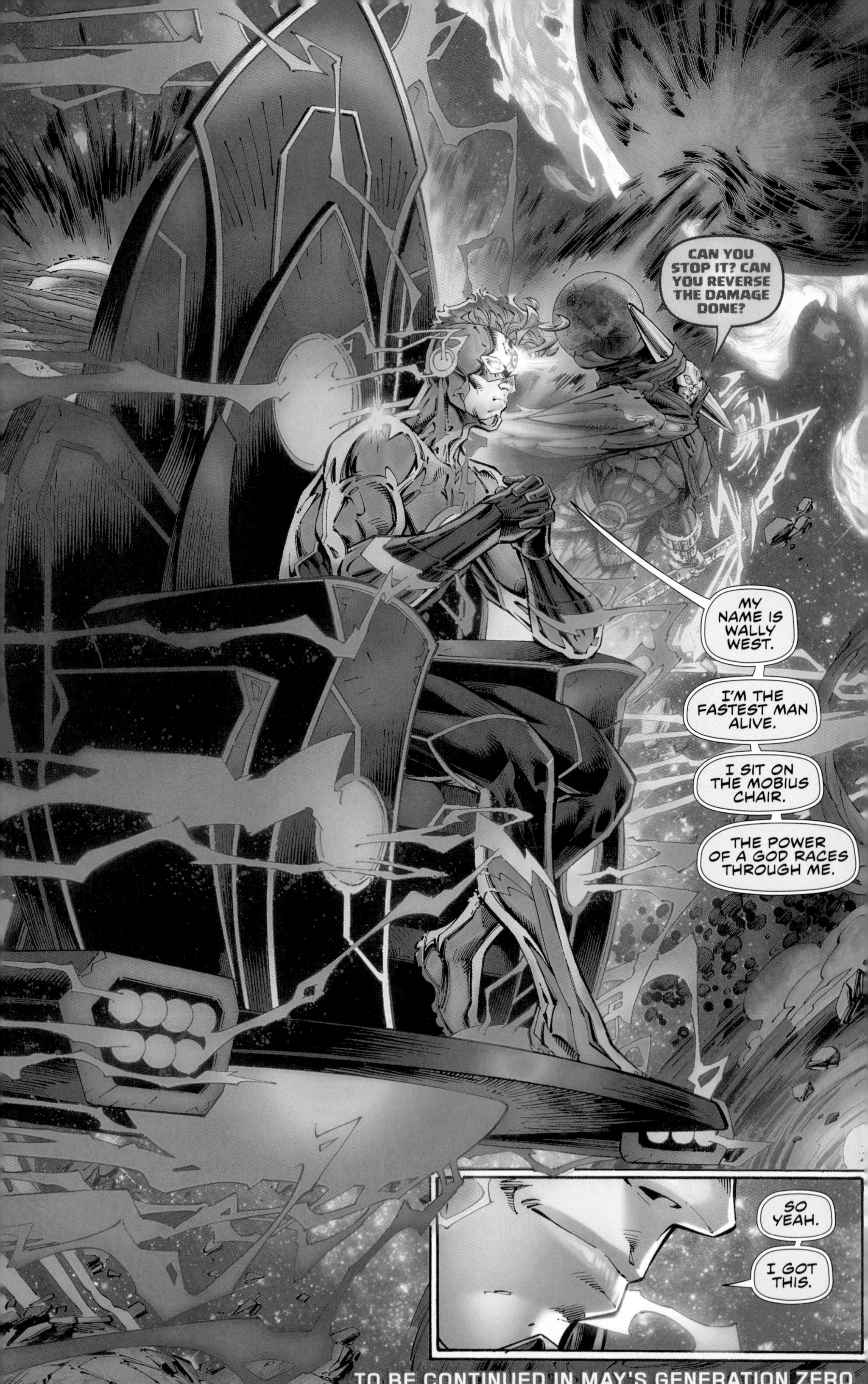
CAN YOU STOP IT? CAN YOU REVERSE THE DAMAGE DONE?
MY NAME IS WALLY WEST.
I'M THE FASTEST MAN ALIVE.
I SIT ON THE MOBIUS CHAIR.
THE POWER OF A GOD RACES THROUGH ME.
SO YEAH.
I GOT THIS.

TO BE CONTINUED IN MAY'S GENERATION ZERO

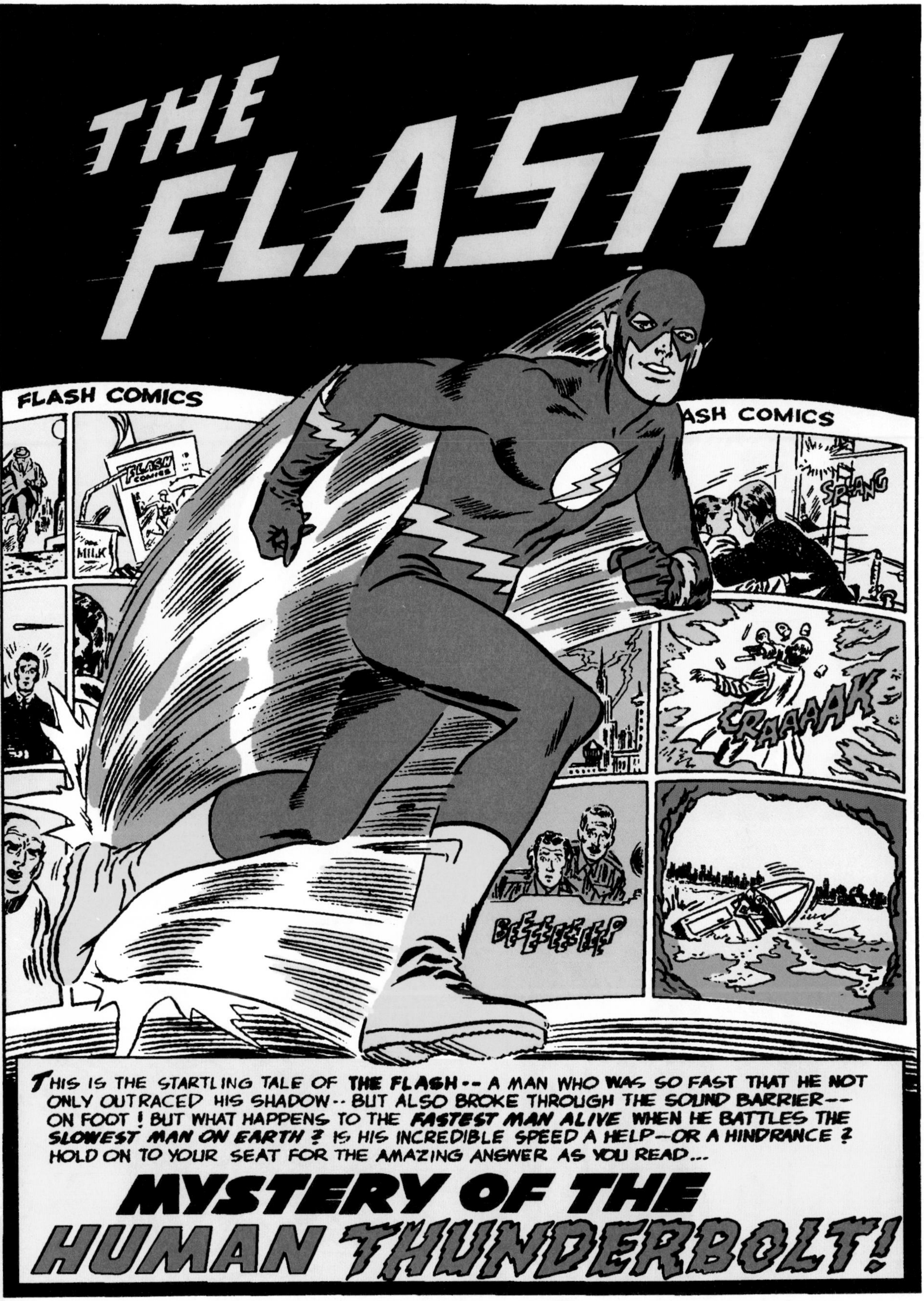
THE FLASH
FLASH COMICS
FLASH COMICS
FLASH COMICS
MILK
SPLANG
CRAAAAK
BEEEEEP
THIS IS THE STARTLING TALE OF THE FLASH -- A MAN WHO WAS SO FAST THAT HE NOT ONLY OUTRACED HIS SHADOW -- BUT ALSO BROKE THROUGH THE SOUND BARRIER -- ON FOOT ! BUT WHAT HAPPENS TO THE FASTEST MAN ALIVE WHEN HE BATTLES THE SLOWEST MAN ON EARTH ? IS HIS INCREDIBLE SPEED A HELP--OR A HINDRANCE ? HOLD ON TO YOUR SEAT FOR THE AMAZING ANSWER AS YOU READ...
MYSTERY OF THE HUMAN THUNDERBOLT!

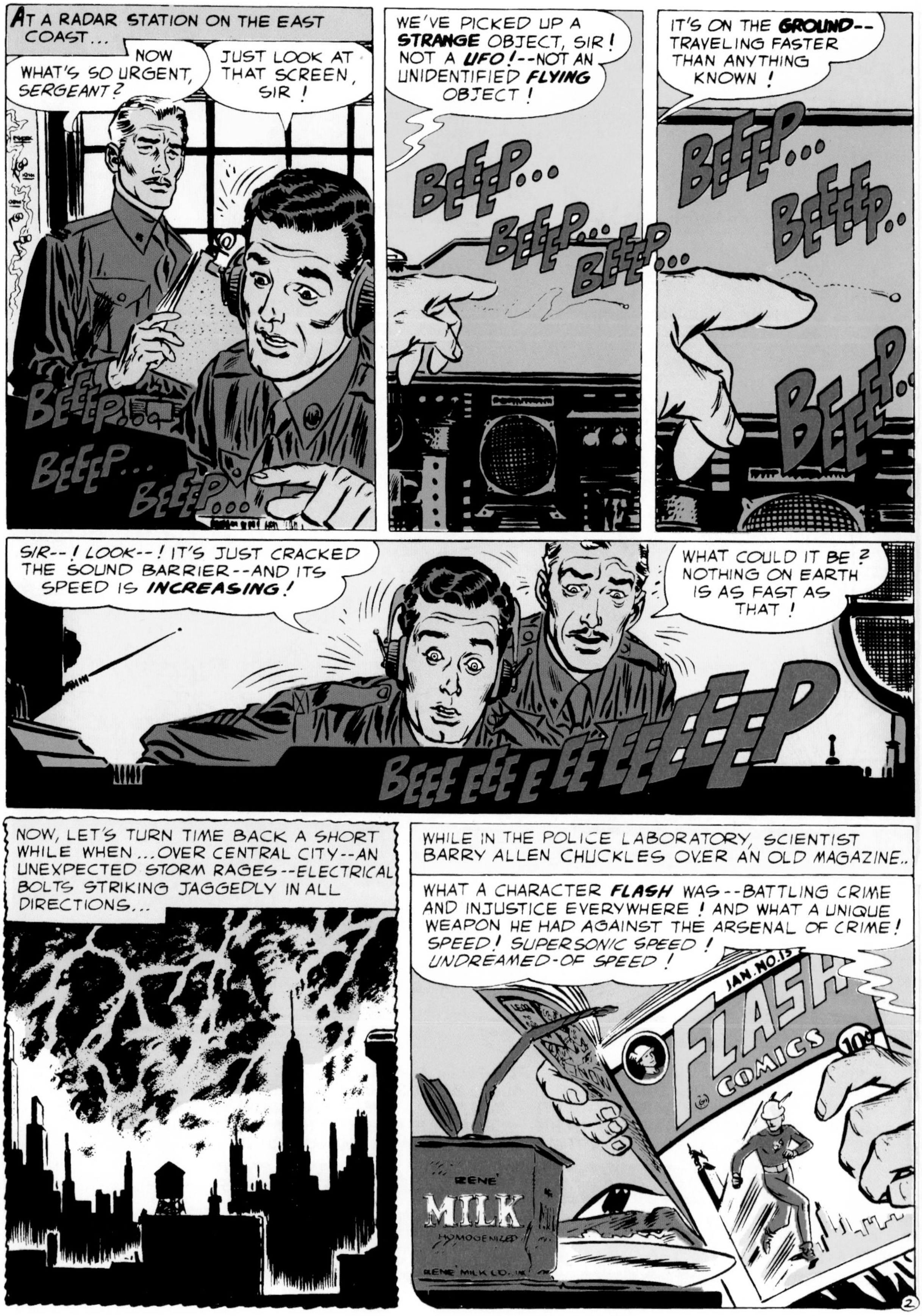

AT A RADAR STATION ON THE EAST COAST...
NOW WHAT'S SO URGENT, SERGEANT?
JUST LOOK AT THAT SCREEN, SIR!
BEEEP...
BEEEP...
BEEEP...
WE'VE PICKED UP A STRANGE OBJECT, SIR! NOT A UFO!--NOT AN UNIDENTIFIED FLYING OBJECT!
BEEEP...
BEEEP...
BEEEP...
IT'S ON THE GROUND--TRAVELING FASTER THAN ANYTHING KNOWN!
BEEEP...
BEEEEP...
BEEEP...
SIR--! LOOK--! IT'S JUST CRACKED THE SOUND BARRIER--AND ITS SPEED IS INCREASING!
WHAT COULD IT BE? NOTHING ON EARTH IS AS FAST AS THAT!
BEEE EEE E EE EEEEEEP
NOW, LET'S TURN TIME BACK A SHORT WHILE WHEN...OVER CENTRAL CITY--AN UNEXPECTED STORM RAGES--ELECTRICAL BOLTS STRIKING JAGGEDLY IN ALL DIRECTIONS...
WHILE IN THE POLICE LABORATORY, SCIENTIST BARRY ALLEN CHUCKLES OVER AN OLD MAGAZINE..
WHAT A CHARACTER FLASH WAS--BATTLING CRIME AND INJUSTICE EVERYWHERE! AND WHAT A UNIQUE WEAPON HE HAD AGAINST THE ARSENAL OF CRIME! SPEED! SUPERSONIC SPEED! UNDREAMED-OF SPEED!
JAN. NO. 13
FLASH COMICS
10¢
RENE'
MILK
HOMOGENIZED
RENE' MILK CO. INC.
2

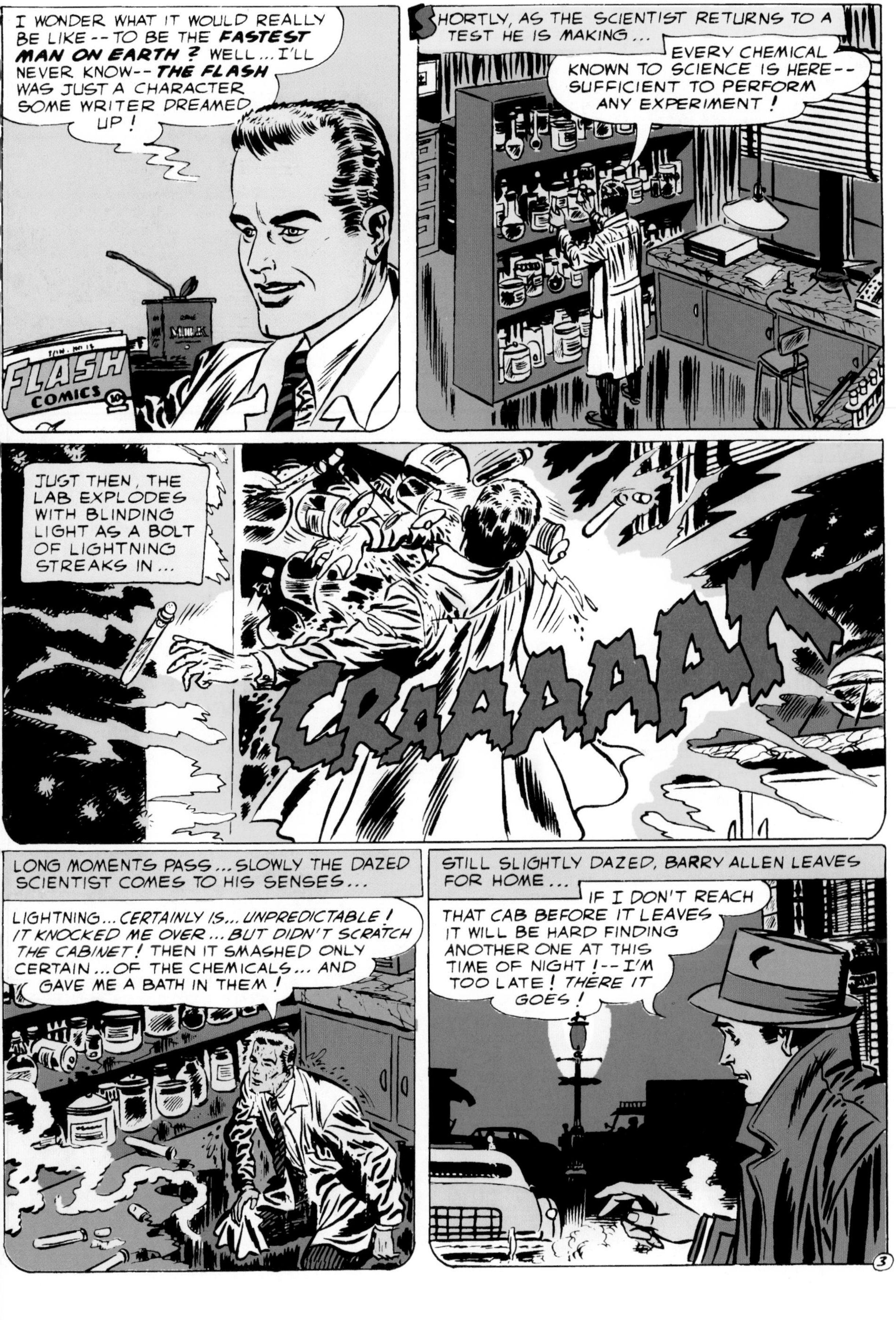
I WONDER WHAT IT WOULD REALLY BE LIKE -- TO BE THE FASTEST MAN ON EARTH? WELL... I'LL NEVER KNOW -- THE FLASH WAS JUST A CHARACTER SOME WRITER DREAMED UP!
FLASH COMICS
SHORTLY, AS THE SCIENTIST RETURNS TO A TEST HE IS MAKING...
EVERY CHEMICAL KNOWN TO SCIENCE IS HERE -- SUFFICIENT TO PERFORM ANY EXPERIMENT!
JUST THEN, THE LAB EXPLODES WITH BLINDING LIGHT AS A BOLT OF LIGHTNING STREAKS IN...
CRAAAAAK
LONG MOMENTS PASS... SLOWLY THE DAZED SCIENTIST COMES TO HIS SENSES...
LIGHTNING... CERTAINLY IS... UNPREDICTABLE! IT KNOCKED ME OVER... BUT DIDN'T SCRATCH THE CABINET! THEN IT SMASHED ONLY CERTAIN... OF THE CHEMICALS... AND GAVE ME A BATH IN THEM!
STILL SLIGHTLY DAZED, BARRY ALLEN LEAVES FOR HOME...
IF I DON'T REACH THAT CAB BEFORE IT LEAVES IT WILL BE HARD FINDING ANOTHER ONE AT THIS TIME OF NIGHT! -- I'M TOO LATE! THERE IT GOES!
3

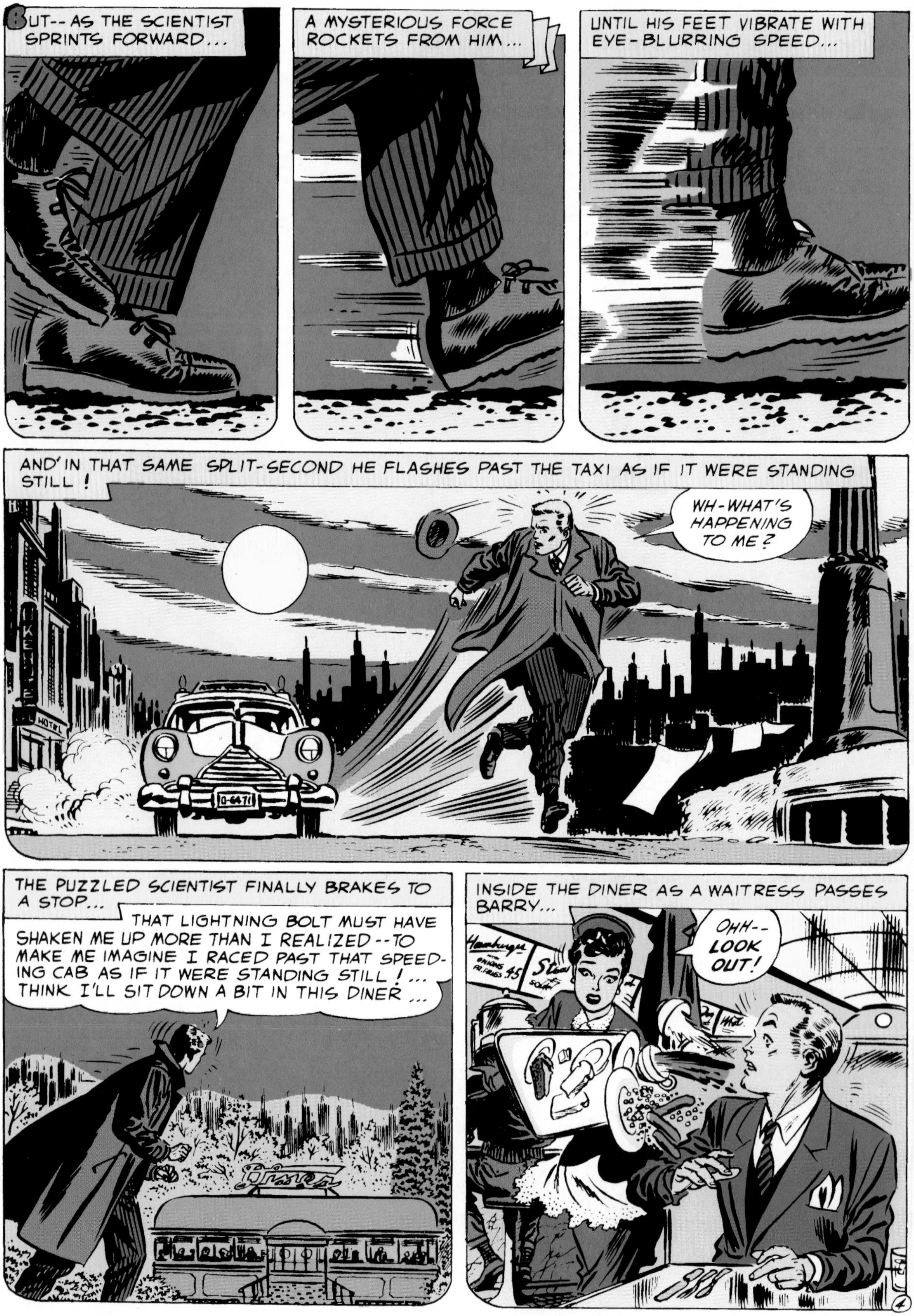
BUT-- AS THE SCIENTIST SPRINTS FORWARD...
A MYSTERIOUS FORCE ROCKETS FROM HIM...
UNTIL HIS FEET VIBRATE WITH EYE-BLURRING SPEED...
AND IN THAT SAME SPLIT-SECOND HE FLASHES PAST THE TAXI AS IF IT WERE STANDING STILL!
WH-WHAT'S HAPPENING TO ME?
HOTEL
THE PUZZLED SCIENTIST FINALLY BRAKES TO A STOP...
THAT LIGHTNING BOLT MUST HAVE SHAKEN ME UP MORE THAN I REALIZED--TO MAKE ME IMAGINE I RACED PAST THAT SPEEDING CAB AS IF IT WERE STANDING STILL!... THINK I'LL SIT DOWN A BIT IN THIS DINER...
INSIDE THE DINER AS A WAITRESS PASSES BARRY...
OHH-- LOOK OUT!
4

INSTINCTIVELY SHRINKING FROM THE FALLING OBJECTS, BARRY IS STARTLED TO SEE...

WHY--IT LOOKS AS IF THEY'VE **STOPPED** FALLING ! IT CAN'T BE HARD TO CATCH THINGS THAT ARE JUST **HANGING** IN THE AIR--AS IF THEIR **MOTION** IS STOPPED !

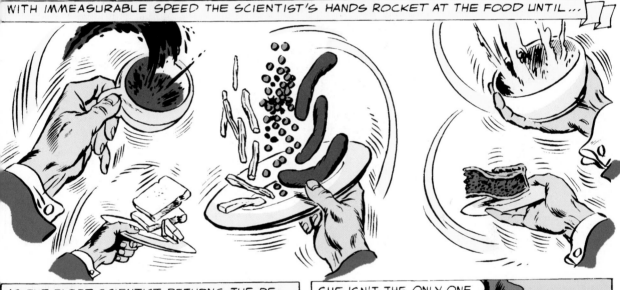

WITH IMMEASURABLE SPEED THE SCIENTIST'S HANDS ROCKET AT THE FOOD UNTIL...

AS THE FLEET SCIENTIST RETURNS THE RE-TRIEVED FOODS TO THE FLABBERGASTED WAITRESS...

I--I MUSN'T BE GETTING ENOUGH SLEEP !... I'M BEGINNING TO SEE TH-THINGS !... I COULD HAVE SWORN I DROPPED EVERY-THING AND Y-Y-YOU--NO ! IT'S IMPOSSIBLE !... EXCUSE ME, SIR !

SHE ISN'T THE ONLY ONE WHO'S SEEING THINGS ! THAT LIGHTNING BOLT TOSSED ME AROUND LIKE A SALAD IN A DRESSING OF CHEMICALS ! I'D BETTER GO HOME AND GET A GOOD NIGHT'S SLEEP !

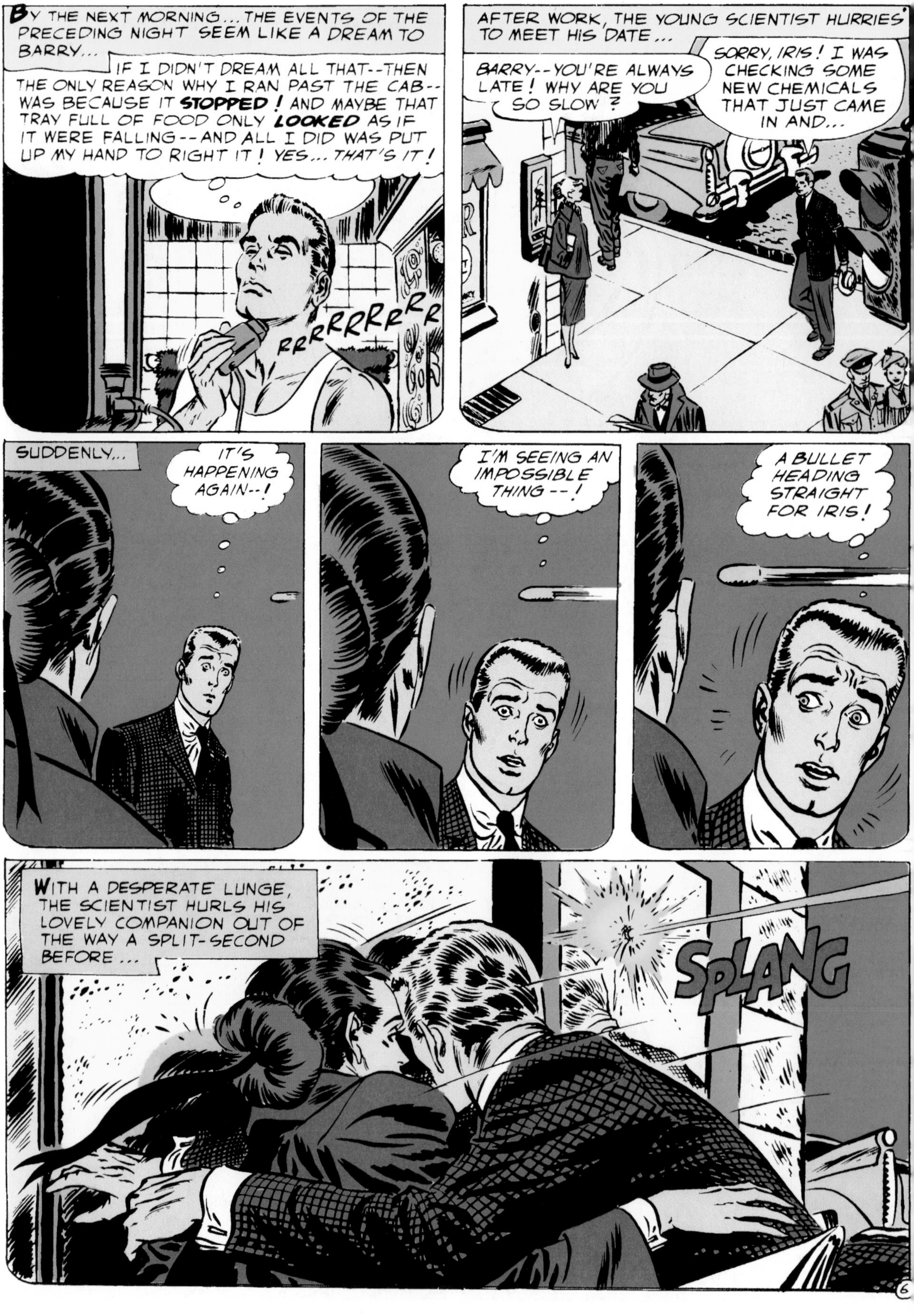
BY THE NEXT MORNING... THE EVENTS OF THE PRECEDING NIGHT SEEM LIKE A DREAM TO BARRY...
IF I DIDN'T DREAM ALL THAT--THEN THE ONLY REASON WHY I RAN PAST THE CAB--WAS BECAUSE IT **STOPPED**! AND MAYBE THAT TRAY FULL OF FOOD ONLY **LOOKED** AS IF IT WERE FALLING--AND ALL I DID WAS PUT UP MY HAND TO RIGHT IT! YES... THAT'S IT!
RRRRRRRRRR
AFTER WORK, THE YOUNG SCIENTIST HURRIES TO MEET HIS DATE...
BARRY--YOU'RE ALWAYS LATE! WHY ARE YOU SO SLOW?
SORRY, IRIS! I WAS CHECKING SOME NEW CHEMICALS THAT JUST CAME IN AND...
SUDDENLY...
IT'S HAPPENING AGAIN--!
I'M SEEING AN IMPOSSIBLE THING--!
A BULLET HEADING STRAIGHT FOR IRIS!
WITH A DESPERATE LUNGE, THE SCIENTIST HURLS HIS LOVELY COMPANION OUT OF THE WAY A SPLIT-SECOND BEFORE...
SPLANG
6

BARRY--IF Y-YOU H-HADN'T ACCIDENTALLY STUMBLED AGAINST ME J-JUST BEFORE THAT STRAY BULLET STRUCK--I WOULD HAVE BEEN H-HIT!

GLAD YOU FOLKS WEREN'T HURT! THAT STRAY WAS FIRED BY THE *TURTLE MAN*--MAKING A GETAWAY!

THE *TURTLE MAN?* THAT'S THE CRIMINAL CALLED "*THE SLOWEST MAN ON EARTH*"!

LATER... BARRY RETURNS TO THE LAB...

THERE'S NO DOUBT OF IT NOW! BY A FREAK ACCIDENT--CAUSED BY THAT LIGHTNING STRIKING A STRANGE COMBINATION OF CHEMICALS--I WAS DRENCHED WITH A SOLUTION WHICH MUST HAVE CHANGED MY MOLECULAR STRUCTURE! I AM NOW... *THE FASTEST MAN ON EARTH!*

THERE MUST BE **SOME** WAY I CAN USE THIS UNIQUE SPEED TO HELP HUMANITY!... HMMM--THIS GIVES ME AN IDEA!

JAN. NO. 12
FLASH COMICS
10¢

SOMETIME LATER... AT THE LAB...

THE REMOTE CONTROL HOOKUP I'VE FIXED UP WITH THE ALARM SYSTEM AT HEADQUARTERS IS PAYING OFF! IT'S SIGNALLING THAT THE BURGLAR ALARM AT THE CENTRAL BANK HAS BEEN TRIPPED!

BZZZZZZ BZZZZZZ

THE SCIENTIST INSTANTLY PRESSES HIS RING--A COVER ON IT SPRINGS OPEN AND...

IT WORKS! THE CHEMICAL SOLUTION--

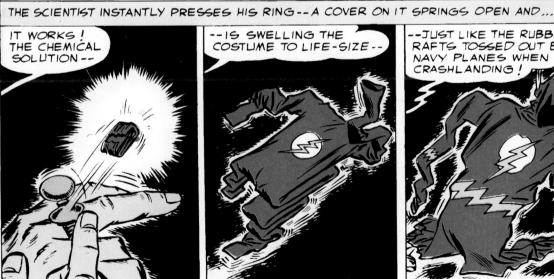

--IS SWELLING THE COSTUME TO LIFE-SIZE--

--JUST LIKE THE RUBBER RAFTS TOSSED OUT BY NAVY PLANES WHEN CRASHLANDING!

⑦

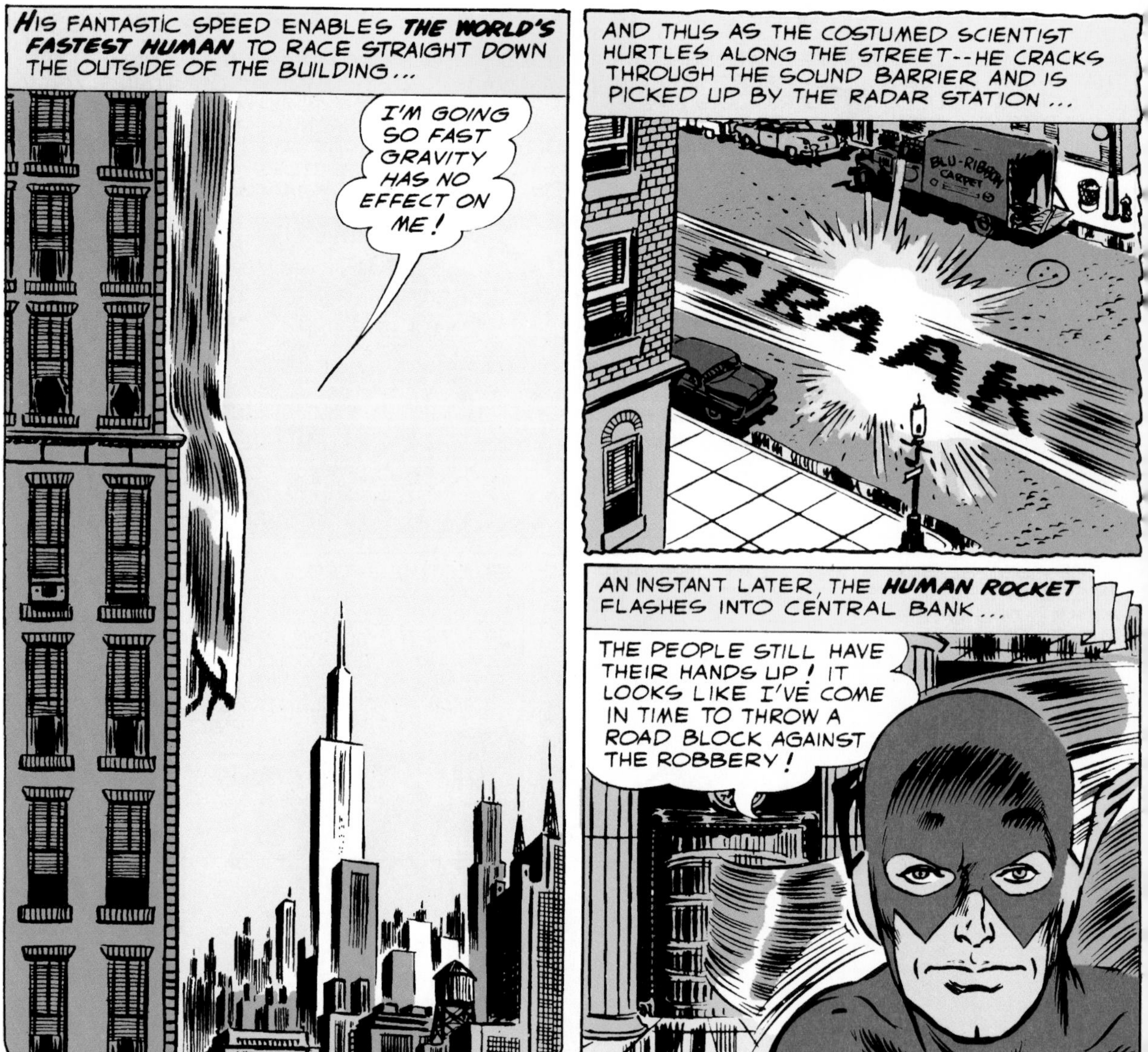

HIS FANTASTIC SPEED ENABLES THE WORLD'S FASTEST HUMAN TO RACE STRAIGHT DOWN THE OUTSIDE OF THE BUILDING...
I'M GOING SO FAST GRAVITY HAS NO EFFECT ON ME!
AND THUS AS THE COSTUMED SCIENTIST HURTLES ALONG THE STREET--HE CRACKS THROUGH THE SOUND BARRIER AND IS PICKED UP BY THE RADAR STATION...
BLU-RIBBON CARPET
CRAAK
AN INSTANT LATER, THE HUMAN ROCKET FLASHES INTO CENTRAL BANK...
THE PEOPLE STILL HAVE THEIR HANDS UP! IT LOOKS LIKE I'VE COME IN TIME TO THROW A ROAD BLOCK AGAINST THE ROBBERY!
THERE'S THE BANK VAULT!--OPEN!--THE CROOKS MUST BE INSIDE!
BUT TO THE SPEEDY SCIENTIST'S ASTONISHMENT...
GREAT THUNDER! THE VAULT'S EMPTY! NO ONE IS HERE! AND--NOTHING HAS BEEN TOUCHED!
8

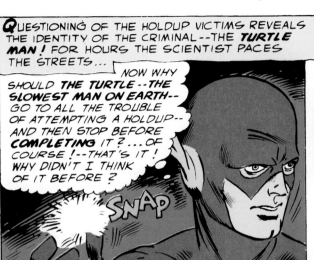

QUESTIONING OF THE HOLDUP VICTIMS REVEALS THE IDENTITY OF THE CRIMINAL--THE *TURTLE MAN*! FOR HOURS THE SCIENTIST PACES THE STREETS...

NOW WHY SHOULD *THE TURTLE*--THE *SLOWEST MAN ON EARTH*--GO TO ALL THE TROUBLE OF ATTEMPTING A HOLDUP--AND THEN STOP BEFORE *COMPLETING* IT?...OF COURSE!--THAT'S IT! WHY DIDN'T I THINK OF IT BEFORE?

SNAP

IN THE BLINK OF AN EYE, BARRY STREAKS TOWARD THE BANK...

THE REASON WHY *THE SLOWEST MAN ON EARTH DIDN'T* COMPLETE THE CRIME--WAS THAT HE WAS DOING IT IN *TWO* STAGES! THE SECOND--*AFTER* EVERYONE WAS OFF GUARD! AND THERE HE IS!

AT EYE-BLURRING SPEED...

THE SCIENTIST REACHES OUT FOR THE STATIONARY VILLAIN...

ONLY TO DISCOVER...

HE TRICKED ME--THIS IS JUST A PAINTED SILHOUETTE--NOT A REAL SHADOW!

SO GREAT IS THE *HUMAN WHIRLWIND'S* SPEED--HE BORES THROUGH THE SOLID BRICK WALL LIKE A GIGANTIC DRILL... AS THE *TURTLE MAN* TAUNTS...

HE...DOESN'T...KNOW...I...ANTICIPATED...HIS... RETURN...AFTER...I...SAW...HIM...ENTER... THE...VAULT...WHERE...I...WAS...HIDING... HA...HA...HA...

KRUNNG

⑨

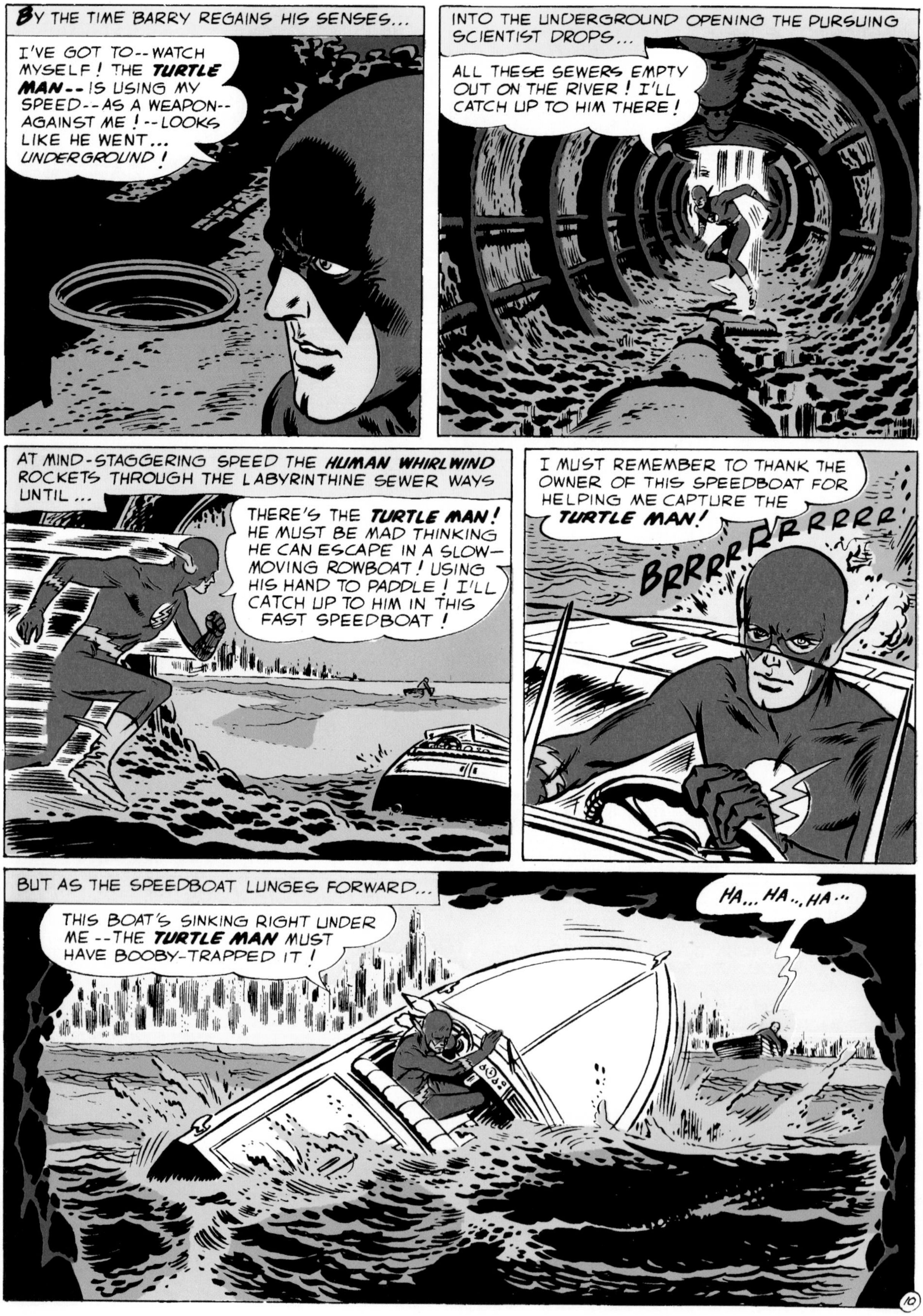
BY THE TIME BARRY REGAINS HIS SENSES...
I'VE GOT TO--WATCH MYSELF! THE TURTLE MAN--IS USING MY SPEED--AS A WEAPON--AGAINST ME!--LOOKS LIKE HE WENT... UNDERGROUND!
INTO THE UNDERGROUND OPENING THE PURSUING SCIENTIST DROPS...
ALL THESE SEWERS EMPTY OUT ON THE RIVER! I'LL CATCH UP TO HIM THERE!
AT MIND-STAGGERING SPEED THE HUMAN WHIRLWIND ROCKETS THROUGH THE LABYRINTHINE SEWER WAYS UNTIL...
THERE'S THE TURTLE MAN! HE MUST BE MAD THINKING HE CAN ESCAPE IN A SLOW-MOVING ROWBOAT! USING HIS HAND TO PADDLE! I'LL CATCH UP TO HIM IN THIS FAST SPEEDBOAT!
I MUST REMEMBER TO THANK THE OWNER OF THIS SPEEDBOAT FOR HELPING ME CAPTURE THE TURTLE MAN!
BRRRRRRRRRRR
BUT AS THE SPEEDBOAT LUNGES FORWARD...
THIS BOAT'S SINKING RIGHT UNDER ME--THE TURTLE MAN MUST HAVE BOOBY-TRAPPED IT!
HA... HA... HA...
10

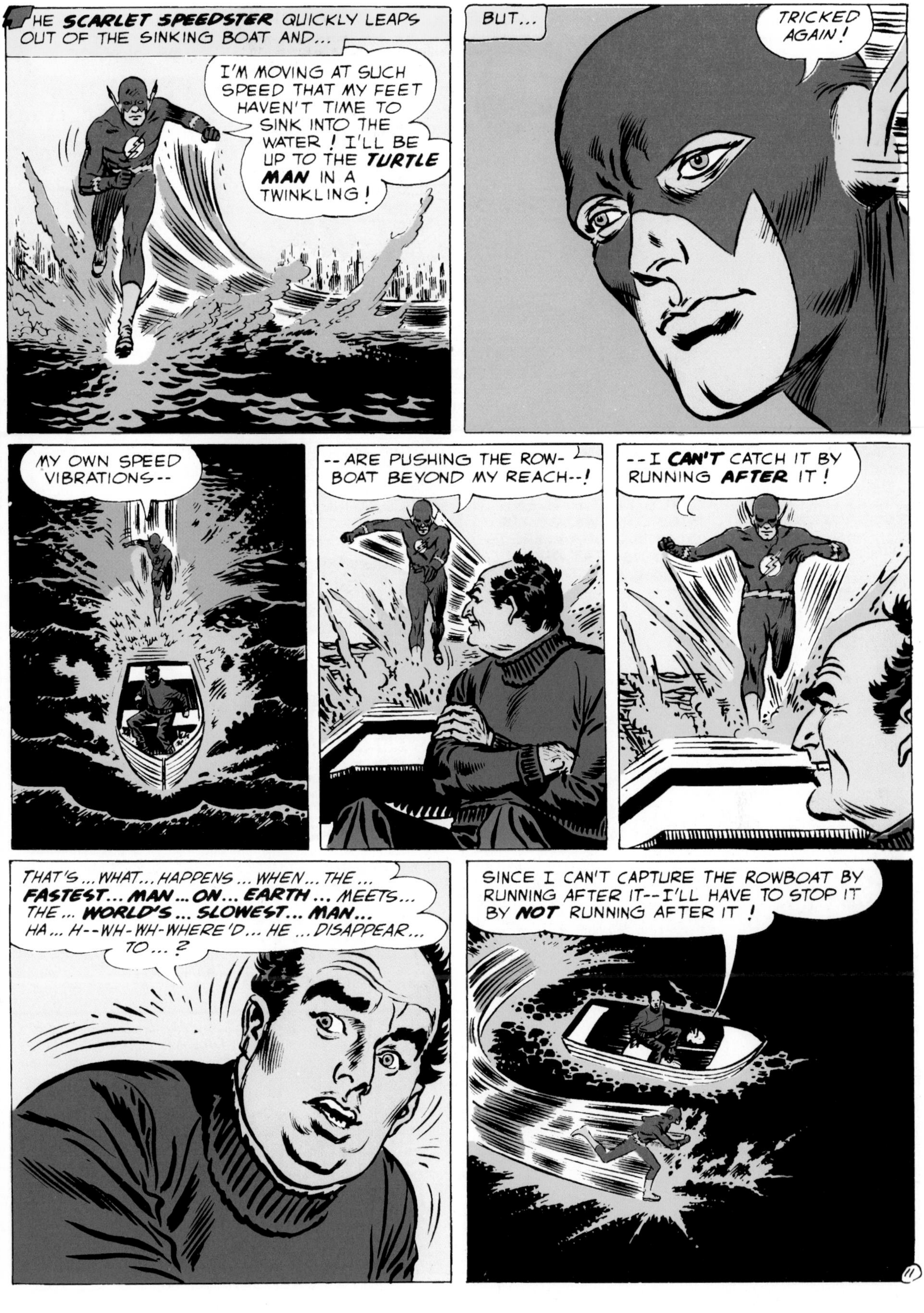
THE SCARLET SPEEDSTER QUICKLY LEAPS OUT OF THE SINKING BOAT AND...
I'M MOVING AT SUCH SPEED THAT MY FEET HAVEN'T TIME TO SINK INTO THE WATER ! I'LL BE UP TO THE TURTLE MAN IN A TWINKLING !
BUT...
TRICKED AGAIN !
MY OWN SPEED VIBRATIONS--
--ARE PUSHING THE ROW-BOAT BEYOND MY REACH--!
--I CAN'T CATCH IT BY RUNNING AFTER IT !
THAT'S ... WHAT ... HAPPENS ... WHEN ... THE ... FASTEST ... MAN ... ON ... EARTH ... MEETS ... THE ... WORLD'S ... SLOWEST ... MAN ... HA ... H--WH-WH-WHERE'D ... HE ... DISAPPEAR ... TO ... ?
SINCE I CAN'T CAPTURE THE ROWBOAT BY RUNNING AFTER IT--I'LL HAVE TO STOP IT BY NOT RUNNING AFTER IT !
11

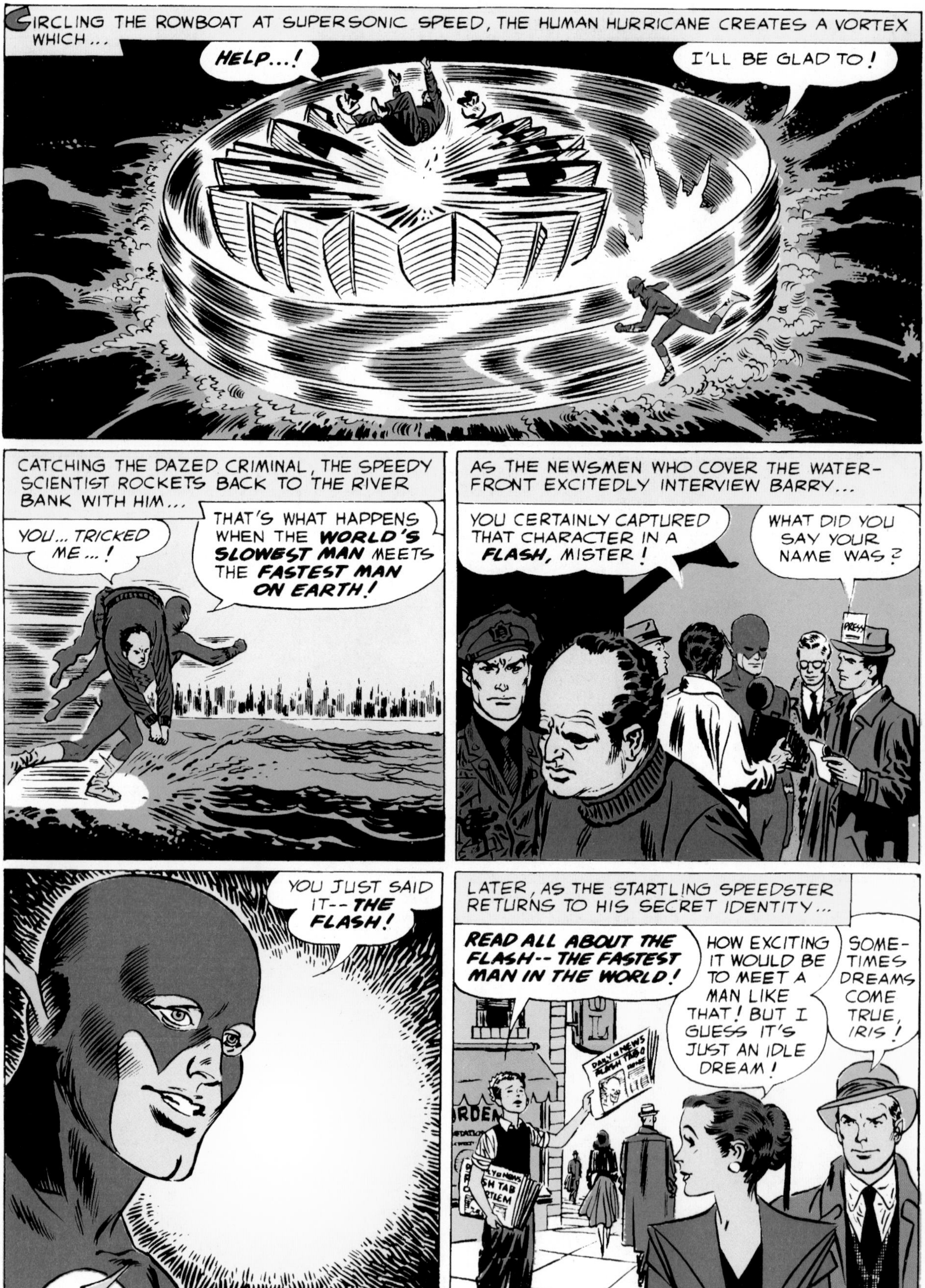
CIRCLING THE ROWBOAT AT SUPERSONIC SPEED, THE HUMAN HURRICANE CREATES A VORTEX WHICH...
HELP...!
I'LL BE GLAD TO!
CATCHING THE DAZED CRIMINAL, THE SPEEDY SCIENTIST ROCKETS BACK TO THE RIVER BANK WITH HIM...
YOU... TRICKED ME...!
THAT'S WHAT HAPPENS WHEN THE WORLD'S SLOWEST MAN MEETS THE FASTEST MAN ON EARTH!
AS THE NEWSMEN WHO COVER THE WATER-FRONT EXCITEDLY INTERVIEW BARRY...
YOU CERTAINLY CAPTURED THAT CHARACTER IN A FLASH, MISTER!
WHAT DID YOU SAY YOUR NAME WAS?
PRESS
YOU JUST SAID IT-- THE FLASH!
LATER, AS THE STARTLING SPEEDSTER RETURNS TO HIS SECRET IDENTITY...
READ ALL ABOUT THE FLASH-- THE FASTEST MAN IN THE WORLD!
HOW EXCITING IT WOULD BE TO MEET A MAN LIKE THAT! BUT I GUESS IT'S JUST AN IDLE DREAM!
SOMETIMES DREAMS COME TRUE, IRIS!
12

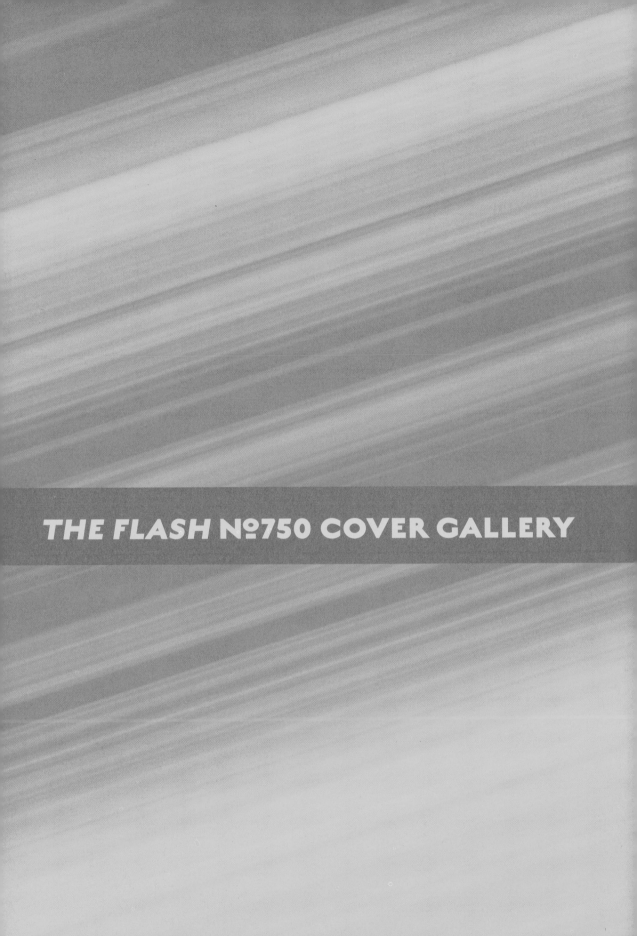

THE FLASH №750 COVER GALLERY

1940s variant cover by NICOLA SCOTT and ANNETTE KWOK

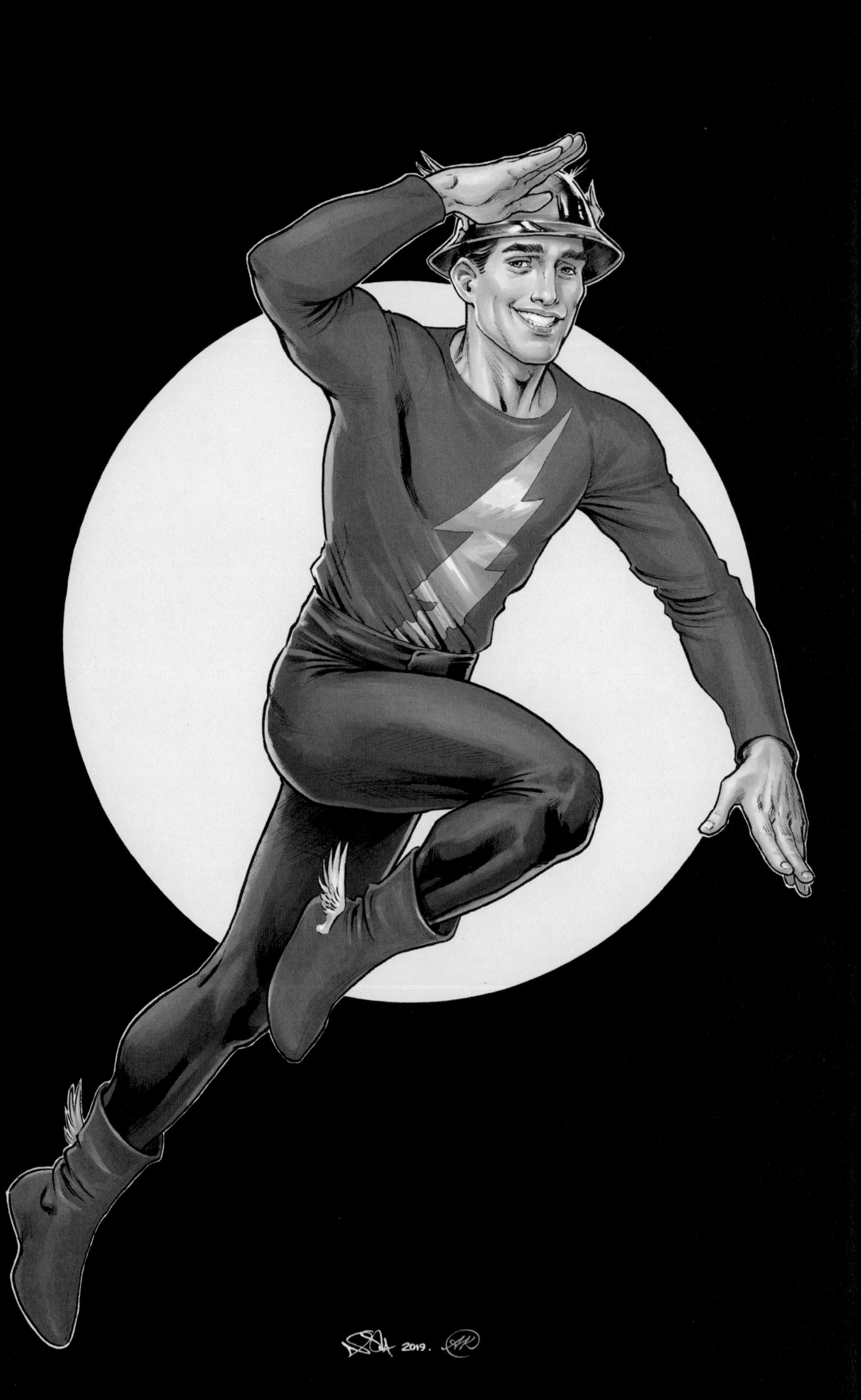
2019.

1950s variant cover by GARY FRANK and BRAD ANDERSON

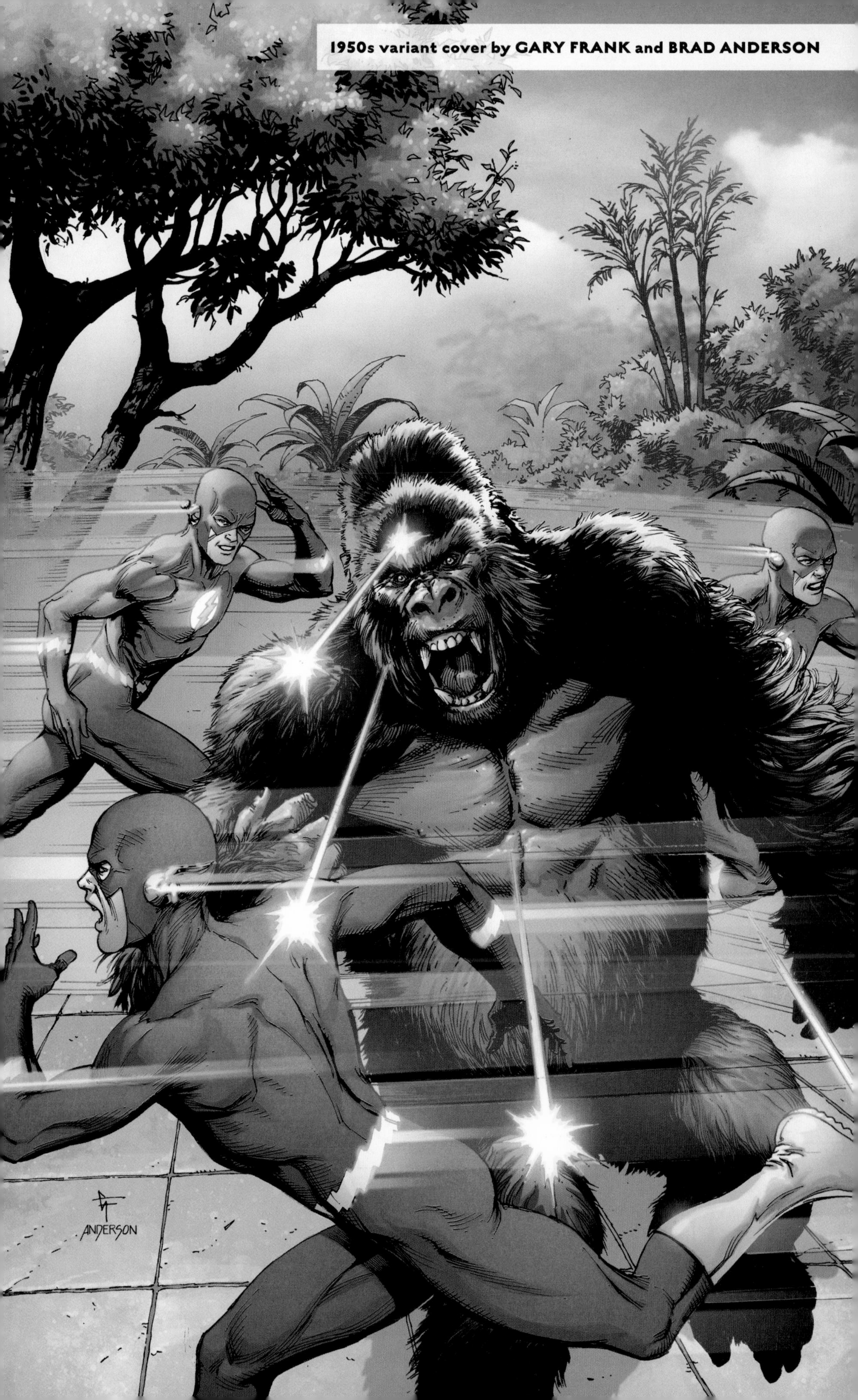
ANDERSON

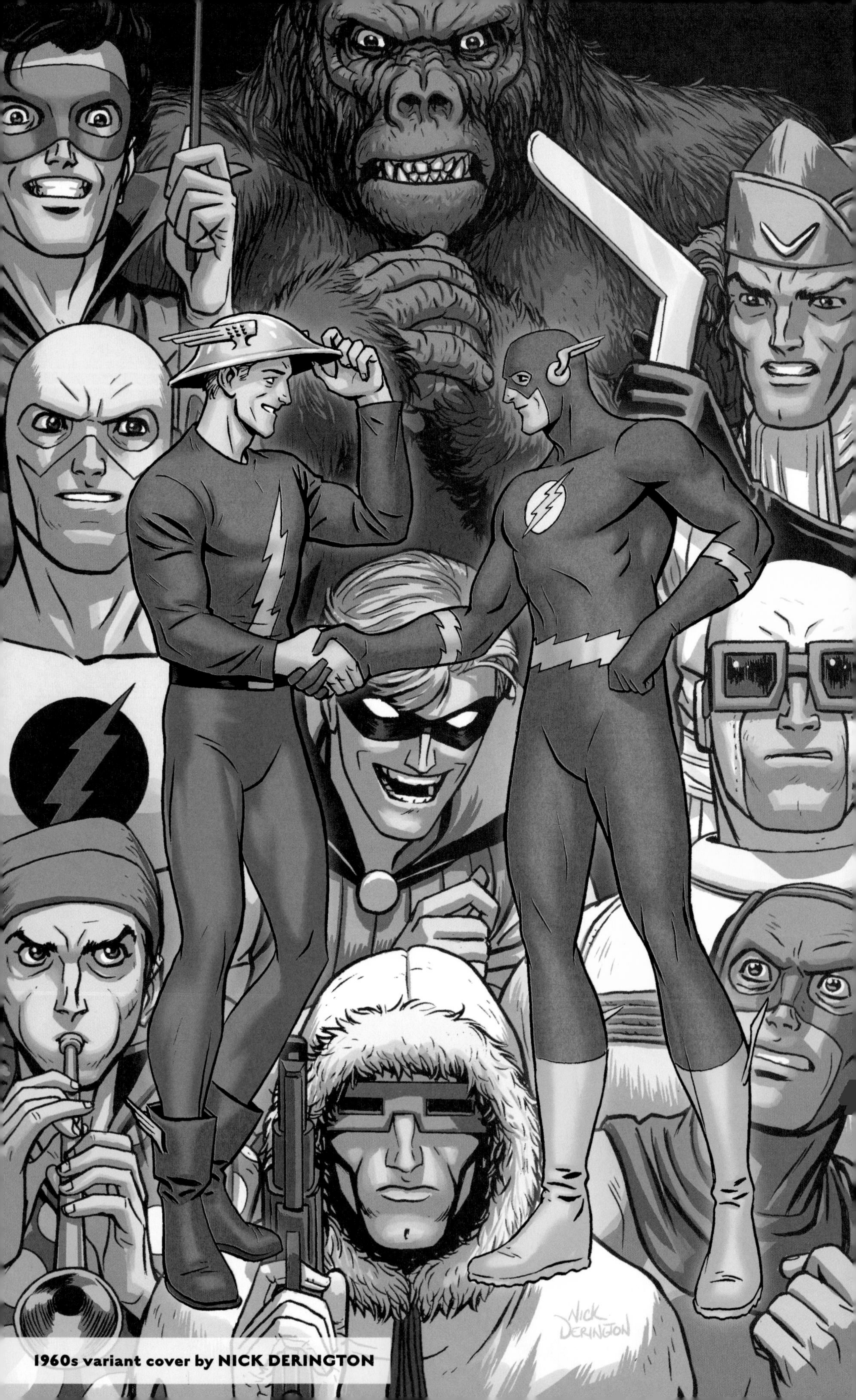
NICK DERINGTON

1960s variant cover by NICK DERINGTON

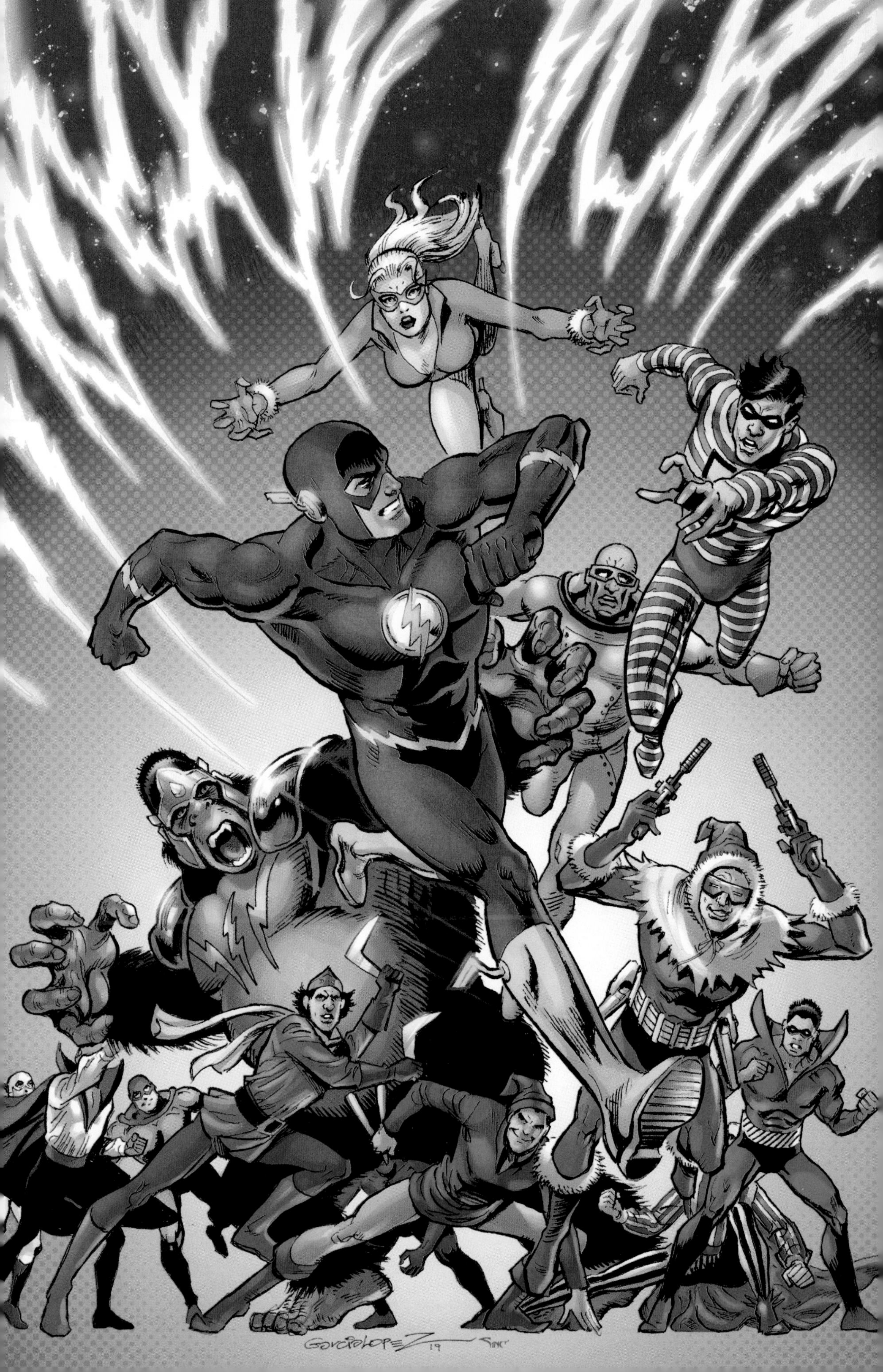

1970s variant cover by **JOSÉ LUIS GARCÍA-LÓPEZ** and **ALEX SINCLAIR**

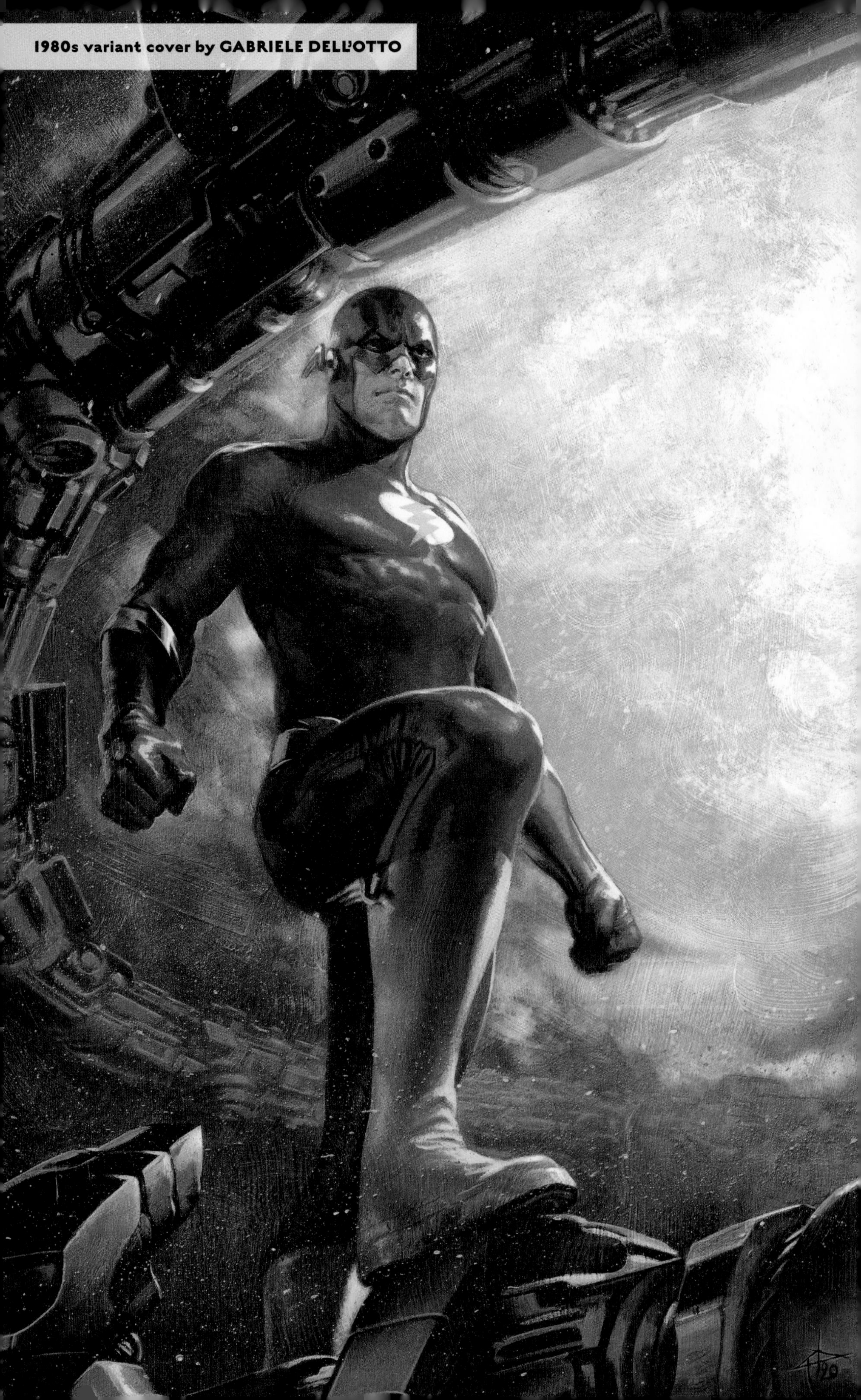

1980s variant cover by GABRIELE DELL'OTTO

1990s variant cover by FRANCESCO MATTINA

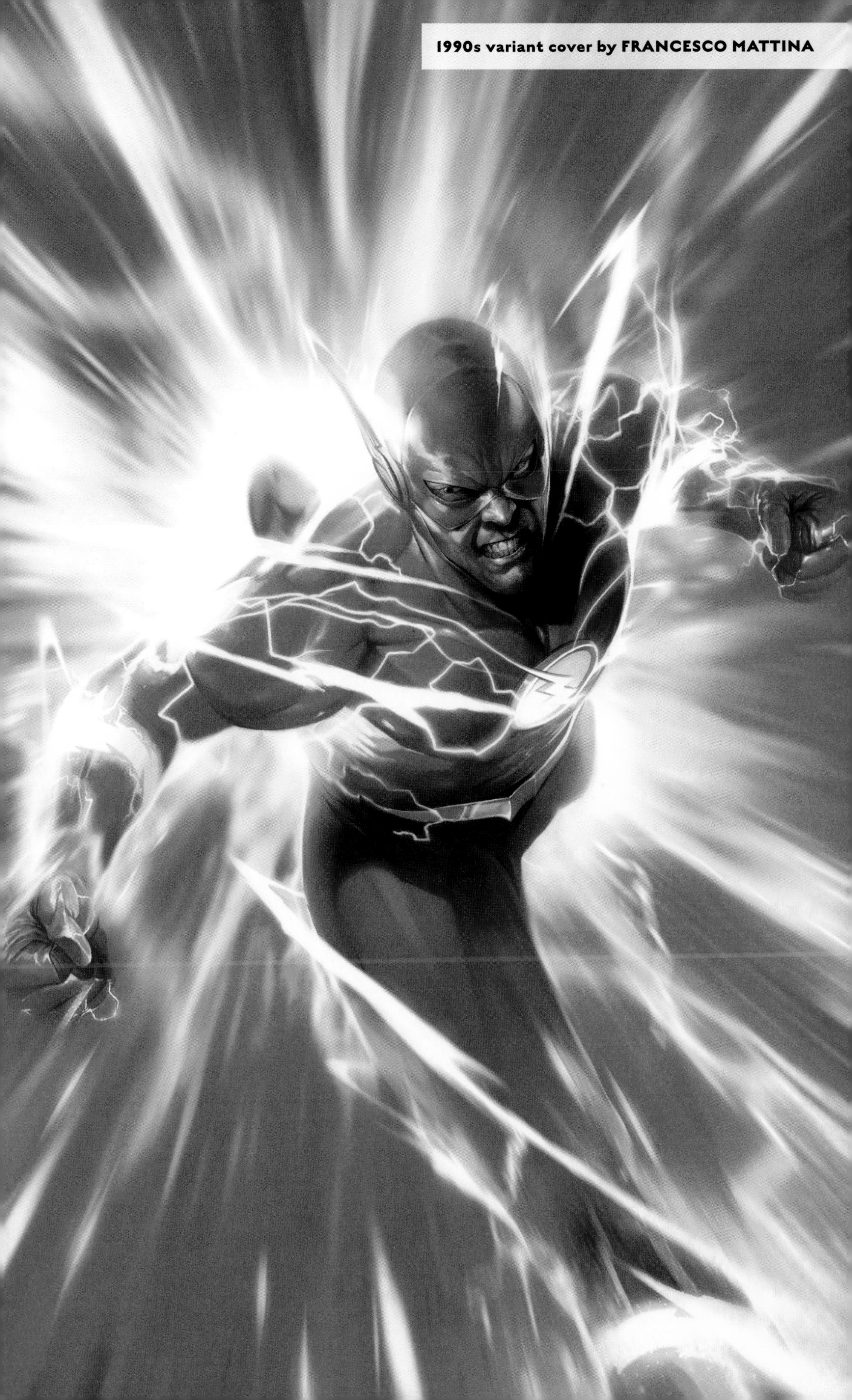

2000s variant cover by JIM LEE, SCOTT WILLIAMS, and ALEX SINCLAIR

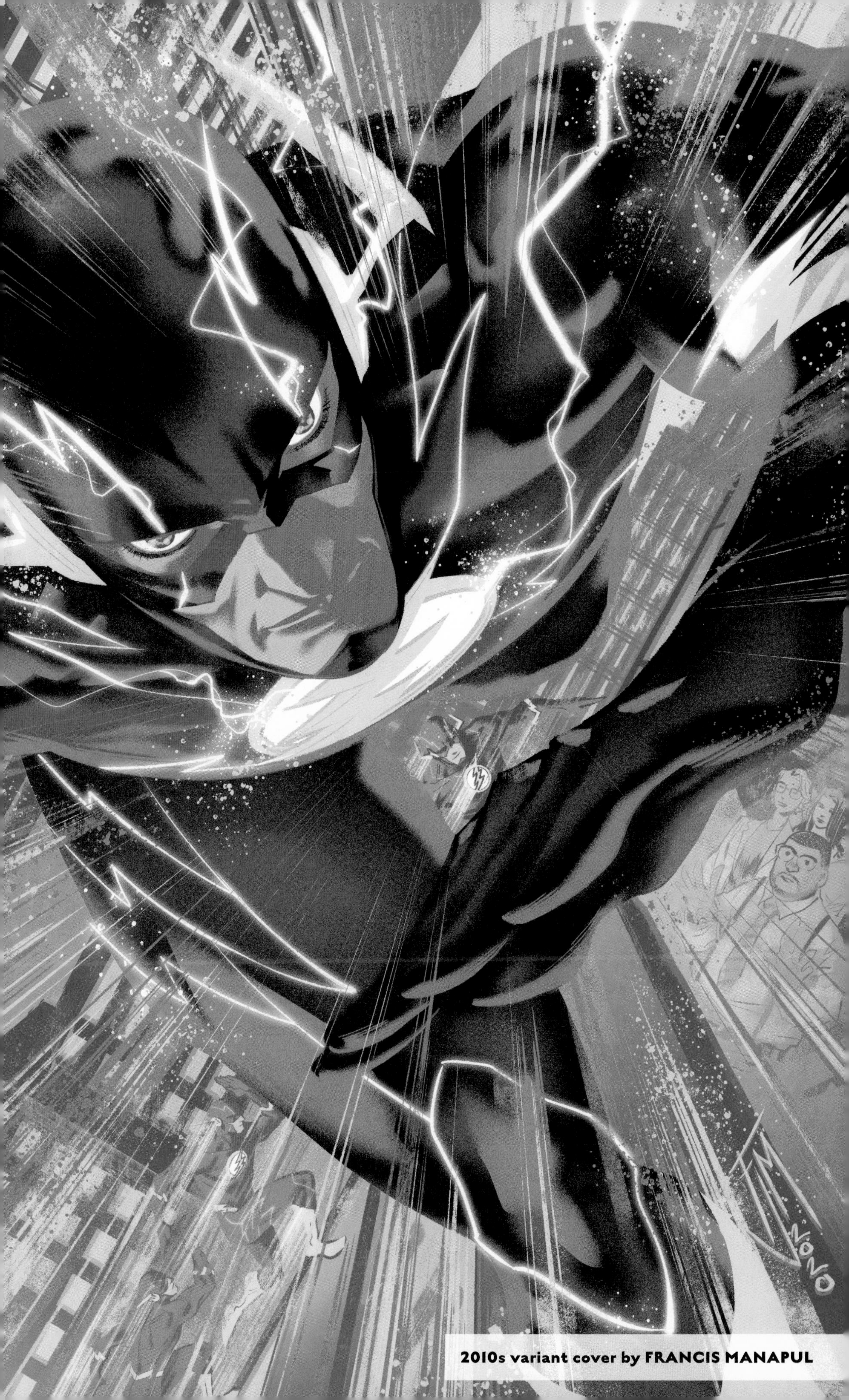

2010s variant cover by **FRANCIS MANAPUL**

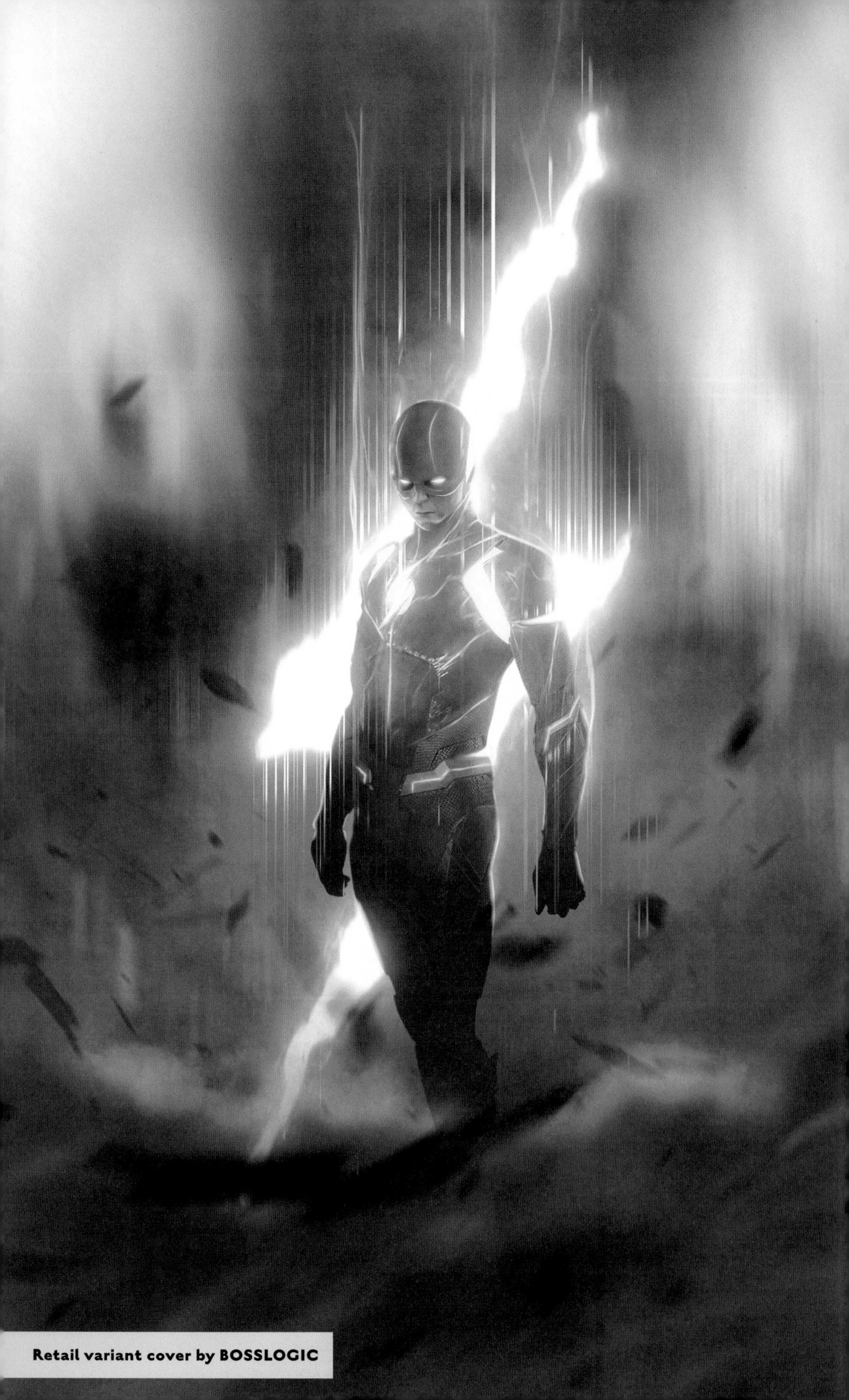

Retail variant cover by BOSSLOGIC

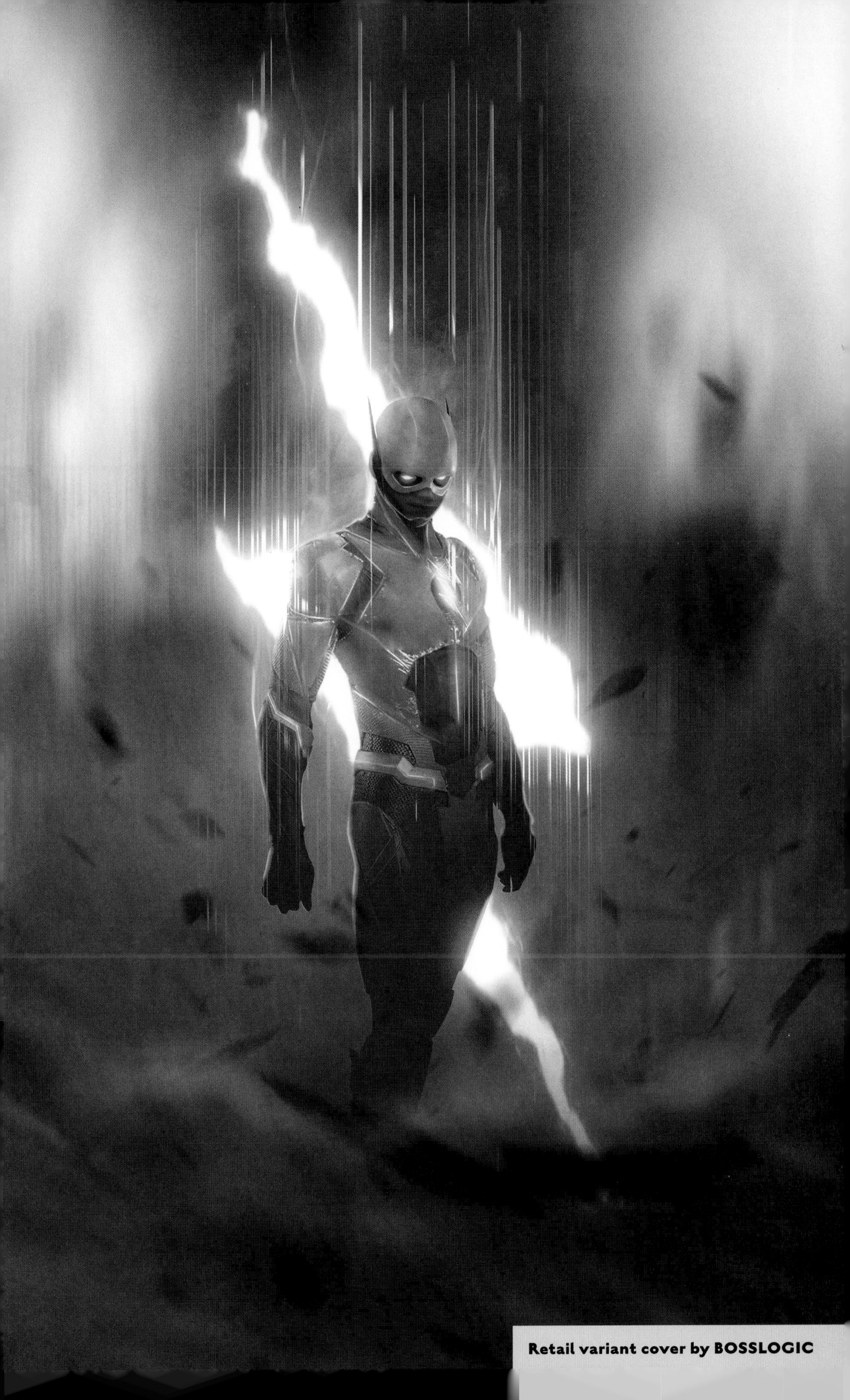

Retail variant cover by BOSSLOGIC

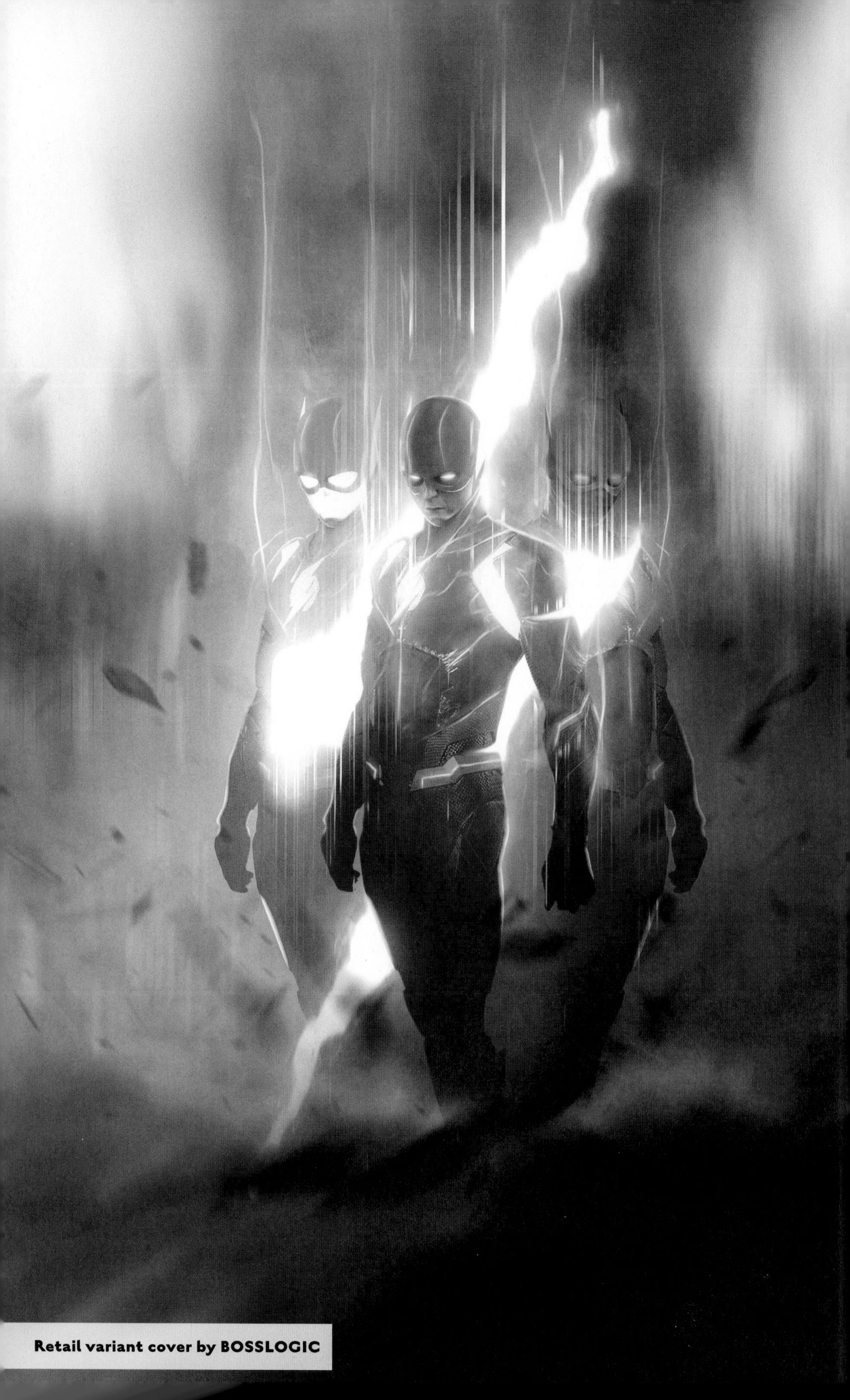

Retail variant cover by BOSSLOGIC